Centre for Educational Research and Innovation

Brian Fleming Research & Learning Library
Ministry of Education
Ministry of Training, Colleges & Universities
900 Bay St. 13th Floor, Mowat Block
Toronto, ON M7A 1L2

Formative Assessment

IMPROVING LEARNING
IN SECONDARY CLASSROOMS

ORGANISATION FOR ECONOMIC CO-OPERATION AND DEVELOPMENT

ORGANISATION FOR ECONOMIC CO-OPERATION AND DEVELOPMENT

The OECD is a unique forum where the governments of 30 democracies work together to address the economic, social and environmental challenges of globalisation. The OECD is also at the forefront of efforts to understand and to help governments respond to new developments and concerns, such as corporate governance, the information economy and the challenges of an ageing population. The Organisation provides a setting where governments can compare policy experiences, seek answers to common problems, identify good practice and work to co-ordinate domestic and international policies.

The OECD member countries are: Australia, Austria, Belgium, Canada, the Czech Republic, Denmark, Finland, France, Germany, Greece, Hungary, Iceland, Ireland, Italy, Japan, Korea, Luxembourg, Mexico, the Netherlands, New Zealand, Norway, Poland, Portugal, the Slovak Republic, Spain, Sweden, Switzerland, Turkey, the United Kingdom and the United States. The Commission of the European Communities takes part in the work of the OECD.

OECD Publishing disseminates widely the results of the Organisation's statistics gathering and research on economic, social and environmental issues, as well as the conventions, guidelines and standards agreed by its members.

> This work is published on the responsibility of the Secretary-General of the OECD. The opinions expressed and arguments employed herein do not necessarily reflect the official views of the Organisation or of the governments of its member countries.

Also available in French under the title:
L'évaluation formative
POUR UN MEILLEUR APPRENTISSAGE DANS LES CLASSES SECONDAIRES

Photo credit: with the permission of *The Times Educational Supplement*.

PISA™, OECD/PISA™ and the PISA logo are trademarks of the Organisation for Economic Co-operation and Development (OECD). All use of OECD trademarks is prohibited without written permission from the OECD.

© OECD 2005

No reproduction, copy, transmission or translation of this publication may be made without written permission. Applications should be sent to OECD Publishing: *rights@oecd.org* or by fax (33 1) 45 24 13 91. Permission to photocopy a portion of this work should be addressed to the Centre français d'exploitation du droit de copie, 20, rue des Grands-Augustins, 75006 Paris, France (*contact@cfcopies.com*).

IN MEMORIAM

This report is dedicated to
Caroline St. John-Brooks (1947-2003)
one of the pioneers of the "What Works in Innovation in Education" series,
who worked in OECD/CERI between 1994 and 1996.

Foreword

Formative assessment – the frequent, interactive assessments of student understanding and progress to identify learning needs and shape teaching – has become a prominent issue in education reform. This approach is frequently contrasted with "summative" assessment – the more familiar, and much more newsworthy, tests and examinations that seek to provide summary statements of students' capabilities.

Since 2002, the OECD Centre for Educational Research and Innovation (CERI) has analysed the formative approach. It has examined exemplary practice in secondary schools in eight countries (Australia [Queensland], different provinces in Canada, Denmark, England, Finland, Italy, New Zealand and Scotland), has brought together literature reviews from different linguistic research traditions, relating all this to the broader current policy environment. The resulting study combines these elements to clarify the concept of, and approaches to, formative assessment and its relation to teaching strategies. It offers pointers for policies to support this direction of reform in schools and classrooms.

Each of the education systems participating in this study has promoted the practice of formative assessment in the conviction that it is an important area of reform for promoting student achievement, equity of student outcomes, and "learning to learn". In spite of these very encouraging findings, there are still major barriers to wider practice. There are those who feel that the resource and organisational implications make it impractical; there are tensions with the accountability demands of certain highly visible "summative" tests of student performance; and a frequent lack of coherence between assessments at the classroom, school and system level. The study addresses the barriers to suggest ways forward. The focus on lower secondary schooling has been deliberate as the barriers tend to be most acutely felt at this level, compared with the primary cycle that precedes it and the upper secondary cycle that follows – innovations "that work" are thus particularly revealing of what can be achieved.

This "What Works"[1] study complements other educational work in OECD, including PISA (Programme for International Student Assessment), which measures students' "knowledge and skills for life" at age 15 and related explanatory factors, and the recently-completed publication *Teachers Matter: Attracting, Developing and Retaining Effective Teachers*. The next "What Works" study will maintain the focus on formative assessment while extending the purview to adult learners.

Within the CERI Secretariat, the report was prepared by Janet Looney, with the assistance of Jennifer Cannon and Delphine Grandrieux and advice from other colleagues. This report is published on the responsibility of the Secretary-General of the OECD.

The Centre for Educational Research and Innovation was created in June 1968 by the Council of the Organisation for Economic Co-operation and Development and all member countries of the OECD are participants.

The main objectives of the Centre are as follows:

– analyse and develop research, innovation and key indicators in current and emerging education and learning issues, and their links to other sectors of policy;

– explore forward-looking coherent approaches to education and learning in the context of national and international cultural, social and economic change; and

– facilitate practical co-operation among member countries and, where relevant, with non-member countries, in order to seek solutions and exchange views of educational problems of common interest.

The Centre functions within the Organisation for Economic Co-operation and Development in accordance with the decisions of the Council of the Organisation, under the authority of the Secretary-General. It is supervised by a Governing Board composed of one national expert in its field of competence from each of the countries participating in its programme of work.

---

[1] The Programme "What Works in Innovation in Education" was initiated in 1993 to provide timely studies of significant innovations in education. The series is aimed at a broad OECD-wide audience of educational policy-makers, practitioners, and the public. Each study in this series focuses on an area of importance for policy and practice, to examine concrete examples of innovations in a small number (between 5 and 10) of countries and to identify issues for policy and implementation.

ACKNOWLEDGEMENTS

This study would not have been possible without the substantial contributions made by the participating countries. It has enjoyed extensive inputs from dedicated experts located in each. We wish to acknowledge their invaluable contribution, while recognising that many others in each country helped make this study possible. *Canada:* Marian Fushell, Department of Education, Newfoundland and Labrador; Martine Gauthier, Direction de la recherche, statistiques et indicateurs, ministère de l'Éducation du Québec; Rick Johnson, Saskatchewan Learning. *Denmark:* Lejf Moos and Poul Skov, Danish University of Education. *England:* Dylan Wiliam, King's College, London. *Finland:* Helena Kasurinen, Finnish National Board of Education. *Italy:* Cosimo Laneve, the University of Bari, and Maria Teresa Moscato, University of Bologna. *Scotland:* Ernest Spencer, education consultant and University of Glasgow. *New Zealand:* Jenny Poskitt, Massey University. *Queensland, Australia:* Graham Maxwell with Michael Staunton, Queensland Studies Authority.

This "What Works" study went much further than previous volumes in the series to compile literature reviews which are included below as specific chapters. For these, we are particularly indebted to, for the English-language research review, Paul Black, Professor Emeritus, King's College, London and Dylan Wiliam (above); for the French-language review, Linda Allal and Lucie Mottier Lopez, University of Geneva; and, for the German-language review, Olaf Köller, University of Erlangen-Nuremberg.

We also wish to acknowledge the work of a dedicated team of consultants who undertook country visits and wrote reports together with the country experts: Judy Sebba, University of Sussex; Anne Sliwka, University of Mannheim; John Townshend, education consultant; Joke Voogt, University of Twente. David Hopkins, of the DfES in London, provided invaluable guidance at the design stage of the study.

Table of Contents

Executive Summary 13

PART I. THEMATIC DISCUSSION

Chapter 1. The Case for Formative Assessment 21
Meeting goals for lifelong learning 22
Addressing barriers to wider practice 24
Study goals and methodology 27

Chapter 2. Policy Frameworks 31
Legislation promoting the practice of formative assessment 32
Encouraging the use of summative data for formative purposes at school
 and classroom levels 33
Guidelines on effective teaching and assessment practices embedded in national
 curriculum and other materials 36
Provision of tools and teaching resources to support formative assessment 38
Special initiatives and innovative programmes 39
Investments in teacher professional development 40
Developing stronger policy strategies 41

**Chapter 3. The Elements of Formative Assessment: Case Study Findings
 and Supporting Research** 43
The elements of formative assessment 45
Element 1: establishment of a classroom culture that encourages interaction
 and the use of assessment tools 46
Element 2: establishment of learning goals, and tracking of individual
 student progress toward those goals 47
Element 3: use of varied instruction methods to meet diverse student needs 48
Element 4: use of varied approaches to assessing student understanding 49
Element 5: feedback on student performance and adaptation of instruction
 to meet identified needs 50
Element 6: active involvement of students in the learning process 50
Creating powerful frameworks 51

Chapter 4. Formative Assessment in Practice 55
Element 1: establishment of a classroom culture that encourages interaction
  and the use of assessment tools 55
Element 2: establishment of learning goals, and tracking of individual
  student progress toward those goals 58
Element 3: use of varied instruction methods to meet diverse student needs 60
Element 4: use of varied approaches to assessing student understanding 61
Element 5: feedback on student performance and adaptation of instruction
  to meet identified needs 63
Element 6: active involvement of students in the learning process 64
Learning from experience 68

Chapter 5. Benefits and Barriers 69
Addressing barriers and realising benefits at the classroom level 70
Direct benefits in classrooms 72
School leaders' strategies for initiating, sustaining and deepening changes
  in school and teacher practice 73
School-wide benefits 77
Addressing challenges and sustaining innovations 79

Chapter 6. Policy Implications 83
Policy principle 1: keep the focus on teaching and learning 84
Policy principle 2: align summative and formative assessment approaches 85
Policy principle 3: ensure that data gathered at classroom, school and system levels
  are linked and are used formatively, to shape improvements at every level
  of the system 86
Policy principle 4: invest in training and support for formative assessment 88
Policy principle 5: encourage innovation 89
Policy principle 6: build stronger bridges between research, policy and practice 90

PART II. THE CASE STUDIES

Canada: Encouraging the Use of Summative Data for Formative Purposes 97
by Anne Sliwka, Marian Fushell, Martine Gauthier and Rick Johnson
Overview 97
Highlights from the case studies 97
Case study 1: Les Compagnons-de-Cartier, Ste-Foy 98
Case study 2: Sacred Heart Community School, Regina 104
Case study 3: Xavier School, Deer Lake 109

Denmark: Building on a Tradition of Democracy and Dialogue in Schools 117
by John Townshend, Lejf Moos and Poul Skov
Overview 117
Highlights from the case studies..118
Case study 1: Statens Pædagogiske Forsøgscenter (SPF)..............................118
Case study 2: Snejbjerg Skole 125

England: Implementing Formative Assessment in a High Stakes Environment ...129
by Janet Looney and Dylan Wiliam
Overview 129
Highlights from the case studies..132
Case study 1: Lord Williams's School 133
Case study 2: Seven Kings High School 138
Case study 3: Brighton Hill Community College 141
Case study 4: The Clere School..144

Finland: Emphasising Development instead of Competition and Comparison 149
by Joke Voogt and Helena Kasurinen
Overview 149
Highlights from the case studies..150
Case study 1: Tikkakoski Upper Comprehensive School............................150
Case study 2: Meilahti Upper Comprehensive School 156

Italy: A System in Transition..163
by Janet Looney, Cosimo Laneve and Maria Teresa Moscato
Overview 163
Highlights from the case studies..164
Case study 1: the Michelangelo School..165
Case study 2: the Testoni Fioravanti Unified School 171

New Zealand: Embedding Formative Assessment in Multiple Policy Initiatives ..177
by Janet Looney and Jenny Poskitt
Overview 177
Highlights from the case studies..179
Case study 1: Waitakere College 179
Case study 2: Rosehill College 184

Queensland, Australia: An Outcomes-based Curriculum 191
by Judy Sebba and Graham Maxwell
Overview 191
Highlights from the case studies..192
Case study 1: Our Lady's College 192
Case study 2: Woodridge State High School..198

Scotland: Developing a Coherent System of Assessment 205
by Anne Sliwka and Ernest Spencer
Overview 205
Highlights from the case studies 207
Case study 1: Forres Academy 207
Case study 2: John Ogilvie High School 214

PART III. THE LITERATURE REVIEWS

**Changing Teaching through Formative Assessment: Research and Practice
The King's-Medway-Oxfordshire Formative Assessment Project** 223
by Paul Black and Dylan Wiliam
Introduction 223
The research review 223
Moving into action 227
Reflections on the outcome 231
Research and practice 234
References 237

Formative Assessment of Learning: A Review of Publications in French 241
by Linda Allal and Lucie Mottier Lopez
Coverage of the review 242
Conceptualisation of formative assessment 243
Empirical research on formative assessment 252
Conclusion 256
References 256

**Formative Assessment in Classrooms: A Review of the Empirical
German Literature** 265
by Olaf Köller
Introduction and databases 265
Historical roots of formative assessment in Germany 266
Measures of alternative assessment in German schools 267
Marks vs. reports as assessment measures 269
Additional studies in Germany on formative assessment 271
Summary and some remarks on future directions in research on formative
    assessment in Germany 275
References 276

Executive Summary

Assessment is integral to the education process. The most visible assessments are summative, measuring what students have learnt through testing and examination, or holding schools accountable for student performance. But assessment can also be "formative". Formative assessment refers to frequent, interactive assessments of student progress and understanding. Teachers are then able to adjust teaching approaches to better meet identified learning needs.

Formative assessment differs from summative assessment in that the information gathered in the formative process is used to shape improvements, rather than serve as a summary of performances. The principles of formative assessment may be applied at the school and policy levels to identify areas for improvement and to promote constructive cultures of evaluation throughout education systems. Studies show that formative assessment is one of the most effective strategies for promoting high student performance. It is also important for improving the equity of student outcomes and developing students' "learning to learn" skills. But formative assessment is not practised systematically, particularly in lower secondary schools – the focus of this study – where barriers to innovation and change are often more difficult to overcome. These barriers include perceived tensions between classroom-based formative assessments and highly visible summative tests for school accountability (teachers tend to teach to the test), and a lack of connection between systemic, school and classroom approaches to assessment and evaluation.

This study looks at the practice of formative assessment in classrooms and schools in eight education systems: Australia (Queensland), Canada, Denmark, England, Finland, Italy, New Zealand and Scotland. It focuses on classroom practice to a greater degree than is usual in OECD studies. In taking this approach, the study gives shape to the concept of formative assessment as practised across these countries, and analyses how policies supporting the use of formative assessment can develop. It also suggests ways in which policy could better support the wider practice of formative assessment.

There are three major parts to the study:

- **Part I** offers the OECD analysis of case study findings and international research on formative assessment. The key findings are highlighted under the subheadings below.

- **Part II** presents the case study evidence gathered in each of the participating countries. The schools featured in the case studies were chosen because they provide useful examples of highly effective formative assessment in practice, and are therefore illustrative of what is possible. While there are common elements across the case studies, they also take a range of approaches to teaching and learning, including, for example, a co-operative learning programme in Scotland, a school focused on the use of ICT to re-shape teaching and learning in Québec, a programme designed to meet the cultural and learning needs of Maori students in New Zealand, and approaches to promoting democracy in Danish schools. Each case study begins with an overview of the policy context within which schools are working, describes teaching and assessment in classrooms and examines the ways in which school leaders guided the change process in their schools.

- **Part III** includes English, French and German literature reviews describing the context of formative assessment research in their respective traditions. The English literature review by Paul Black and Dylan Wiliam summarises findings from their highly influential 1998 review, and their subsequent experience in working with teachers to translate research into practice in a pilot programme. They observe that while much is known about the kinds of classrooms that promote effective learning, less is known about making it happen on a broader basis.

The review of the French language literature by Linda Allal and Lucie Mottier-Lopez has a particular focus on the concept of "regulation" (how teachers orchestrate learning for and with students). They emphasise the importance not only of providing students with feedback, but of adapting instruction to meet a variety of student needs and of providing them with skills and tools for self-assessment.

The review by Olaf Köller explores the German literature in educational psychology, primarily concerned with how students respond to various forms of feedback, a key element in formative assessment. The findings point to the greater impact of feedback based on individual progress toward learning goals, rather than comparison with other students.

Introducing the concept of formative assessment

Chapter 1 defines the concept of formative assessment and presents evidence regarding its effectiveness in improving student achievement, equity of educational outcomes, and learning to learn skills. The chapter suggests that the principles of formative assessment may be applied to identify areas for improvement and to promote effective and constructive cultures of evaluation from individual classrooms through to whole systems. The chapter concludes with an overview of the study scope and methodology.

Exploring the range of policy approaches

Chapter 2 introduces the range of policies the case study countries have developed to promote the broader practice of formative assessment. Transforming teaching and assessment approaches across education systems requires strong policy leadership, serious investment in training and professional development and innovative programmes, as well as appropriate policy incentives. The chapter builds a framework for analysing policy approaches. There is *legislation* promoting and supporting the practice of formative assessment and establishing it as a priority. There are efforts to encourage *the use of summative data for formative purposes*. *Guidelines* on effective teaching and formative assessment have been embedded in the national curriculum and other materials. There is the *provision of tools and exemplars* to support effective formative assessment. There are important *investments in special initiatives and innovative programmes* incorporating formative assessment approaches. There is also investment in *teacher professional development* for formative assessment. All education systems will need to strengthen the policy mix and to make deeper investments if they are to promote real changes in teaching and assessment throughout education systems.

Understanding the elements of formative assessment

Chapter 3 examines the elements of formative assessment as identified in the case study research and in the international literature, with the following six elements of classroom practice emerging consistently:

- Establishment of classroom cultures that encourage interaction and the use of assessment tools.

- Establishment of learning goals and tracking individual student progress toward goals.
- Use of varied instruction methods to meet diverse student needs.
- Use of varied approaches to assess student understanding.
- Feedback on student performance and adaptation of instruction to meet identified needs.
- Active involvement of students in the learning process.

Teachers in the case study schools in all eight countries had incorporated each of the six elements of formative assessment into regular practice, using the elements as a framework for teaching and learning. Many said they had made fundamental changes in their teaching – in their interactions with students, the way they set up learning situations and guided students toward learning goals, even how they thought about student success. Research also points to the importance of *how* teachers apply each of the elements in making an impact on student achievement.

Analysing formative assessment in practice

Chapter 4 provides vivid descriptions of each of the elements of formative assessment in practice. The examples, which are drawn from a diversity of settings, help to move the discussion of formative assessment from broad principles to a more concrete understanding of the changes formative approaches entail. The chapter describes specific approaches and techniques that teachers have used to encourage greater classroom interaction, to better gauge levels of student understanding, and to develop students' skills of self- and peer-assessment. Formative assessment requires hard work, as well as shifts in how teachers view their own roles and that of their students.

Addressing benefits and barriers in the school and classroom

Chapter 5 addresses the concerns of educators who may be sceptical about the ability of teachers and schools in general to take on formative assessment in the face of logistical challenges. The chapter draws on the case study material to show how teachers, after experimenting with a variety of techniques, were able to develop straightforward and ingenious solutions to problems such as large class size and extensive curriculum requirements. With experience, they also began to use formative assessment methods with students they considered as more challenging. The chapter also examines the vital role of school leaders in initiating, deepening and sustaining changes.

Meeting the policy challenges

Chapter 6 examines policy implications of the case study findings and identifies the ways in which policy can facilitate and encourage the wider practice of formative assessment. System-wide changes in teaching and assessment require strong policy leadership. This means that policy makers and officials need to send consistent messages about the importance of quality teaching and learning, of adapting teaching to meet diverse student needs, and of promoting students' skills for "learning to learn". Policy focused on teaching and learning should recognise complexity, be concerned with the *process* of learning, and draw upon a broad range of indicators and outcome measures to better understand how well schools and teachers are performing. The six policy principles discussed in the chapter are to:

- Keep the focus on teaching and learning.
- Align summative and formative assessment approaches.
- Ensure classroom, school and system level evaluations are linked and are used formatively to shape improvements at each level
- Invest in training and support for formative assessment.
- Encourage innovation.
- Build stronger bridges between research, policy and practice.

Part I
Thematic Discussion

Chapter 1
The Case for Formative Assessment

> Formative assessment refers to frequent, interactive assessments of student progress and understanding to identify learning needs and adjust teaching appropriately. This chapter shows how formative assessment promotes the goals of lifelong learning, including raising levels of student achievement, greater equity of student outcomes, and improved learning to learn skills. The chapter also discusses barriers to wider practice of formative assessment and ways in which those barriers can be addressed, and concludes with an outline of the study scope and methodology.

Assessment is vital to the education process. In schools, the most visible assessments are summative. Summative assessments are used to measure what students have learnt at the end of a unit, to promote students, to ensure they have met required standards on the way to earning certification for school completion or to enter certain occupations, or as a method for selecting students for entry into further education. Ministries or departments of education may use summative assessments and evaluations as a way to hold publicly funded schools accountable for providing quality education. Increasingly, international summative assessments – such as OECD's Programme for International Student Assessment (PISA) – have been important for comparing national education systems to developments in other countries.

But assessment may also serve a formative function. In classrooms, formative assessment refers to frequent, interactive assessments of student progress and understanding to identify learning needs and adjust teaching appropriately. Teachers using formative assessment approaches and techniques are better prepared to meet diverse students' needs – through differentiation and adaptation of teaching to raise levels of student achievement and to achieve a greater equity of student outcomes. But there are major barriers to wider practice, including perceived tensions between classroom-based formative assessments, and high visibility summative tests to hold schools accountable for student achievement, and a lack of connection between systemic, school and classroom approaches to assessment and evaluation.

The principles of formative assessment may be applied at the school and policy levels, to identify areas for improvement and to promote effective and constructive cultures of evaluation throughout education systems. More consistent use of formative assessment throughout education systems may help stakeholders address the very barriers to its wider practice in classrooms.

This chapter shows how formative assessment promotes the goals of lifelong learning, including higher levels of student achievement, greater equity of student outcomes, and improved learning to learn skills. The chapter then discusses barriers to wider practice of formative assessment and ways in which those barriers can be addressed, and outlines the study scope and methodology.

MEETING GOALS FOR LIFELONG LEARNING

Each of the national and regional governments participating in this study promotes formative assessment as a means to meeting the goals of lifelong learning. They are motivated by quantitative and qualitative evidence that teaching which incorporates formative assessment has helped to raise levels of student achievement, and has better enabled teachers to meet the needs of increasingly diverse student populations, helping to close gaps in equity of student outcomes. Teachers using formative assessment approaches guide students toward development of their own "learning to learn" skills – skills that are increasingly necessary as knowledge is quickly outdated in the information society.

Promoting high-performance: raising levels of student achievement

Formative assessment methods have been important to raising overall levels of student achievement. Quantitative and qualitative research on formative assessment has shown that it is perhaps one of the most important interventions for promoting high-performance ever studied. In their influential 1998 review of the English-language literature on formative assessment, Black and Wiliam concluded that:

> "... formative assessment does improve learning. The gains in achievement appear to be quite considerable, and as noted earlier, among the largest ever reported for educational interventions. As an illustration of just how big these gains are, an effect size of 0.7, if it could be achieved on a nationwide scale, would be equivalent to raising the mathematics attainment score of an 'average' country like England, New Zealand or the United States

into the 'top five' after the Pacific Rim countries of Singapore, Korea, Japan and Hong Kong." (Beaton *et al.*, 1996, Black and Wiliam, 1998, p. 61)

These findings provide a strong foundation for further research on effective teaching, learning and assessment strategies (including the present study).

Promoting high-equity: education for all

The "What Works" case studies support the idea that formative assessment methods may help create greater equity of student outcomes. Although Black and Wiliam (1998 and in Part III of this study) note that research on the effectiveness of formative assessment is lacking in regard to underachieving students or students' race, class, or gender, it is worth noting that several of the case study schools with large percentages of "disadvantaged" students had moved from "failing" to exemplary status over the past several years. Case study schools featuring programmes specifically targeted to the needs of underachieving students also yielded positive results.

Teachers in the case study schools used formative assessment to establish factors lying behind the variation in students' achievements in specific subjects, and to adapt teaching to address identified needs. Such approaches represent a move away from models of equity that suggest that all children should receive exactly the same inputs (they are "indifferent to difference", Perrenoud suggests [1998]), or "deficit" models that identify certain children as "disadvantaged". Instead, teachers adjust methods to recognise individual, cultural, and linguistic differences between children (see for example, Bruner 1996; Bishop and Glynn, 1999).

Building students' skills for learning to learn

Formative assessment builds students' "learning to learn" skills by:

- Placing emphasis on the *process* of teaching and learning, and actively involving students in that process.
- Building students' skills for peer- and self-assessment.
- Helping students understand their own learning, and develop appropriate strategies for "learning to learn".

Students who are actively building their understanding of new concepts (rather than merely absorbing information), who have developed a variety of strategies that enable them to place new ideas into a larger context, and who are learning to judge the quality of their own and their peer's work against well-defined learning goals and criteria, are also developing skills that are invaluable for learning throughout their lives.

ADDRESSING BARRIERS TO WIDER PRACTICE

The major (although not the only) barriers to wider practice of formative assessment that emerged from the case studies include:

- The tension between classroom-based formative assessments of student learning, and high visibility summative tests – that is, large-scale national or regional assessments of student performance that are intended to hold schools accountable for meeting standards, and that may hold particular consequences for low or underperforming schools. Too often, highly visible summative tests used to hold schools accountable for student achievement drive what happens in classrooms.

- A lack of connection between systemic, school and classroom approaches to assessment and evaluation. Too often, information gathered through national or regional monitoring systems, or even in school-based evaluations, is seen as irrelevant or unhelpful to the business of teaching. Too often, information gathered in classrooms is seen as irrelevant to the business of policy making.

Addressing the formative-summative tension

While teachers often express ambivalence or resistance to external summative tests, there is nothing inherent in summative assessment to prevent teachers from using formative methods. Indeed, summative results can be used formatively. Yet, in several countries, summative assessments have dominated political debate over education. Often, schools with poor results on public examinations face major consequences, such as threatened shut-downs, reconstitution, or firing of teachers.

In environments where summative tests have high visibility, teachers often feel compelled to "teach to the test", and students are encouraged to meet performance goals (to perform well on tests) at the expense of learning goals (that is, to understand and master new knowledge). Many – if not most – teachers perceive these external assessments as being in conflict with – or even inimical to – the practice of formative assessment. Poorly designed external tests, media league tables which use a narrow set of data to compare performance across schools, and lack of connection between tests and curriculum can also inhibit innovation.

Note that, for the purposes of this study, assessment refers to judgments of student performance, while evaluation refers to judgements of programme or organisational effectiveness. In all cases, the use of data to inform teacher planning of future classroom activities, or at the national level to inform and adapt policies, might be considered as secondary levels of formative assessment. (See the distinction in Allal and Mottier Lopez, included in Part III of this study, between primary use of formative assessment which directly benefits the students who were assessed and secondary uses which foster broader transformations of instruction.)

Strengthening cultures of evaluation

One of the particular interests for this study has been in examining how teachers and school leaders create or strengthen cultures of evaluation. In a culture of evaluation, teachers and school leaders use information on students to generate new knowledge on what works and why, share their knowledge with colleagues, and build their ability to address a greater range of their students' learning needs.

A culture of evaluation refers to the development of a shared language regarding the goals of learning and teaching, as well as a shared understanding of the purposes of evaluation in meeting these goals. Several OECD countries support school-based evaluation as a key component, either as the primary or only form of school-level evaluation, or as a complement to external testing, inspections and programme evaluation. All education stakeholders are thus focused on developing strategies for school improvement. School-based evaluation helps school leaders and teachers to focus their attention on resources and organisational challenges, and to develop solutions appropriate to their circumstances.

The idea of school-based evaluation is quite appealing because it involves school staff directly, incorporates local knowledge, and potentially, directly shapes school improvement. However, school-based evaluation is not always well aligned with the work of schools. Evaluation tools may be more suited to the needs of policy officials than they are to schools and teachers. Moreover, the skills required for gathering and interpreting school or programme level data are quite different than those required for classroom assessment (Monsen, 2002; Simmons, 2002; Lander and Ekholm, 1998).

Some countries that do not now have external examinations and/or inspection systems are considering adopting such approaches to ensure greater school accountability. By contrast, a few countries that have promoted external examinations are paying greater attention to the potential for school-based evaluation to shape school improvement. Policy officials can learn much from the experiences of their counterparts. No matter which approach is chosen, assessment and evaluation are only really effective if the data gathered at different levels are taken into account throughout systems.

Ideally, information gathered in assessments and evaluations is used to shape strategies for improvement at each level of the education system. At the classroom level, teachers gather information on student understanding, and adjust teaching to meet identified learning needs. At the school level, school leaders use information to identify areas of strength and weakness across the school, and to develop strategies for improvement. At the policy level, officials use information gathered through national or regional tests, or through monitoring of school performance, to guide investments in training and support for schools and teachers, or to set broad priorities for education. In this way, summative information is used formatively at each level of the system (see Figure 1.1). Teachers, school leaders and policy officials are more likely to use assessment information when assessments are well coordinated, and it is clear why and how the information is relevant to their work.

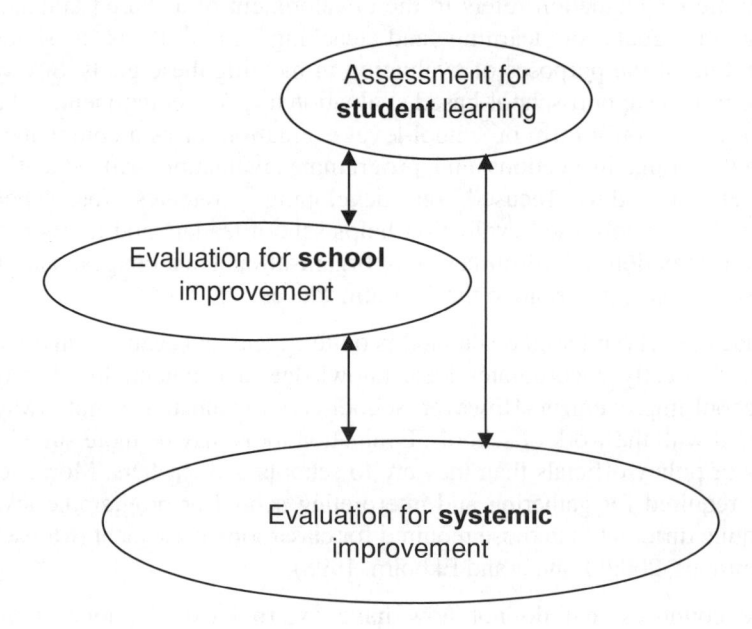

Figure 1.1. Coordinating assessment and evaluation

Assessment for **student** learning

Evaluation for **school** improvement

Evaluation for **systemic** improvement

Note: Information gathered at each level of the system can be used to identify strengths and weaknesses, and to shape strategies for improvement.

Source: Authors.

Formative assessment – while not a "silver bullet" that can solve all educational challenges – offers a powerful means for meeting goals for high-performance, high-equity of student outcomes, and for providing students with knowledge and skills for lifelong learning. Systems that address tensions that prevent wider practice of formative assessment and that foster cultures of evaluation are likely to make much greater progress toward these goals.

STUDY GOALS AND METHODOLOGY

What can be done to address major barriers to formative assessment? How can policies promote stronger evaluation cultures so that data are used to shape improvements throughout the system (in teaching, in school and in policy leadership)? This study aims to address these questions and to give more shape to the concept of formative assessment as practiced across the participating countries by:

- Bringing together findings from English, French and German-language research reviews on formative assessment (Part III of this study). The international literature reviews have helped to identify common threads among various approaches to teaching and student assessment across countries with different education traditions.

- Examining the range of policy approaches to promoting formative assessment across the case study countries, and the barriers to and opportunities for wider practice.

- Learning more about how teachers have taken on policies and research, and have adapted and made them their own.

International researchers note that, as of yet, there is no "theory of formative assessment". Understanding the elements of effective formative processes is therefore still very much an inductive endeavour. The study aims to clarify and strengthen concepts of formative assessment through international analysis. The study also delineates a framework for understanding the range of policy approaches to promoting formative assessment.

Because the study is international, it presents a broad array of conceptual and policy approaches to formative assessment. The study also helps to reinforce those elements that stand out most consistently as essential to quality teaching and student assessment. Cross-country analysis provides the opportunity to share lessons regarding how teachers, school leaders and policy officials have addressed barriers and realised benefits through formative assessment.

The study includes 19 case studies from exemplary, lower secondary schools in: Canada, Denmark, England, Finland, Italy, New Zealand, Scotland, and the state of Queensland in Australia. Country experts helped to identify suitable cases for the "What Works" study. Criteria for case study selection were as follows:

- To focus on formative assessments used in connection with *deliberate instructional strategies*, illustrating examples of coordinated teaching and assessment strategies that responded to learning styles, skills, interests, and student motivations. Where possible, the case studies needed also to illustrate strategies that promote teachers' abilities to diagnose learning needs, their assessment literacy, and, importantly, their knowledge and capacity to use this in their teaching, individually and collectively.

- To provide *evidence* of "what works". To the extent possible, the cases needed to provide evidence that learning was significantly enhanced by the approach taken.

- To be from the *lower secondary* level. The study was particularly interested in identifying schools that had made significant strides in overcoming powerful bureaucratic constraints – most often found in lower secondary schools – to promote innovation. In addition, students in lower secondary schools are often more vulnerable to developing poor images of their own learning skills, and losing motivation for learning. (Note, however, that formative assessment teaching methods are relevant to students of all ages, including the very young and adult learners.)

- To *involve "whole-school" approaches*. The intention here was to ensure that studies of "what works" in innovation were not limited to one or a few classrooms in the schools visited. Case studies had to illustrate how schools had built their capacity to share knowledge and to influence and build each other's practice.

- To be *embedded in a policy process* or broader initiative that could offer lessons for "scaling-up". Often, policy reforms are limited to a few classrooms, or to a few very high functioning schools.

- To offer lessons of *relevance to the majority* of schools, rather than apply only to very specific sections of the secondary student population. The schools examined needed to offer lessons that would also be applicable to mainstream schools – and not just part of a special initiative with no hope for scaling-up or further dissemination.

The international case studies and literature reviews conducted for the "What Works" study have allowed a thorough examination of the concepts underlying formative assessment, the range of related policy approaches, and common barriers and benefits across countries. While there are inevitable challenges to promoting wider practice of formative assessment across education systems or to addressing organisational and logistical challenges at the school level, the rewards are also likely to be considerable. Formative assessment holds significant promise for improving educational outcomes for individual students, as well as transforming cultures of evaluation across education systems.

References

Beaton, A.E. *et al.* (1996), *Mathematics Achievement in the Middle School Years*, Boston College, Boston, MA.

Bishop, R. and T. Glynn (1999), *Culture Counts: Changing Power Relations in Education*, Dunmore Press, Palmerston North, New Zealand.

Black P. and D. William (1998), "Assessment and Classroom learning", *Assessment in Education: Principles, Policy and Practice,* CARFAX, Oxfordshire, Vol. 5, No.1, pp. 7-74.

Bruner, J. (1996), *The Culture of Education*, Harvard University Press, Cambridge, MA.

Lander, R. and M. Ekholm (1998), "School Evaluation and Improvement: A Scandinavian view" in A. Hargreaves, A. Lieberman, M. Fullan and D. Hopkins (eds.), *International Handbook of Educational Change*, Kluwer Academic Publishers, Dondrecht, the Netherlands, pp. 1119-1134.

Monsen, L.I. (2002), "School-based Evaluation in Norway: Why is it so Difficult to Convince Teachers of its Usefulness?" in D. Nevo (ed.), *School-based Evaluation: An International Perspective*, JAI Press, Oxford, pp. 73-88.

Perrenoud, P. (1998), "From Formative Evaluation to a Controlled Regulation of Learning Processes. Towards a Wider Conceptual Field", *Assessment in Education: Principles, Policy and Practice*, CARFAX, Oxfordshire, Vol. 5, No. 1, pp. 85-102.

Simmons, H. (2002), "School Self-evaluation in a Democracy", *School-Based Evaluation* in D. Nevo (ed.), *School-based Evaluation: An International Perspective*, JAI Press, Oxford, pp. 17-34.

Chapter 2
Policy Frameworks

> Transformation of teaching and assessment approaches across education requires strong policy leadership, serious investments in training and professional development and in innovative programmes, and incentives for change. This chapter introduces the range of policy approaches case study countries have developed to promote broader practice of formative assessment. All countries will need to strengthen the mix of strategies they are using and to make deeper investments if they are to promote real changes in teaching and assessment throughout education systems.

Teachers face many competing pressures on a daily basis. Without support and special opportunities to test innovative approaches, it is difficult for them to take on new and more demanding approaches to teaching and formative assessment. At a minimum, teachers need support from colleagues and school leaders as they make changes to their practice. But transformation of teaching and assessment approaches across education systems also requires strong policy leadership, serious investments in training and professional development and in innovative programmes, and appropriate policy incentives.

Policies can encourage and facilitate, but cannot mandate the kinds of deep changes in teaching and formative assessment discussed in this study. The policies, therefore, focus on building teachers' and school leaders' capacity, creating opportunities for innovation, and providing incentives for change. This chapter delineates a framework for understanding the range of policy approaches to promoting effective formative assessment, drawing on examples from the case study countries.

Each of the case study countries has made important strides in advancing the practice of formative assessment. Countries that use a mix of approaches and that make important investments in promoting change and building capacity are likely to push changes much further. The primary policy approaches, which are explored in more detail in the following pages, are:

- *Legislation* supporting the practice of formative assessment and establishing it as a priority.

- Efforts to *encourage the use of summative data for formative purposes* at the school and classroom levels.

- *Guidelines* on effective teaching and formative assessment practices embedded in national curriculum and other materials.

- *Provision of tools and exemplars* to support effective formative assessment.

- Investment in *special initiatives and innovative programmes* incorporating formative assessment approaches.

- Investment in *teacher professional development* for formative assessment.

It should be noted that change is easier in smaller systems, where communication is more direct. But all systems can learn from the experiences of the case study countries – which include both large and small education systems – in their efforts to balance formative and summative assessments, and to better link assessment and evaluation at each level of the system.

LEGISLATION PROMOTING THE PRACTICE OF FORMATIVE ASSESSMENT

In **Denmark** and **Italy,** formative assessment is accorded high visibility in legislation promoting its regular use. The Act governing the Danish *Folkeskoler* system requires schools to make comprehensive and versatile assessments of the "benefits of schooling", and to share these with parents and pupils. According to the Act, assessments are to be integrated into teaching, should serve as the basis for guidance that teachers give to individuals students, and shape the adaptation of teaching methods. The Act stresses that students should be active participants in the assessment process.

The Danish Ministry has more recently proposed the development of national learning standards, and student achievement tests to be administered at key points in students' school careers. Education stakeholders are making efforts to balance effective formative practices with the more recent focus on school accountability and the drive to raise levels of student achievement.

Italy first placed formative assessment on the national agenda in 1977 with legislation introducing the national "valuation form". Teachers are required to use the valuation form to compile data on their students, including information on what has been taught, any discipline issues, and results of assessment (including social, behavioural, cognitive and metacognitive factors). The form is intended to facilitate communication between school leaders, teachers and students. Students are to be kept informed of the preliminary planning of the subjects and of the teaching schedule, and of marks when they are reported in the register. For primary and lower secondary students, marks are qualitative rather than quantitative.

Nevertheless, Ministry officials note that teaching remains fairly "traditional" in the majority of secondary schools. As a recent Ministry report notes, "[a]ctive didactics, group work, *cooperative learning* are forms that are beginning to be more frequent in nursery and primary school, while they are still rare experiences in the secondary school … [T]he impression is that teachers are aware of the need of innovation and, at the same time, they resist in front of tasks for which they do not feel professionally prepared". (Ministry of Instruction and University Research, 2003, "Attracting, Developing and Retaining Effective Teachers", Country Background Report on Italy, OECD, Paris, *www.oecd.org/dataoecd/54/7/17997702.pdf*, p. 107)

More recent legislation may help remedy these problems. Legislation authorised in March 2003 is aimed at reinforcing the use of formative assessment in classrooms. The reform incorporates the principle of "personalisation". Personalisation refers to differentiation of curricular content and tasks to address learning and cultural differences and special or different educational needs. The reform promotes the "learning laboratory" as a way to tailor teaching methods by providing students with the chance to integrate learning from different classes, engage in hands-on learning and group work, and to study subjects in more depth. The 2003 reform also creates the position of tutor/co-ordinator for each class. The co-ordinators, who are to have teacher training, will be responsible for gathering data from students and talking with families. The teacher can adapt interventions according to the student's needs.

ENCOURAGING THE USE OF SUMMATIVE DATA FOR FORMATIVE PURPOSES AT SCHOOL AND CLASSROOM LEVELS

The use of data for planning of *future* classroom activities (or at the policy level, for adjustment of policies) might be considered as a secondary level of formative assessment (see the distinction in Allal and Mottier Lopez, in Part III of this study, between primary use of formative assessment which directly benefits the students who are assessed and secondary uses which foster broader transformations of instruction). These approaches come closest to reflecting the 3-tiered model introduced in Chapter 1, which links evaluation for systemic improvement, evaluation for school improvement, and assessment for student learning. Countries promote this objective through various means.

Denmark and **Finland** have placed primary emphasis on the importance of school and student self-evaluation. In 1999, the Danish Ministry's Quality in the *Folkeskole* programme published a number of school self-evaluation tools on the web for schools to use at their discretion. Schools are encouraged to use these tools to assess their own performance in a formative way. In addition to looking at students' performance, teachers are encouraged to evaluate the breadth and content of their own teaching. If teaching is limited, then formative assessments of students' work will give a limited picture of students' potential, so the web-based tools are intended to help teachers with this level of evaluation.

The Danish Ministry is now exploring ways to encourage more rigorous approaches and to further develop evaluation cultures in schools. The Danish Evaluation Institute (EVA) has noted, for instance, that there is confusion about evaluation methods and tools that are appropriate for continuous evaluation in classrooms. Potential remedies will include the introduction of standards for student achievement, which will provide schools with better benchmarks (standards are now under development), and further professional development for teachers on appropriate use of data for planning and strategy development.

In **Finland**, the main idea behind school and student self-evaluation is that it is more important to focus on school development through self-assessment than comparison (among schools or among students). Not only the outcomes of evaluation are important, but also the process, because the results of evaluation can serve as a foundation for further development. Therefore, in 1993, Finland's National Board of Education launched a project to develop school self-evaluation practices. The aim of the project is to develop suitable self-evaluation models for different types of educational institutions. The models allow for diversity in educational institutions, but also offer means to municipalities and schools to systematically evaluate the processes of teaching and learning and achievement outcomes. This project could be considered the start of the recognition of self-evaluation as a core concept in the Finnish education system.

The Finnish Ministry of Education monitors the extent to which the objectives set in statutes, education policy decisions and national core curricula are achieved. The purpose of the national evaluation system is to produce information on the quality of learning outcomes. The results of these evaluations are utilised in the development of the education system and core curricula, as well as in practical teaching work. The national evaluation system also supports educational institutions and teachers in the continuous reform of education, on the one hand, and the production and dissemination of diverse, up-to-date and reliable information on the functionality and results of the institutions and the entire education, on the other hand.

In **Canada**, all provinces and territories participate in a national assessment programme to assess student achievement in mathematics, reading and writing, and science on a four-year cycle. Each province and territory receives its own results as well as an analysis by sub-test. Provinces may then conduct a secondary analysis to shape teaching practices. The three Canadian provinces participating in the study, Newfoundland and Labrador, Saskatchewan, and Québec, encourage schools to use school-level data in school planning.

Before 2002, when **Saskatchewan** Learning in Canada began an Assessment for Learning pilot, no large-scale assessment data for individual schools or school divisions had been made available to schools or to the public. Prior to that time not every school in Saskatchewan gathered assessment data, and not all those who did made use of the data in a systematic fashion. In the face of growing pressure from parents and communities for greater educational accountability, the province started to gather assessment data. However, most educators and administrators in Saskatchewan are strongly convinced that change has to occur at the individual school level. For this reason, the debate about the meaning of any assessment data should primarily take place in each school itself.

Due to the comprehensive and detailed nature of the data provided to schools, local school boards provide resources for each schools' leadership team to attend data-interpretation workshops. No data are given to a school whose leadership team has not attended the data interpretation workshop. These workshops are clearly focused on the idea of assessment for school learning. Schools can use data to help set goals, allocate resources and plan interventions in areas that require improvement, as well as celebrate areas of strength and improvement.

Since 2001, the Department of Education in **Newfoundland and Labrador** has tested student performance in language arts and mathematics on an annual basis. The Department advocates that the results of provincial tests be explicitly linked to school development. In some districts, schools are required to respond to the test data by completing a written analysis of how the school will use the data to improve the quality of instruction and which specific targets the school sets for itself using the data analysis. Testing has changed the culture of communication about school achievement in Newfoundland and Labrador and has triggered communication at various levels. Slightly more than ten years ago, assessment was hardly talked about in schools; now it is driving the change and school development process, and there is little resistance to it. All school districts are using the test results in a formative manner.

In the early 1990s Her Majesty's Inspectors of Education in **Scotland** published school self-assessment and development planning guidelines that schools could use on a voluntary basis. Since 2001, all schools have been required to use these guidelines to develop school plans. The plans are to refer to data on student performance as gathered in national examinations for 16-year-olds and on attainment levels for students between the ages of 5 and 14 (as established in official targets). School plans are expected to evaluate and improve learning and teaching practices. The plans are shared with parents and published in school outreach materials and on websites.

In **New Zealand**, schools are required to develop their own charters, and to set benchmarks for performance. The national Education Review Office (ERO) inspects schools, monitoring their effectiveness and whether they are meeting commitments made in individual school charters. Schools typically view ERO reviews as an opportunity to reflect on their strategy and practice, and welcome inspectors into the schools. In turn, the ERO invites teachers from other schools to participate in the ERO process. Teachers view their participation in ERO as an opportunity for professional development.

Italian schools are required to evaluate the success of prior efforts and to plan for the next year in an annual Plan of Formative Offer (POF). The POF is to include a description of: the organisation of teaching time; school-based research and development; and, teaching methodologies to be used in meeting educational objectives. The POF is formally approved by the *consiglio di circolo* (boards of school, students and families' representatives).

GUIDELINES ON EFFECTIVE TEACHING AND ASSESSMENT PRACTICES EMBEDDED IN NATIONAL CURRICULUM AND OTHER MATERIALS

Several countries have introduced new curriculum guidelines that incorporate advice on integrating formative assessment into lessons on a systematic basis. England, New Zealand, Scotland and the state of Queensland, Australia, provide valuable examples of this approach.

In 2000, the Department for Education and Skills (DfES) in **England** introduced the Assessment for Learning (AfL) programme, targeting pilots to Key Stage 3 schools – that is, lower secondary schools. AfL provides teachers, school leaders, local education authorities and other stakeholders with guidance and resources on the principles of good classroom assessment, as supported in research. DfES promises also to provide a repertoire of teaching strategies and tools from which schools and teachers may choose, based on students' needs and the school's goals and priorities.

In **New Zealand**, assessment for learning has been a key part of the national assessment strategy since 1999. The National Assessment Strategy is designed to help teachers gather and use high quality assessment information to raise achievement and reduce educational inequities. It is embedded in multiple national policies, including guidance in the curriculum framework and the National Administration Guidelines (NAGS). The guidelines establish learning goals ("achievement objectives"), and describe the importance of diagnostic and formative assessment for enhancing teaching and learning. Achievement objectives are intended to provide the basis for planning programmes, assessing student progress, and providing students with clear concepts of learning goals.

Scotland has introduced its own version of the Assessment is for Learning (AiFL) development programme. The AiFL builds on national guidelines on assessment for 5-14 year-old students which were first published in 1990. The guidelines encourage teachers to think systematically about assessment as an integrated part of learning and teaching. They advise that summative judgments should occur only occasionally and should be based on a large amount of class work. In English language and mathematics, when it is clear that a student shows full command of the subject for his or her level, the teacher selects a National Assessment from an electronic bank available from the Scottish Qualifications Authority (SQA). The results of this test are intended to confirm the teacher's judgment. Teachers administer a National Assessment test when they consider it appropriate; there is no "test day" for all at the same time.

The Scottish Executive Education Department (SEED) is now extending the new concept of "Personal Learning Planning" (PLP). PLP emphasises the importance of interaction between student and teacher, and of building students' skills of reflection. Students, with the support of teachers and parents, are expected to take greater responsibility for their own progress toward individually established learning aims.

Almost all of the assessment in **Queensland** schools for all year levels (P-12) is school-based (teacher designed and managed). This applies even for the end-of-school certificate awarded on the basis of study in Years 11 and 12. There have been no external examinations in Queensland since 1972. For the end-of-school certificate, a system of moderation based on panels of expert teachers provides advice to schools on the quality of their assessment procedures and the quality of their judgments of performance standards. Over the two years leading to the certificate, assessment is continuous and all assessments are used formatively. In these years, schools have highly developed feedback processes, including rubrics for providing students with feedback on the standards of their performance on the assessment tasks. These processes foster conversations between teachers and students about what represents a good performance, how well student have performed, and what they can do to improve further.

A key concept is the integration of formative and summative uses of assessment. In addition to their formative uses, assessments also contribute summatively to the student's final result. Student portfolios are selectively updated over time. This means that earlier performance is replaced by later (improved) performance relating to the same learning outcomes. Students therefore have an incentive to learn from feedback. The students' final results depend on the latest evidence of their performance across all course requirements.

This form of integration of formative and summative assessment is also practiced in the primary and lower secondary years to some extent, and is supported by professional networks and "copying" of senior secondary practice, and is promoted in recently introduced key learning area syllabuses. At all year levels, teacher-directed assessments are used for feedback and for reporting to parents. Existing guidelines emphasise strongly that assessment should be integral to teaching and learning, include feedback to students about their progress, and assist in the development of self-directed learners. Semester reports involve summative judgements based on the accumulated evidence of student performance.

PROVISION OF TOOLS AND TEACHING RESOURCES TO SUPPORT FORMATIVE ASSESSMENT

To enhance assessment literacy in the system the Department of Education in **Newfoundland and Labrador, Canada,** disseminates rubrics for use in primary, elementary, and intermediate schools. Rubrics provide specific guidelines and criteria for evaluating student work. For example, a rubric for an essay might tell students that their work will be judged on organisation, purpose, detail, vocabulary and "mechanics" (spelling, punctuation, grammar). A good rubric also describes levels of quality for each of the criteria, usually on a point scale. In other words, rubrics help students and teachers define quality. Developing rubrics takes time but in the long run, the rubrics save time because they force teachers to reflect carefully on learning objectives and criteria.

The **New Zealand** Ministry of Education has also supported the development of a number of tools for formative assessment. These include Assessment Tools for Teaching and Learning (asTTle) for assessing literacy and numeracy from years 5 to 10, in English and te reo Maori, and national curriculum exemplars for students in years 1-10 in all curriculum areas. The asTTle are a key component of both the government's literacy and numeracy assessment strategies. Teachers use the tools to evaluate the impact of teaching approaches on student achievement, and when necessary, to adjust teaching to better meet student needs. The national exemplars include annotated work samples and feature sample teacher-student dialogues and written teacher comments, showing how teachers might assess the student work in a formative manner, and in a way that is sensitive to different learning and communication styles of students. They are available in print form and on-line. Many are also supported by video clips.

SPECIAL INITIATIVES AND INNOVATIVE PROGRAMMES

Several schools included in the case study countries participated in pilot or other special projects before deciding to adopt formative assessment teaching methods. Certainly, their participation in special projects signals that these are schools that are more open to innovation and change, and is likely one of the reasons the schools have come to the attention of researchers. Their participation in these projects also helped to prepare the ground for further change.

As participants in special projects, teachers have, in many cases, received additional professional development opportunities, and occasionally, benefited from additional resources. For example, teachers involved in the Maori Mainstream Programme (MMP, *Te Kotahitanga*, in the Maori language) at Waitakere College in **New Zealand** have had a half-time, on-site facilitator. The facilitator works with experts on Maori education at the University of Waikato, brings readings and relevant research to teachers involved in the programme, shares practical ideas on how to address challenges in the classroom, and observes classes. The facilitator is also formative in her own interactions with the teachers. The programme represents a heavy expenditure on the part of the Ministry, however, and policy makers have implemented a variety of professional development models in schools participating in the MMP in order to determine the optimal level of investment.

Teachers at the Bologna School in Bari, **Italy**, played an important role in piloting the national valuation form. Between 1985 and 1995, the Michelangelo School was among a small number of schools selected by the Italian Ministry of Education to participate in a project to revise the national valuation form, which had been in use since 1977. Several of the teachers who participated in the demonstration project recall that the experience of working on this project was key to shaping a strong working relationship among them. In 1995, the current valuation form became a part of regular practice in Italian schools. Teachers at Bari have continued to discuss and revise their approaches to assessment as a group.

INVESTMENTS IN TEACHER PROFESSIONAL DEVELOPMENT

Formative assessment requires deep changes in overall approaches to teaching and assessment, as well as the development of new habits and integration of new techniques into daily teaching. Teachers greatly benefit from professional development, mentoring and peer feedback when making these types of changes.

In 1998, the **New Zealand** Ministry introduced the Assess to Learn (AToL) professional development programme. AToL encourages teachers to review current assessment practices, and to incorporate recently developed national assessment tools into their practice in formative ways. AToL programmes are intended to support implementation of new curriculum statements or programmes that meet high priority goals of the Ministry (such as the Ministry's literacy and numeracy programme, and the new National Certificate Examination Award). Apart from these special programmes, however, the Ministry does not require teachers to update their skills on a regular basis.

Queensland has a variety of in-service workshops and professional development opportunities for teachers on assessment. At the senior secondary school level, professional workshops assist teachers in implementing assessment in the subjects they teach. Teacher practice is supported by strong professional networks and professional subject-based organisations. Service on moderation panels (discussed above) is recognised as providing powerful professional development for panellists, and many schools encourage their staff to seek panel membership. Feedback from moderation panels to schools involves teachers in discussions on their assessment practices, both within their school and with the relevant panel. Being wholly responsible for student assessment, teachers continually reflect on their assessment practice and consider how it can be improved. Assessment practice is therefore always evolving.

The situation in the earlier years (primary and lower secondary) is much less externally directed. There is no formal certificate issued to students in these years. Consequently, leverage for professional improvement is weaker. However, regular workshops for teachers and schools are offered by the Queensland Studies Authority (QSA) on teaching and assessing students using the recently introduced key learning area syllabuses. In addition, the three education sectors (State schools, Catholic schools and Independent schools) run their own workshops for teachers and support programmes for schools directed at improving the quality of teachers' use of assessment to assist student learning.

DEVELOPING STRONGER POLICY STRATEGIES

Each of the case study countries has established formative assessment as a high priority. These policies recognise that much of the hard work of reform takes place at the school and classroom level, and that change also requires policy leadership as well as the development of specific tools and support to carry this work through.

Several of the countries use a mix of strategies to promote wider practice of formative assessment. Yet, all countries will need to strengthen the mix of policies and to make deeper investments if they are to promote real changes in teaching and assessment throughout education systems. The greater the range of strategies included in any country's policy mix, the more consistent the messages regarding the importance of formative assessment will be, the more strategic the investment of resources, and the more likely change in culture at all levels of the education system.

Chapter 3
The Elements of Formative Assessment:
Case Study Findings and Supporting Research

> Several key elements emerged consistently in the case study classrooms and in international research on formative assessment. When teachers regularly draw upon each of these key elements, they create new frameworks for teaching and learning. The chapter refers to selected research to illustrate the importance of each of the elements in promoting learning. *How* teachers apply the elements of formative assessment is also important to impact.

Many teachers already incorporate aspects of formative assessment in their practice – regularly interacting with students, and adjusting teaching to meet identified student needs. But, as teachers in several of the case study schools confessed, prior to establishing formative assessment as an overall framework for teaching, their own use of formative methods had been somewhat haphazard.

School leaders and teachers in the case study schools were motivated to bring discipline to their use of formative assessment through their participation in research or pilot projects, or in response to national or regional policies promoting formative assessment. Many said they had made fundamental changes in their approaches to teaching – in their interactions with students, the way they set up learning situations and guided students toward learning goals – even in the way they thought about student success.

Because the case study countries do not share a common definition of formative assessment, "What Works" national experts used a broad definition of formative assessment in locating exemplary schools. They identified cases where teachers were using coordinated teaching and assessment strategies to respond to student predispositions, learning styles, skills, interests, and/or motivations.

The key elements that have emerged from the case studies and related research are:

1. Establishment of a classroom culture that encourages interaction and the use of assessment tools.
2. Establishment of learning goals, and tracking of individual student progress toward those goals.
3. Use of varied instruction methods to meet diverse student needs.
4. Use of varied approaches to assessing student understanding.
5. Feedback on student performance and adaptation of instruction to meet identified needs.
6. Active involvement of students in the learning process.

What is most striking about the case study findings is that in all cases, teachers had incorporated each of the six elements into regular practice. While teachers may have placed different emphases on the various elements (for example, some teachers placed greater stress on providing students with feedback; other teachers were more focused on providing students with a variety of learning opportunities), they used each of these elements to shape teaching and assessment. Teachers thus created a framework, language and tools, using the elements of formative assessment to shape their approach to teaching and learning.

This chapter looks more closely at each of the elements of formative assessment as identified in the case study schools. The chapter refers to selected supporting research for each of the elements. The research also points to the importance of *how* teachers apply the elements of formative assessment to their impact on student achievement, including underachieving students, and in helping students to develop learning to learn skills.

Across the case study schools, teachers referred to research as they built their facility with formative assessment. They paid particular attention to how they were using formative approaches and the impact of new methods on student learning. The formative assessment methods spurred teachers' interest in exploring learning theories in more depth, and in experimenting with new teaching methods. Research in the area of formative assessment (and related teaching strategies) has had an unusually strong impact on practice.

The Elements of Formative Assessment

The case study findings are consistent with elements identified in English and French language literature reviews in Part III of this study (also see Black and Wiliam, 1998). Black and Wiliam in their extensive review of the English-language literature on formative assessment, "Assessment and Classroom Learning" (1998), consider formative assessment as involving four elements:

- Establishment of a standard or expected level of student performance.
- Gathering of information on a student's current performance.
- Development of a mechanism to compare the two performance levels.
- Development of a mechanism to alter the gap.

Assessment is "formative" when the information gathered is actually used to alter the student's performance gap.

Allal and Mottier Lopez extend this definition in their review of the French-language literature (Part III of this study) by placing a particular emphasis on how teachers organise and orchestrate learning as an important element of formative assessment. This includes:

- The actions that teachers and students actually carry out to alter a learning gap or to arrive at a shared vision of learning objectives.
- The degree of student involvement in the assessment process.
- The meaning attributed by teachers and students to assessment practices and to their effects.

These elements situate formative assessment in a classroom culture involving interaction among teachers and students and the use of assessment tools (Allal and Mottier Lopez, Part III of this study).

Figure 3.1 summarises the understanding of formative assessment developed through the "What Works" case studies and the literature reviews informing this study.

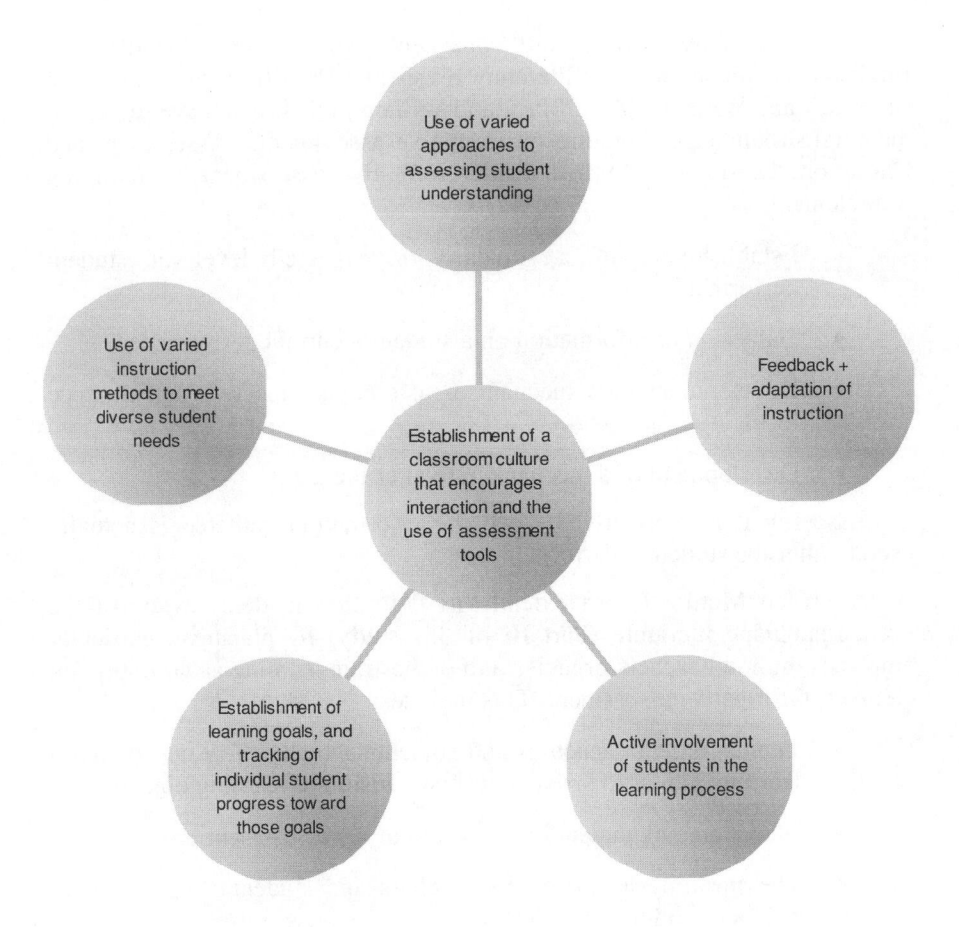

Figure 3.1. The six key elements of formative assessment

- Use of varied approaches to assessing student understanding
- Use of varied instruction methods to meet diverse student needs
- Feedback + adaptation of instruction
- Establishment of a classroom culture that encourages interaction and the use of assessment tools
- Establishment of learning goals, and tracking of individual student progress toward those goals
- Active involvement of students in the learning process

Note: Teachers across the case study schools used formative assessment as a framework for teaching and learning. Culture change was central to creating and sustaining regular practice of formative assessment. Teachers drew upon each of these elements to create a dynamic teaching and learning environment and to move students toward learning goals.

Source: Authors.

ELEMENT 1: ESTABLISHMENT OF A CLASSROOM CULTURE THAT ENCOURAGES INTERACTION AND THE USE OF ASSESSMENT TOOLS

The concept of formative assessment was first introduced in 1971 by Bloom, Hastings and Maddaus. They formally introduced the idea that assessment needs not be used solely to make summative evaluations of student performance, arguing that teachers should include episodes of formative assessment following phases of teaching. During these episodes teachers should provide students with feedback and correction as a way to remediate student work. Most experts now consider formative assessment as an *ongoing* part of the teaching and learning process. Formative assessment thus becomes a central element in teaching and learning.

Teachers across the case study schools have integrated formative assessment into their teaching, establishing classroom cultures that encourage interaction and use of assessment tools. In each of the case studies, teachers noted the importance of helping students to feel safe to take risks and make mistakes in the classroom. This is, in part, simply practical: children who feel safe to take risks are more likely to reveal what they do and don't understand, an essential feature of the formative process.

Research also highlights the importance of focusing students' attention on mastering tasks, rather than on competition with peers, and in developing emotional competencies. Emotional competencies, such as self-awareness, self-control, compassion, co-operation, flexibility, and the ability to make judgments on the value of information serve students well in school and throughout their lives (OECD, 2002, p. 58). Emotions also affect the student's self-esteem, motivation and ability to regulate his or her own learning.

ELEMENT 2: ESTABLISHMENT OF LEARNING GOALS, AND TRACKING OF INDIVIDUAL STUDENT PROGRESS TOWARD THOSE GOALS

Several OECD countries have established general standards for student achievement, and monitor students' progress toward those standards. Teachers in several of the case study schools worked together to define the standards in more detail, developing and sharing criteria with colleagues and students, and developing new internal systems to track individual student progress.

Teachers in the case study schools look to these objective standards to set out learning goals for students, sometimes scaffolding these goals for weaker students. The teachers have also moved away from traditional systems of marking – which tend to rely on "social comparison" of student performance (that is, comparison of each students' performance with that of their peers) toward methods that allowed them to track an individual student's progress toward the learning goals, as judged through established criteria.

International research supports idea that tracking a student's progress toward objective learning goals is more effective than is comparison with peers' progress (Cameron and Pierce, 1994; Kluger and DeNisi, 1996; Heckhausen, 1989; and Rheinberg and Krug, 1999). In situations of comparison, weaker students absorb the idea that they lack ability, and thus lose motivation and confidence. Ames (1992) notes that teachers' beliefs about the importance of effort, rather than ability, also play an important role in students' beliefs about themselves. Appropriate reference to an individual student's progress and opportunities to improve work based on feedback can help counter the negative impact of social comparisons.

Mischo and Rheinberg (1995) and Köller (2001) also found positive effects in several experimental and field studies where teachers referred to student progress over time. Positive effects were identified for students':

- Intrinsic motivation.
- Self-esteem.
- Academic self-concept.
- Causal attributions.
- Learning (see particularly Krampen [1987]).

The establishment of learning goals and tracking of student progress toward those goals makes the learning process much more transparent; students do not need to guess what they need to do to perform well. Teachers also help students to track their own progress and to build confidence.

ELEMENT 3: USE OF VARIED INSTRUCTION METHODS TO MEET DIVERSE STUDENT NEEDS

Teachers in the case study schools adjust their teaching methods to meet the needs of a variety of students. In some cases, this means that they adjust teaching to recognise different emotional styles. Teachers note that more vulnerable students need help in developing greater emotional competency. (For a more detailed discussion on emotions and cognition, see OECD, 2002.) These teachers are concerned with building students' confidence in their own skills and knowledge and in their ability to manage their own learning.

Social and cognitive psychologists, anthropologists and other social scientists have increasingly recognised that the knowledge and experiences children bring to school shape their learning experiences (Bruner, 1996; Bransford et al., 1999). Such prior knowledge is shaped, in part, by learners' ethnicity, culture, socio-economic class, and/or gender. Teachers can help students learn new concepts and ideas in ways that connect to their prior understandings and ways of looking at the world. Teachers who are attuned to variations in cultural communication patterns and sensitive to individual ways of communicating are more likely to draw out what children understand, and how they develop their understanding of new ideas (Bishop and Glynn, 1999).

Research has found that parents can play an important role here, too, because they share their children's life experiences, are well acquainted with their abilities and interests, and can help their children make connections between ideas (Bransford *et al.*, 1999).

Swiss education scholar Philippe Perrenoud proposes that:

"… [t]o the extent that pupils do not have the same abilities, nor the same needs or the same way of working, an optimal situation for one pupil will not be optimal for another …. One can write a simple equation: diversity in people + appropriate treatment for each = diversity in approach". (Perrenoud, 1998, p. 93-94)

Early research findings suggest that there is a need for a fundamental re-thinking of approaches to reaching equitable student outcomes. But there is also a need for more refined research on the impact of formative assessment methods for different students. Such research might address whether and how formative assessment can address the needs of students based on individual differences, such as emotional style, or ethnicity, culture, socio-economic class, and/or gender

ELEMENT 4: USE OF VARIED APPROACHES TO ASSESSING STUDENT UNDERSTANDING

Teachers in the case study schools use varied approaches to assessing individual student progress over time, in realistic settings, and in a variety of contexts. Students who may not perform well in certain tasks have the opportunity to demonstrate their knowledge and skills in others. Such varied assessments also draw out information on students' ability to transfer learning to new situations – a skill emphasised as important to learning to learn – and on how student understanding might be corrected or deepened. These varied assessments may include tests and other summative forms of assessment, so long as the information on student performance gathered in the tests is used to inform further learning.

Summative results, when embedded in the wider teaching and learning environment, are more likely to be used formatively. They also help to lower the stress of tests, which can have a have negative impact on the self-esteem of lower achieving students (See for example, a study conducted by the EPPI – Centre at the Institute of Education, University of London, June 2002).

ELEMENT 5: FEEDBACK ON STUDENT PERFORMANCE AND ADAPTATION OF INSTRUCTION TO MEET IDENTIFIED NEEDS

Feedback is vital to formative assessment, but not all feedback is effective. Feedback needs to be timely and specific, and include suggestions for ways to improve future performance. Good feedback is also tied to explicit criteria regarding expectations for student performance, making the learning process more transparent, and modelling "learning to learn" skills for students.

In their review of the English-language literature, Black and Wiliam (1998) identified a number of studies, conducted under ecologically valid circumstances (that is, controlled experiments conducted in the student's usual classroom setting and with their usual teacher) to support this point of view. For example, "ego-involving" feedback (even in the form of praise) rather than feedback on the task at hand appears to have a negative impact on performance (Boulet *et al.*, 1990). Students also obtain better results when they are working toward process goals rather than product goals, and when tracking progress toward overall goals of learning (Schunk, 1996). Grades may actually undermine the positive help of specific feedback on tasks (Butler, 1995).

Teachers also benefit from the feedback process. When providing feedback, teachers pay closer attention to what students do and do not understand well, and are better able to adjust teaching strategies to meet identified student needs.

ELEMENT 6: ACTIVE INVOLVEMENT OF STUDENTS IN THE LEARNING PROCESS

Ultimately, the goal of formative assessment is to guide students toward the development of their own "learning to learn" skills (also sometimes referred to as "metacognitive" strategies). Students are thus equipped with their own language and tools for learning and are more likely to transfer and apply these skills for problem solving into daily life; they develop their ability to find answers or develop strategies for addressing problems with which they are not familiar. In other words, they have developed strong "control" strategies for their own learning.

"Metacognition" involves awareness of how one goes about learning and thinking about new subject matter and is sometimes referred to as "thinking about thinking". The student who has an awareness of how he or she learns is better able to set goals, develop a variety of learning strategies, and control and evaluate his or her own learning process. As evidence of this, PISA 2000 found that:

> "... Within each country, students who use... [metacognitive and control strategies] more frequently tend to perform better on the combined PISA reading literacy scale than those who do not (although whether the learning strategies cause the better results cannot be established). ... [T]he strategies are essential for effective self-regulation of learning because they help students to adapt their learning to particular features of the task on which they are working. Schools may need to give more explicit attention to allowing students to manage and control their learning in order to help them all to develop effective strategies, not only to support their learning at school but also to help them with the tools to manage their learning later in life". (OECD, 2001, p. 110)

Importantly, PISA also found that students are unlikely to use control strategies if they lack motivation or self-confidence (OECD, 2003). Students' personal judgments about their ability to carry out a task ("self-efficacy") also significantly influence task performance (Pajares, 1996). Thus, a key role for teachers is to help children build confidence, and develop a variety of learning strategies.

Teachers in the case study schools model such learning behaviour, teach self-assessment skills and help students to analyse of how well different learning strategies have worked for them in the past. Such teaching approaches may be particularly important for children who do not have extra support for learning at home (OECD, 2003; Bransford *et al.*, 1999).

CREATING POWERFUL FRAMEWORKS

The above discussion illustrates how each of the elements of formative assessment as identified in the international case studies and research, is important to raising levels of student achievement, helping to close achievement gaps, and building students' learning to learn skills. When the elements are used together as an overall framework for teaching and learning, they are especially powerful. Teachers are better able to organise their thinking about how they set up learning situations, uncover student understanding of new concepts, guide students toward learning goals, and involve them more actively in the learning process.

The importance of each of the elements is supported in research. In turn, the overall framework provides a way for teachers to further organise their thinking about student learning, and to make more directed inquiries into research-based methods on improving student learning. Teachers increase their facility with these methods when they pay particular attention to the impact of the methods they are using on student learning.

References

Ames, C. (1992), "Classrooms: Goals, Structures, and Student Motivation", *Journal of Educational Psychology*, Vol. 84, pp. 261-271.

Bishop, R. and T. Glynn (1999), "Culture Counts: Changing Power Relations in Education", Dunmore Press, Palmerston North, New Zealand.

Black P. and D. Wiliam (1998), "Assessment and Classroom Learning", *Assessment in Education: Principles, Policy and Practice*, CARFAX, Oxfordshire, Vol. 5, No. 1, pp. 7-74.

Bloom, B. *et al.* (1971), *Handbook on Formative and Summative Evaluation of Student Learning*, McGraw-Hill Book Co., New York.

Boulet, M.M. *et al.* (1990), "Formative Evaluation Effects on Learning Music", *Journal of Educational Research*, Vol. 84, pp. 119-125.

Bransford, J.D. *et al.* (eds.) (1999), *How People Learn: Brain, Mind, Experience, and School*, National Academy of Sciences, National Academy Press, Washington D.C.

Bruner, J. (1996), *The Culture of Education*, Harvard University Press, Cambridge, MA.

Butler, D.L. and P.H. Winne (1995), "Feedback and Self-regulated Learning: A Theoretical Synthesis", *Review of Educational Research*, Vol. 65, No. 3, pp. 245-281.

Cameron, J. and D.P. Pierce (1994), "Reinforcement, Reward, and Instrisic Motivation: A Meta-analysis", *Review of Educational Research*, Vol. 64, pp. 363-423.

EPPI – Centre at the Institute of Education, University of London (2002), "A Systematic Review of the Impact of Summative Assessment and Tests on Students' Motivation for Learning", June.

Heckhausen, H. (1989), *Motivation und Handeln*, Springer, Berlin.

Kluger, A.N. and A. DeNisi (1996), "The Effects of Feedback Interventions on Performance: A Historical Review, a Meta-Analysis, and a Preliminary Feedback Intervention Theory", *Psychological Bulletin*, Vol. 119, pp. 254-284.

Köller, O. (2001). "Mathematical World Views and Achievement in Advanced Mathematics: Findings from the TIMSS Population III", *Studies in Educational Evaluation*, Vol. 27, pp. 65-78.

Krampen, G. (1987), "Differential Effects of Teacher Comments", *Journal of Educational Psychology*, Vol. 79, No. 2, pp. 137-146.

Mischo, C. and F. Rheinberg (1995), "Erziehungsziele von Lehrern und individuelle Bezugsnormen der Leistungsbewertung", *Zeitschrift für Pädagogische Psychologie*, Vol. 9, pp. 139-151.

National Board of Education (2002), "Assessing Learning-to-learn: A Framework", *Evaluation 4/2002*, National Board of Education, Helsinki.

OECD (2001), *Knowledge and Skills for Life*, OECD, Paris.

OECD (2002), *Understanding the Brain: Towards a New Learning Science*, OECD, Paris.

OECD (2003), *Learners for Life: Student Approaches to Learning: Results from PISA 2000*, OECD, Paris.

Pajares, F. (1996), "Self-efficacy Beliefs in Academic Settings", *Review of Educational Research*, Vol. 66, pp. 543-578.

Palincsar, A.S. and A.L. Brown (1984), "Reciprocal Teaching of Comprehension Monitoring Activities", *Cognition and Instruction*, Vol. 1, pp. 117-175.

Perrenoud, P. (1998), "From Formative Evaluation to a Controlled Regulation of Learning Processes. Towards a Wider Conceptual Field", *Assessment in Education: Principles, Policy and Practice*, CARFAX, Oxfordshire, Vol. 5, No. 1, pp. 85-102.

Rheinberg, F. and S. Krug (1999), *Motivationsförderung im Schulalltag* (2. Auflg.), Hogrefe, Göttingen, Germany.

Scardamalia, M. *et al.* (1984), "Teachability of Reflective Processes in Written Composition", *Cognitive Science*, 8, pp. 173-190.

Schoenfeld, A.H. (1983), "Problem Solving in the Mathematics Curriculum: A Report, Recommendation and an Annotated Bibliography", *Mathematical Association of America Notes*, No. 1.

Schoenfeld, A.H. (1985), *Mathematical Problem Solving*, Academic Press, Orlando, FL.

Schoenfeld, A.H. (1991), "On Mathematics as Sense-making: An Informal Attack on the Unfortunate Divorce of Formal and Informal Mathematics", in J.F. Voss, D.N. Perkins and J.W. Segal (eds.), *Informal Reasoning and Education*, Erlbaum, Hillsdale, pp. 311-343.

Schunk, D.H. (1996), "Goal and Self-evaluative Influences during Children's Cognitive Skill Learning", *American Educational Research Journal,* 33, pp. 359-382.

Chapter 4
Formative Assessment in Practice

> The "What Works" case studies provide vivid examples of formative assessment in practice. Teachers in the case study schools changed the culture of their classrooms in order to encourage greater interaction, and to incorporate the use of assessment tools. The formative assessment framework allowed them to integrate and create new approaches and techniques into their regular teaching practice.

The countries, provinces and schools contributing to this study provide vivid examples of formative assessment in practice. These examples are of interest to both policy officials and practitioners, as they move the discussion from broad principles – such as rhetoric regarding the importance of "child-centred learning" – to concrete descriptions regarding the changes such approaches entail. The following discussion follows the framework established in Chapter 3 and summarised in Figure 3.1, to illustrate the different ways teachers made formative assessment an integral part of their daily teaching.

ELEMENT 1: ESTABLISHMENT OF A CLASSROOM CULTURE THAT ENCOURAGES INTERACTION AND THE USE OF ASSESSMENT TOOLS

Teachers in the case study schools changed the culture of their classrooms in order to encourage greater interaction, and to incorporate the use of assessment tools. Themes which emerged consistently across the case studies were:

- Helping students to feel safe and confident in the classroom.
- Recognising students' individual and cultural differences.
- Planning for student learning, rather than merely planning activities.

Teachers across the case studies also noted that they needed to share their power with students in order to create a real culture change within the classroom.

Helping students feel safe and confident in the classroom

In each of the case studies, teachers placed emphasis on helping students feel safe and confident in the classroom. Students demonstrated the success of these approaches when, for example, they told case study researchers that "it's okay to make mistakes – that's how we learn".

At the Statens Pædagogiske Forsøgscenter School (SPF) (the National Centre for General Education) in Copenhagen, Denmark, teachers emphasised that students must feel self-confident in class if they are to dare to show and use what they are able to do. Activities to facilitate this in the school are: reading and telling stories, writing stories, use of logbooks and diaries, listening to music, interviewing other people, and inviting guest teachers. Humour and fun are developed through play, games, video production, role plays, etc. Through these techniques, teachers are able to engage students and help them feel secure and confident in the classroom environment. At the same time, students develop their own verbal competencies. The oral tradition is quite important in Danish education.

Several teachers in the English case study schools mentioned that they worked hard to keep the classroom a safe place for taking risks. While teachers often follow a "no hands up policy" to avoid calling only on more confident and outgoing students, teachers provide students with enough time to think before they answer a question in order not to embarrass a student who is less sure of him or herself. Teachers sometimes give students the chance to discuss answers in pairs or in small groups prior to opening class discussion. Teachers sometimes also seek to bring quieter students into the discussion, asking them if they agree with another student's answer.

Recognising individual and cultural differences

Teachers who understand their own cultural preconceptions and allow students to express their own identities and cultures in classrooms are better able to meet a diversity of learning needs. As an example of this, the New Zealand Ministry of Education is sponsoring the Maori Mainstream Programme (MMP, also known as *Te Kotahitanga* programme) to respond to the needs of Maori students, who have traditionally performed less well than other groups – even in well-off schools. While the programme was designed to meet the needs of a specific group, its principles are generally relevant to educators, particularly as classrooms are increasingly diverse, and there are notable differences in the equity of educational outcomes for minority or disadvantaged students.

The MMP is built on principles of Kaupapa Maori, which is based on a critical analysis of the unequal power relations within society (Bishop and

Glynn, 1999).[1] Within this framework, the importance of culture is paramount. The MMP encourages teachers to understand their own cultural preconceptions and to create environments in which children can safely bring "who they are" into the learning situation.

Maori researchers Bishop and Glynn note that:

"... many Maori children ... had been socialised into family, community and peer groups where both group competition and cooperation were valued, where both group achievement and peer solidarity were dominant, where the complementary nature of abstract and concrete thought, physical and social achievements, and religion and culture were emphasised. Socialisation of Maori children emphasised the interdependence of the group and the individual". (Bishop and Glynn, 1999, p. 36)

The MMP therefore emphasises group work, co-construction of knowledge, and peer solidarity. (One student told case study researchers that they feel like they were brothers and sisters growing up together.) A teacher in the MMP noted, "You are often told as new teachers to be tough and keep it quiet, individuals in their seats, and to have quiet classrooms. But in this programme you can have noisy engaged learning and it is not a discipline problem". The school is known for being relatively strict – so noisy learning in the MMP classrooms gets noticed. But, the MMP teachers noted that they have fewer discipline problems than other teachers who follow the stricter approach to teaching. Students told us that they relate to their teachers better in the MMP classes.

In another example, teachers at the Italian Michelangelo School in Bari use varied approaches to getting to know students and to better understand their abilities, acquired knowledge, and approaches to learning. Because students are increasingly diverse with regard to knowledge and competencies, cultural and ethnic identities and backgrounds, using formative assessment has been important for both students and teachers in understanding what they need to do to, respectively, to improve their learning, and to adjust lessons.

Planning for student learning, rather than merely planning activities

Teachers in the case study schools noted that their lesson plans have changed, placing greater focus on what students *learn* in class, as opposed to what students *do* in class. One teacher noted, "Rather than thinking of which

---

[1] Bishop, R. and T. Glynn (1999), *Culture Counts: Changing Power Relations in Education,* Dunmore Press, Palmerston North, New Zealand.

article in the newspaper or which page in the text I'm going to use, I'm really thinking of which formative assessment I'm going to use, or a bit of both. ... But you've got to have the energy to do it".

Teachers in the Michelangelo School in Italy noted that they draw upon learning theories as they set up new situations, but that they are also careful to pay attention to the impact of different approaches. They said that they "... don't think they have sure and absolute recipes" and are "humbly aware in every moment of the complexity in working with human subjects whose answers are not always foreseeable". Teachers at the school try to be creative, flexible, and self-critical in their work. They are engaged in ongoing action research, and update teaching tools according to experiences and the changing needs of students.

ELEMENT 2: ESTABLISHMENT OF LEARNING GOALS, AND TRACKING OF INDIVIDUAL STUDENT PROGRESS TOWARD THOSE GOALS

A common theme in classrooms studied in the case study countries is the importance of establishing learning goals, tracking student progress toward those goals, and in some cases adjusting learning goals to better meet student needs. Teachers thus make the learning process more transparent. In several of the case study systems, teachers draw upon nationally or regionally-established standards for student achievement. The standards are usually broad, so teachers in the case study schools have developed more specific learning objectives and criteria by which they can judge the quality of student work. In Italy, where there are not yet nationally-defined learning standards, teachers in the case study schools have developed their own objectives and standards, and they regularly discuss teaching approaches. Teachers have found this process helpful to their own process of working through what they should expect from students.

While not a universal practice, the majority of teachers interviewed for the case studies regularly share learning goals, criteria and standards with students. Typically, the teachers share objectives for the day's lesson early in the class period (usually written on the board, and shared orally), tying the goals to earlier learning in order to place the lesson in context. They may also engage students in a discussion of what criteria for a quality piece of work should include, and may provide examples of exemplary student products.

Some teachers, however, said that they are wary of following the same format all the time – one teacher interviewed said that she sometimes waits until the end of the class to ask students, "Why did I do that?".

Teachers in the schools visited in Italy had mixed reactions to the idea of sharing criteria for performance with students. Some teachers fear that establishing criteria might stifle students' creativity. That is, if students have a set of criteria handed to them, they might adhere to those criteria as they do their work, and might not call upon their own ideas. Teachers in England and New Zealand also had mixed reactions as to whether they should provide students with exemplars – fearing that students might hold too closely to the model without exploring the ideas for themselves. Several of the teachers agreed that it is acceptable to share exemplary work products so long as the students do not have too much time with them.

Tracking student progress

Teachers in the case study schools have found that tracking student progress is important to the formative process. At the Testoni Fioravanti school in Italy, teachers keep personalised booklets on each student's progress. In this way, they can get to know each student better and can also pass on a portrait of the student to other teachers. Teachers in several of the case study schools also keep graphs and tables to track students' acquisition of knowledge, and their ability to comprehend, analyse, synthesise, and to express themselves. They are able to compare their assessments of how students are doing with other teachers during the class council discussions. The graphs and discussions among teachers also help to ensure that they are treating students equitably.

In several of the case study schools visited, teachers have grappled with the value of providing students with marks. In most cases, they have found that if they notify parents of what they are doing and why, parents accept the new, formative approach to tracking their child's progress. Parents across several of the case study schools expressed their views that comments-only or rubric marking are actually quite helpful, and that they have a better idea of what their children are doing and how they might be able to help them with their school work. But it is not always easy to drop marks. Sometimes students still want to know how they are doing in relation to other students and parents are also interested in the relative position of their child in the school.

Adjusting learning goals

In some cases, programmes have been designed to provide teachers with greater flexibility, allowing them to adjust learning goals to better suit student needs. The Québec Ministry of Education's reform was developed to provide learners of different ability with the opportunity to learn things that they can apply in useful ways once they have left school. The idea behind the programme is that schools can reduce failure rates by ensuring that learning is more relevant to the student's needs. This has been important not only for students at risk of failure, but also for high-achieving students. For example, a high achieving student at Sainte-Foy PROTIC programme in Québec commented that "Compared to my old school there is a lot more pride here about our work, not about grades, but about the results of what we do in the projects".

ELEMENT 3: USE OF VARIED INSTRUCTION METHODS TO MEET DIVERSE STUDENT NEEDS

Teachers across the case study schools diversify instruction to meet a variety of student needs. They ensure that lessons include a variety of approaches to explaining and helping students to understand new concepts. Teachers sometimes work together to ensure that the overall school schedule provides students with a mix of activities in each school day.

Teachers in the Maori Mainstream Programme at Waitakere College in New Zealand try to reach students with different learning styles by providing them with several options for classroom work. Students do task work the majority of the time they are in class, and the teachers are able to wander around and work with students individually. Teachers in the programme are conscious of the need to be flexible and try to use different approaches to explaining a concept, or encourage students who have done well to help fellow students.

Students at Our Lady's in Queensland, Australia, suggested that active lessons with plenty of variety of activities and in which teachers stick to the point, help them to learn. One student suggested that a good teacher is one that "doesn't put you to sleep" while they all agreed that copying off the board or out of books was least likely to help learning.

Students at Our Lady's reported that teachers give more time to those who needed help but that "brainy" people are still given time and made to think. The school leader noted that she would like to fast-track more students, and set up more opportunities for peer tutoring to ensure that diverse needs are being met.

At the Tikkakoski School in Finland, teachers set up the class schedule together. They make sure that students have at least one practical, or optional, class every day. Not all subjects are covered in every term due to the course system. The students said that they like this approach, and that they are able to concentrate better when there is variety in the schedule. The school also provides several optional courses, which students say they appreciate.

Teachers at the Tikkakoski School are able to either fast track students who are doing very well, or provide extra help for those students who need it. Students with severe difficulties in a subject get extra help in separate classes. Students with less severe difficulties can take advantage of individual remediation instead of optional remedial courses.

ELEMENT 4: USE OF VARIED APPROACHES TO ASSESSING STUDENT UNDERSTANDING

Teachers in the case study schools use a variety of approaches to assessing student understanding. In some cases, they use the assessments diagnostically, for instance, when students first enter the school, or at specified times during the school term. During classroom interactions, however, teachers most often use questioning techniques to reveal what students understand. Students' written products also provide opportunities for teachers to assess student understanding and to enter into written dialogues with them.

Using diagnostic assessment

Teachers in several of the case study schools use diagnostic assessment to gauge each student's abilities as he or she enters the school, and at specific stages during the school year. At the Italian Testoni Fioravanti school in Bologna, students making the transition from primary to lower secondary school are asked to take diagnostic tests in a range of subjects. Teachers use test results to determine the student's level upon entry to the school. They also use a grid listing various aspects of the child's prior scholastic success, attitudes, aspirations, and habits which also serve to guide their discussions with parents. The school uses information on all incoming students to form classes that mix students by ability and personality.

At the SPF in Copenhagen, students participate in diagnosing their learning styles. At the beginning of the school year, students are introduced to basic learning theory, including Howard Gardner's concept of multiple intelligences. On that basis students write a profile that is both a self-description in relation to the multiple intelligences and a description of their expectations and goals for learning for the next two years in the school.

Questioning

While diagnostic assessments are conducted when students are entering a new school, or during specified times, teachers also assess student understanding through questioning in the normal course of teaching. They use a variety of questioning strategies.

The *types* of questions teachers ask are very important to revealing students' levels of understanding. At Lord Williams's School in England, for example, teachers in the science department discovered that a very good task to uncover students' misconceptions was to pose a question about the direction of causality in a process they are just learning about. Teachers found, for example, that by asking what would happen if chlorophyll stopped working that students commonly thought that all the world would be dark.

In Bologna, one teacher commented that she asks "why" questions so often that the students had start to groan when hearing this line of questioning. She persists with this approach, though, as she has found it to be a very effective method for revealing whether and how students understand the new concepts.

Techniques

Teachers across the case study schools developed a number of techniques that have been helpful in discovering what students actually understand when learning new concepts, and that give quieter students a chance to share their views. Through interaction and monitoring of student progress, teachers are better able to diagnose and respond to student needs.

The traffic light

Teachers working with King's-Medway-Oxfordshire Formative Assessment Project (KMOFAP) in England created the traffic light technique. The traffic light provides an easy way for students to indicate their understanding of a concept. At points in the lesson when teachers want to be sure that students understand a concept before moving on, they ask students to hold up a green, amber or red sign to indicate whether they understand, think they understand but are not quite sure, or do not understand at all. The traffic light became a fairly common strategy in the schools visited in England. Teachers said that they spend more time with students showing amber, or work after class with students showing red traffic lights.

Thinking time instead of hands up

Teachers in several of the schools visited enforce a policy of "no hands up" on a fairly regular basis. Often, teachers announce that they are going to give the class a no-hands up question, but also use the more traditional technique of calling on students with raised hands during other parts of the lesson. Using this technique, the teachers pose a question, take a pause ranging from three seconds to several minutes, and then call upon a student. The teachers noted that, when they started using formative assessment techniques, giving students thinking time was perhaps one of the hardest things to get used to. However, they have found that the quality of responses improves a great deal when they are able to enforce the self-discipline of waiting upon themselves as teachers.

Continued

Portfolios, logbooks and rubrics

Portfolios and logbooks provide an opportunity for written dialogues between teacher and student. Portfolios are in fairly common use in the case study schools visited in Denmark, Canada, and to a lesser extent, in Scotland. In a portfolio or logbook, students might include the results of a project that they had enjoyed and done well on, or alternatively, that they felt had been difficult and needed more work. Students might also be asked to use the portfolio to reflect on the learning process. The portfolios are particularly useful for parents, who receive concrete information on what their children are learning, and therefore have a better basis for entering into dialogue with teachers and with their children. Parents can see for themselves some of the outcomes of students' learning and in what ways they might be able to support and encourage their children's education.

Rubrics are specific guidelines used to evaluate student work, that is, scoring tools that list criteria for a good-quality piece of work, usually on a point scale. Students in several of the case study schools use rubrics to judge the quality of their own work, and then to edit and improve it.

ELEMENT 5: FEEDBACK ON STUDENT PERFORMANCE AND ADAPTATION OF INSTRUCTION TO MEET IDENTIFIED NEEDS

Feedback combined with adaptation of instruction is an important feature across the international case studies. For example, in both Our Lady's and Woodridge schools in Queensland, Australia, there are subjects in which there is a strong emphasis on giving effective feedback through comments indicating how to improve the work.

The students interviewed at Woodridge said that teachers give them verbal feedback on written work in class. One student produced a history work booklet which was an assessed assignment with a sheet on the front giving the outcomes-based statements marked as "beginning, working toward or achieved". In addition, the teacher had given a comment indicating what would need to be done to improve the work. The Year 8 students said that grades or marks are never given and they feel that this has helped them work to their own standard and not worry about comparing themselves to other people. They all claimed to read and act upon the comments and suggested that the teacher is always willing to discuss them.

In social studies at Our Lady's, students receive comments on drafts of assessed work. The comments indicate how students can improve their work. Students are given class time to undertake the revisions. The head of science suggested that this also occurs in science and that students are more likely to read the comments on these assessed drafts than on other work.

Teachers at Rosehill College in Auckland, New Zealand noted that they plan lessons carefully in order to create time to talk with students individually during the lesson. Teachers find that they often provide the best feedback spontaneously. Other opportunities to provide feedback occur when students are working on homework. A Rosehill teacher noted that a few of his students send e-mails asking for feedback. The teacher sends back bullet points on issues to consider – which students seem to like and to use. Another teacher noted that he spends quite a bit of time talking with students about what they need to do next to reinforce their knowledge. Teachers at Rosehill commented that, rather than giving students direct feedback, they often suggest that the students research information in their textbook, look for information on the Internet, or look at exemplars produced by their peers.

ELEMENT 6: ACTIVE INVOLVEMENT OF STUDENTS IN THE LEARNING PROCESS

Teachers using formative assessment actively involve students in the learning process, with the goal of helping students to develop their own learning-to-learn skills. Teachers across the case study schools often scaffold learning, allowing students to accomplish as much as possible on their own. They also help students to build a repertoire of learning strategies, and develop skills for peer- and self-assessment.

Scaffolding learning

When teachers scaffold learning for students, they make an assessment of a student's strengths and weaknesses, and on the basis of this assessment, provide the student with an idea of how to proceed with his or her own learning. When scaffolding learning, teachers provide students with hints rather than answers, so that students have the opportunity to get to the answer themselves.

At Forres Academy, in Scotland, where most teachers use co-operative learning techniques emphasising group work, students work on problems together, and only if students don't know how to get ahead or if there is controversy about the solution to a problem, do they refer to their teacher. The teacher might point the group in the right direction, or might ask an additional question to provide students with an idea as to what they need to know in order to solve the problem on their own.

Helping students to develop a repertoire of learning strategies

The promotion of higher order thinking skills is an important goal of formative assessment. Teachers in the case study schools model approaches to problem-solving, introduce tools such as concept maps to help students address complex concepts, and challenge students to reflect on and improve their own work.

At the Michelangelo School in Bari, students are encouraged to develop concept maps to examine the relationships between a new subject and other things they already know. At the beginning of a new unit, the students brainstorm about what they already know about a particular subject, and how it relates to other subjects they have studied. Students said that they do not study in a linear way – instead, they progress through concepts with learning models. Learning models might be textual, descriptive, analytical, or rhetorical. Students and teachers discuss the model thoroughly before starting to work on their own. Students mentioned that teachers are constantly concerned with cause and effect.

Teachers at the Michelangelo School review homework with students, correcting mistakes and guiding students toward the practice of self-correction, reflection on the work process, and review of sources. Teachers give students the opportunity to revise homework. Teachers also use test results formatively, determining what interventions are appropriate to meet students' learning needs. The teachers sometimes help students to diagnose the initial source of a misunderstanding, allowing the student to self-correct and apply these skills to new problems as well.

Building skills for peer- and self-assessment

The ultimate goal of formative assessment is for students to be able to evaluate and revise their own work. It is, as teachers at Rosehill College in Auckland noted, one of the most challenging aspects of teaching in the formative assessment mode. They hope that students will be able to find what is missing on their own, figure out what to do next, and then take responsibility for following through on next steps.

In order to instil these abilities in students, teachers at Rosehill try to model the steps, encouraging students to be specific about what their own work shows, and then taking it a step further to improve the work. The key issue, they find, is in focusing student attention on specifics relating to criteria (in checklist form) for a high quality piece of work. Teachers often try to approach this task by breaking overall learning goals into smaller goals, for example, working with students to write a perfect topic sentence. In other words, the teachers scaffold learning steps.

At the Meilhati School in Finland, teachers have developed a self-evaluation form in response to national requirements for schools to focus on students' individual development process. Students complete the form at the end of each term, four times a year. Teachers give marks (G = good; M = moderate; T = trying and practice needed). During a course the students and teachers fill in a small questionnaire about their study habits. In grade 7 the questionnaire also asks about students' well-being in the school and in class, in grade 8, about behaviour, and, in grade 9, about attitudes toward learning. According to the teachers, students complete these self-evaluations in a realistic way. The evaluations are shared with the parents, who are then able to comment on them.

At the Tikkakoski School in Finland, teachers have also developed their own system for student self-evaluation, based on course reports. Under this system, students receive a course report at the end of each of the five seven-week terms in the school year. Students determine the grade they expect in each subject, assess their study habits and their development in learning. Concepts such as study habits and learning development are explained on the reverse side of the report. After filling in their own mark, the students receive a mark from the teacher. If there is a difference of two points or more, there is a discussion between teacher and student. For the majority of the students, however, their own grade and their teacher's grade match fairly accurately. It is likely that frequent feedback during lessons is helpful for students in gauging the level of their attainment. The course report also includes the previous assessments, enabling the student to follow his or her development over time. If, according to the course report, a student is failing in a subject he or she is responsible for initiating a discussion with the teacher as to how to improve his or her work.

Acquiring *skills* to learn as compared to *things* to learn is also an important element of the approach to curriculum and assessment in Tikkakoski. Assessment focuses not only on student performance, but also on the development of learning-to-learn skills. Tikkakoski's system of student self-assessment therefore attempts to reflect student development. The principal and the teachers do not want to limit the concept of assessment to student performance only.

Student self-assessment is also an important goal in the two Italian schools visited. By Year 3, students are expected to have developed a relatively high level of autonomy, social skills and the ability to make functional decisions regarding their own development. The students provided some evidence that they are indeed learning to be autonomous. As one Year 3 student declared, if she does not understand a new concept, she tries to relate it to another subject in order to understand the context better, or its relation to other ideas. In other words, she develops her own learning scheme. Ultimately, this student told us, "It is up to us to learn". This sentiment was widely echoed among fellow students.

Enhancing students' roles in peer- and self-assessment

Peer evaluation, including peer-feedback and peer-tutoring is a frequent practice in the case study schools visited. Peer evaluation is important because it helps to create a more dynamic learning environment, helps students to build social skills, and lays the ground for the development of self-assessment skills.

Teachers at several of the schools noted that students need careful coaching and practice if they are to provide useful assessments for their peers. Students are often quite critical of each other. Over time, however, students learn how to comment on those things they like in their peers' work, as well as offering constructive criticism. Students also develop a better sense of what they are looking for in their peers' work in order to assess quality, and pay much greater attention to criteria.

At the John Ogilvie High School in Scotland, teachers introduce criteria they have established, along with appropriate evaluative statements for oral presentations and extended writing to the new students at the beginning of the school year. Early in the year, teachers often find that student presentations are relatively poor, but that peer-assessment using the criteria works very well in helping students to improve their work.

Teachers at John Ogilvie further developed the formative assessment process by providing pupils with stick-on labels describing the different evaluative statements for judging a presentation. Students use the stick-on labels to select assessment statements for different aspects of the work presented. This helps students who are not accustomed to the "language" of assessment to choose suitable evaluative statements from a range of statements. Teachers also use a digital video camera to record classroom processes. Students are able to evaluate and comment on the recordings.

A culture of peer tutoring is clearly visible at the Xavier School in Newfoundland, Canada. Students work in pairs, supporting each other in English, mathematics and science lessons. Sometimes they are able to choose who they will work with. At other times, teachers designate which students will work together, making sure that a student who is strong in a particular subject helps another student who is not as strong.

In a grade 9 English class observed at the Xavier School, students were working on their independent research piece for their portfolio. Those who had almost completed their written assignment were given a checklist for peer editing. The teacher put students together in pairs of two. The students read each other's rescarch pieces in turns, using the checklist and a rubric outlining criteria to improve the quality of each other's written text with regards to expression, structure, grammar and spelling. (Rubrics are scoring tools that list criteria for a good-quality piece of work, usually on a point scale.) Most students visibly enjoy working with rubrics. As one student commented, "You can see what you did wrong and how you can fix it. It also makes it a lot easier to set aims for yourself".

Teachers across the case study schools give mixed reviews as to whether peer marking saves time, or takes time away from other activities. Some teachers said they prefer to cover as much content as possible, particularly in content-heavy subjects in the sciences, and do not want to lose time to peer-marking. Other teachers felt that it was more important to prioritise curriculum content, and perhaps cut out some units, as they prefer not to rush through the curriculum. Some teachers believed that by having students mark each other, the teachers are able to save a great deal of their own time. These teachers commented that with some practice, the quality of peer-marking is very close to that of teachers' marking.

LEARNING FROM EXPERIENCE

This chapter has examined lessons from the case study schools, looking more closely at how each of the elements of formative assessment translates into practice. As examples from the case study schools show, formative assessment requires hard work. It also requires that teachers make dramatic shifts in how they view their own roles, as well as that of their students. But effective formative assessment approaches and techniques help to discipline and make transparent the teaching and learning process. Moreover, as students gain skills for "learning to learn" and take more responsibility for their own learning, they are much more effective.

Chapter 5 will look at how teachers addressed important logistical barriers to implementing formative assessment and how school leaders guided change over time. Chapter 6 will look at how policy can promote wider and deeper changes, so that the schools in the study are no longer considered exemplary, but are actually quite commonplace.

Chapter 5
Benefits and Barriers

> Teachers in the case study schools developed creative ways to address logistical barriers to formative assessment, such as large class size, and extensive curriculum requirements. Working closely with colleagues and experimenting with a variety of strategies, they were able to develop some very interesting solutions. Teachers found that formative assessment actually helped them to save time, allowed them to focus on the needs of weaker students and to incorporate varied teaching methods into their repertoire. They noticed direct benefits in their interactions with students. School leaders played an essential role in initiating, sustaining, and deepening changes. The case study schools provided anecdotal evidence of improvements in teaching and learning.

The concept of formative assessment often resonates with teachers, but many protest that it is just not possible to put these ideas into regular practice – that there are too many barriers. Secondary school teachers, in particular, may be quick to protest that it is not so easy to use formative assessment with large classes. Nor is it possible to slow the pace of instruction, particularly when trying to guide a class through important and extensive curriculum requirements. Teachers also protest that it is difficult to use formative assessment with students they consider as more challenging.

Teachers in the case study schools grappled with these challenges. Working closely with colleagues, and experimenting with a variety of strategies, they were able to develop some very interesting solutions. They found that formative assessment, instead of adding logistical challenges to teaching, actually helped them to save time, allowed them to focus on the needs of weaker students, and to incorporate varied teaching methods into their repertoire. In the process, they also found that they were making more fundamental changes in how they thought about their students' abilities, and about teaching and learning itself.

School leaders in the case study schools also played essential roles in creating conditions that allowed teachers to make significant, sustained changes in teaching and assessment. In many of the cases, they had laid the groundwork for change over several years, building collegial cultures, and encouraging innovation. Formative assessment methods enabled these school leaders to push progress even further, focusing and giving discipline to the teachers' discussions on teaching and learning, and using data generated at classroom and school levels to inform improvements.

This chapter describes some of the specific strategies teachers in the case study schools developed as they built formative assessment into their regular practice, and how their interactions with students have changed as a result. The chapter also examines the strategies school leaders used to lead change across schools, and how these changes have contributed to overall improvements in student achievement, equity, and learning to learn skills.

ADDRESSING BARRIERS AND REALISING BENEFITS AT THE CLASSROOM LEVEL

Teachers in the case study schools developed strategies to address logistical barriers to formative assessment that were both straightforward and ingenious. They experimented with a variety of approaches before finding those that seemed to work best for them and their students. Teachers found ways to use formative assessment with larger classes, to balance extensive curriculum requirements, and to work with students they considered as more challenging. Their efforts paid off in improved interactions with students and in student work.

Class size

At the John Ogilvie High School in Hamilton, Scotland, teachers use the technique of "divided classes" in order to gain more time with individual students or with small groups of students. For example, in a mathematics class observed for the case study, the teacher kept one-half of the class busy with independent learning in the computer lab, while working through new concepts with the other half of the class. The teacher then repeated this procedure.

A significant number of teachers at Forres Academy in northeastern Scotland have been using co-operative learning techniques since the mid-1990s. The teachers commented that co-operative learning has enabled them to spend more time with individual students or with small groups of students. In classrooms featuring co-operative learning, students are encouraged to develop skills for peer-assessment, conflict resolution, leadership and teamwork. They also learn to accept others. Students are able to build cognitive and social skills simultaneously.

School leaders and teachers at the Sacred Heart School in Saskatchewan, Canada created mixed age classes to encourage peer mentoring, and to put older students' energies to positive use (thereby addressing discipline problems). Teachers are able to direct their energies differently as older students take on mentoring roles. The mixed classes also mean that teachers need to pay more attention to providing a variety of learning opportunities, and to diversifying their approaches to teaching and assessment in order to meet the different levels and needs of students in the classes. All students benefit from the wider array of choices.

Students across the case study schools were positive about peer mentoring and peer- and self-assessment that occur in co-operative learning situations. Students said that working in small groups helps them to build confidence because they are able to test out their ideas with a smaller group of peers before sharing them with the whole class or with the teacher.

Prioritising curriculum requirements

Teachers in lower secondary schools are faced with extensive curriculum requirements. In several of the case study schools, teachers prioritise curriculum requirements – deciding which concepts are most important to developing students' understanding of the subject. The teachers ensure that students have a good facility with a new concept before moving on. In some cases, this means that some curriculum items are missed, but teachers say that they are more confident that students are retaining information, and learning the subject matter in greater depth.

Changing attitudes about students' abilities

In addition to logistical barriers of classroom management, teachers may find that taking on formative assessment is difficult because it is different. Formative assessment requires that teachers change the way they interact with students, what they think about when they plan lessons, their attentiveness to students' learning differences, and even the way they think about student success.

Teachers at Rosehill College in Auckland, New Zealand said that even though they believe they have always used aspects of formative assessment (in mathematics, teachers built on previous concepts all the time in order to move forward to successive concepts), their teaching has become more effective as they have been more deliberate in their use of formative assessment. These changes include more attention to timing and specificity of feedback they provide to students, more attention to scaffolding of questions, and greater focus on students' learning-to-learn skills. They notice a difference in the quality of students' work products.

Teachers at Seven Kings High School in England noted that they have changed lesson planning to focus on what they want students to learn in the class, and what classroom set-up will create the best conditions for learning. They no longer focus simply on planning classroom activities. They interact with students more, placing emphasis on dialogue, checking for understanding, and giving students more control over their own learning processes. Teachers at Seven Kings remarked that using formative assessment approaches and techniques has made them feel differently about how students can "get from one place to another" in their learning.

Teachers in several of the case study schools noted that integrating formative assessment into their regular practice has involved a process. In some of the schools visited, teachers started using formative assessment with their best students, and with practice, realised that it would be useful and practical with weaker students, as well. Other teachers noted that they pay greater attention to underachieving students when using formative assessment approaches than they might have before.

DIRECT BENEFITS IN CLASSROOMS

Anecdotal evidence gathered in the case study schools shows direct benefits of using formative assessment in classrooms. For example:

- *Improvements in the quality of teaching.* Teachers across several of the case study schools believe that their own teaching has improved as they have developed their ability to scaffold learning goals for students and to adapt instruction to meet individual learning needs. They pay closer attention to teaching approaches that work well and put them into practice more often.

- *Stronger relationships with students and increased contact with parents.* In several of the case study schools, parents commented that they appreciated getting more specific feedback on what their children were learning, and teachers' suggestions as to how they can better support their learning. In one case study school, students commented that instead of just getting grades, they felt they were involved in a process with their teachers.

- *Different and better work products from students.* Students across the case study schools are taking more responsibility for their learning, and taking more pride in their work.

- *Greater student engagement.* Students in the case study schools are making more connections between what they are learning in class and what is happening in their lives outside of school.

Table 5.1 summarises some of the strategies teachers developed to address barriers.

Table 5.1. Teachers across the case study schools developed a variety of strategies to address barriers

Classroom level barriers to change	Strategies to address barriers
Difficulty of managing large classes or working with students teachers consider as more challenging	Divided classes to provide more time with individual students or groups of students
	Mixed age classes to build students' peer mentoring skills, as well as their social skills. Teachers also provide a greater range of materials and choices for learning, and scaffold learning goals to meet needs of students at different ages
	Co-operative learning to build students' peer mentoring and assessment skills, as well as their social skills
Extensive curriculum requirements	Prioritising curriculum requirements in order to place the greatest emphasis on core concepts
Working with students teachers consider as more challenging	Building confidence by using formative assessment with their highest performing students first, and gradually integrating new practices into more challenging classes

SCHOOL LEADERS' STRATEGIES FOR INITIATING, SUSTAINING AND DEEPENING CHANGES IN SCHOOL AND TEACHER PRACTICE

School leaders play an essential role in initiating, sustaining, and deepening changes in school and teacher practice. School leaders across the case study schools emphasised the importance of keeping the focus on teaching and learning. They actively encourage teachers to participate in innovative projects and to take risks, even with underachieving or more challenging students. They also foster school-wide cultures of evaluation, developing opportunities for teachers to provide peer feedback and support, and asking teachers to refer to objective data on the impact of teaching methods on student performance.

Keeping the focus on teaching and learning

School leaders across the case study schools emphasised the importance of keeping the focus on teaching and learning as the best route to influencing classroom change. Several, particularly those in previously low-performing schools, said that the process of change had been quite incremental, and that it had taken several years before they reached a "tipping point" where the majority of teachers were interacting regularly and sharing ideas about quality teaching and student assessment. Their leadership has been essential to bringing staff together to discuss school priorities and in keeping issues of lower priority from distracting teachers from their main work. They have also created high expectations for teacher performance, and in turn, have been asked to meet teachers' expectations for training and support.

While school leaders in the case study schools have been strategic and focused in their efforts to lead change, they are also open to new ideas and to taking advantage of problems and learning from them. For example, the school leader at Rosehill College in Auckland, New Zealand commented that he and the school staff had "… been down blind alleys … done things wrong, and … sweated a lot". He described the process of adopting formative assessment methods throughout the school as having involved "… a lot of discussion, a lot of debate, a lot of philosophical sort of argument". As a result, members of the school staff have developed a shared language and understanding about the purpose and methods of formative assessment.

In some cases, skilled school leaders have been able to parlay unrelated initiatives into changes in approaches to teaching. For example, when a new principal came to the Sacred Heart School in Saskatchewan several years ago, the first change she introduced to the school was a complete re-organisation of playground time. After each break there had been a long line of students in front of her office, sent there because of disciplinary issues. One boy, a victim of bullying, admitted that the thing he feared most in the school was break time. In close collaboration with teachers, the new principal decided to completely restructure the school break. She replaced recess time with two breaks of 20 minutes each, spent with the class either in the gym or outside playing sports and different kinds of games the children enjoyed. The number of disciplinary incidents dropped immediately giving everyone in the school the courage to initiate and support further changes. "You notice", one teacher says, "that there is no end to innovation. You can't just change a little. Once you've made a change and you notice it works, you have to keep growing and changing".

At the Seven Kings High School in England, the head teacher used the school's reconstruction project – bringing the formerly split school site together onto one campus – as an opportunity to encourage changes in teaching and learning. The head teacher recounts that he told the teachers "We're moving, so we have to think about how we might address Religious Education differently in the future". Even for a change that ostensibly had little to do with curriculum, this school leader maintained the focus on teaching and learning.

Encouraging teachers to participate in innovative projects and to take risks

School leaders often find that they need to encourage teachers to participate in innovative projects or to take risks. In some cases, teachers are nervous about how well students will perform on external examinations. Even when new projects are grounded in research findings, teachers are reluctant to risk lower student achievement scores as they are trying out new teaching methods. In many of the cases, school leaders addressed such challenges by allowing teachers to build confidence in their use of formative assessment methods, working first with their higher achieving students, and building their own evidence that the methods are effective. Only after teachers had had a chance to build their confidence with new approaches did school leaders encourage teachers to start using methods with underachieving students.

Formative assessment approaches may also require deep changes in teachers' attitudes about what students are capable of achieving, what types of adaptation and adjustment of teaching are appropriate, and what the purposes of assessment should be. In some cases, this has to do with doubts that schools can really help disadvantaged students to close learning gaps. Other teachers may believe that equity among students is best achieved through equal treatment (that is, all students should be taught the same curriculum, in the same way), rather than a variety of treatments with the goal of achieving greater equity of student outcomes.

Building school-wide cultures of evaluation

School-wide cultures of evaluation are essential to deep change. Teachers who share a language of assessment and track what they have learnt about what works and why are able to push innovations further, and to pass on their knowledge more easily. Formative assessment facilitates this process with its emphasis on the *process* of learning and the need to carefully track student progress. Teachers working in schools with strong evaluation cultures are also able to "triangulate" data (that is, using varied assessments to confirm or challenge the conclusions), and to address potential biases in their own assessments of student performance.

In essence, teachers and schools using school and teacher self-evaluation as a way to shape future planning are using knowledge management techniques. The codification of knowledge is key to this process. A 2004 OECD report on knowledge and innovation in schools points out that:

"Knowledge-based activities emerge when people, supported by information and communication technologies, interact in concerted efforts to co-produce (*i.e.* create and exchange) new knowledge. Typically, this involves three main elements: a significant number of a community's members combine to produce and reproduce new knowledge (diffuse sources of innovation); the community creates a 'public' space for exchanging and circulating the knowledge; new information and communication technologies are intensively used to codify and transmit the new knowledge." (OECD, 2004, p. 20)

The deputy head teacher at The Clere School in England described how the school-wide focus on formative assessment had helped to "… build on the experience of the teachers participating in the [initial pilot] project, reinforced things they were doing instinctively and put a label on it. That helped to clarify and categorise their methods. … Then, they were asked to look at the difference these methods made in student learning". The project also helped to deepen teachers' understanding of how they could enhance student learning by meeting students at their level of development.

School leaders and teachers in several of the case study schools regularly refer to data as they develop school plans. Since 2001, schools in Newfoundland and Labrador have been developing action plans based on the provincial test results. At the Seven Kings High School, in the east London Borough of Redbridge, the school leader noted a dramatic change from past school practices, commenting that schools used to "let a thousand flowers bloom". No one looked at data to see if innovations were actually working or not. Now, data are regularly used in the development of school strategies.

Because teachers are engaged in the learning process along with students, they sometimes find it difficult to make objective observations and judgments while teaching. They may pay as much or more attention to the success of the instruction process as they do to student outcomes or other evidence of student learning (Airasian and Abrams, 2003) that provides information on how they may need to adapt teaching methods. Even if teachers can automatically predict performance of their students with reasonable accuracy, it helps to have their views confirmed by the data.

There are potential biases in classroom-based assessments. For example, teachers may vary in their interpretation and application of the same performance criteria – either among themselves, or with different students or classes (Kellaghan and Madaus, 2003). They may also develop impressions regarding students early in the year based on incomplete information, or stereotypes. For example, teachers are more likely to give high marks to students who are more like themselves. Alternatively, teachers may make negative judgements of students from different cultural backgrounds, or with different communication styles. Teachers' personalities and characteristics, or varying expectations of different students, may also influence student performance (Airasian and Abrams, 2003).

Teachers in the case study schools address potential biases by working closely with peers. For example, at the Statens Pædagogiske Forsøgscenter School (SPF) in Denmark, teachers discuss the interpretation of student results in teams and how they can be more objective. As one teacher commented, "one sees what one wants to see". These teachers noted that the quality of their assessments has improved as they have worked with other teachers to bring potential biases to light.

Creating opportunities for peer support and observation

Teachers also benefit from observation and feedback when they are making fundamental changes to their teaching practice. The support of peers and school leaders – or at a minimum, of professional networks – is essential to making deep and sustained changes in approaches to teaching. Teachers in several of the case study schools said that working together on student assessment has helped them to develop more collegial cultures and deepened their understanding of those elements most important to formative assessment. In several of the case study schools, teachers participate in training opportunities on formative assessment as a group, or regularly take opportunities to observe each other.

School leaders have taken several approaches to creating opportunities for teachers to observe each other. At Waitakere College in New Zealand, the school supports a half-time mentor who regularly observes teachers participating in the Maori Mainstream (*Te Kotahitanga*) pilot programme, providing feedback and suggestions for improvement. The teachers participating in the programme meet regularly to discuss their own experiences. At Seven Kings High School in England, the school is investing in an observation lab, where teachers are videotaped and have the opportunity to analyse their own teaching.

SCHOOL-WIDE BENEFITS

As noted earlier in this study, a number of case study schools have moved from failing to exemplary status. Such dramatic changes in school performance required time, dedication, crativity, and the willingness to take risks. The case study schools have realised school-wide benefits as they have implemented formative assessment in departments and across schools. Anecdotal evidence of the benefits includes:

- *Improved "learning to learn" skills.* Teachers at the PROTIC programme in Québec said that students show a genuine knowledge of the learning process and share the language of formative assessment with teachers. Teachers at the Michelangelo School in Bari reported that, by their third year at the school (age 14), students are fairly independent, are able to draw relations between new concepts and what they have learnt previously, and are trying to understand the context of new concepts better. In other words, the students are developing individual learning schemes.

- *High value-added.* In the 2001-02 school year (the year prior to the case study visit), the Seven Kings High School in England was recognised as having achieved the second highest value-added in the country. A large percentage of the student population at Seven Kings High School belongs to special needs categories, such as English as an additional language, refugee status, disability, and/or eligibility for free lunch. School leaders at Rosehill College in Auckland, New Zealand, noted that their students are achieving the same or better results as students from schools with higher socio-economic status student populations. At Rosehill, school leaders also noted that high standards have been maintained, in spite of evidence that the writing and reading abilities and the attitudes of incoming students are declining. This suggests that teaching and learning programmes are helping students to close learning gaps effectively.

- *Increased student retention and attendance.* The Maori Mainstream Programme at Waitakere College in Auckland, New Zealand, pointed to better retention and attendance rates as a major advance.

- *Gains in academic achievement, and greater attention to the weakest students.* Teachers at the Xavier School in Newfoundland say that they are able to pay greater attention to the weakest students and are seeing improved learning outcomes for these students. Results from the English case study schools show student achievement gains in externally mandated tests. Researchers from King's College, London noted that the results from departments participating in the project, if replicated across a whole school, would "... raise the performance of a school at the 25th percentile of achievement nationally into the upper half". (Wiliam *et al.*, 2003) Other case study schools point to improved results in ministerial tests, including the PROTIC programme in Québec, and Rosehill College in Auckland, New Zealand.

Table 5.2 summarises some of the strategies school leaders developed to address barriers.

Table 5.2. School leaders across the case study schools developed strategies to initiate, sustain and deepen change

School level barriers to change	Strategies to address barriers
Difficulty of influencing classroom level change	Keeping the focus on teaching and learning Encouraging professional development Encouraging peer support
Lack of innovation or risk-taking with new methods	Using problems as learning opportunities Parlaying unrelated initiatives into changes in approaches to teaching Taking advantage of pilot projects, partnerships with universities
Negative attitudes about student capabilities	Allowing teachers to build confidence in their use of formative assessment before using new methods with lower achieving students
Teacher isolation	Creating opportunities for peer support and observation in classrooms and in videotapes and observation laboratories
Difficulty of sustaining change	Focusing attention on data regarding the impact of teaching practices Developing and disciplining teachers' skills for innovation and creating fertile ground for change

ADDRESSING CHALLENGES AND SUSTAINING INNOVATIONS

Teachers and school leaders in the case study schools worked hard to address logistical barriers to using formative assessment in their classrooms. They found creative ways to address barriers to practice. Evidence from case study schools shows that they realised direct benefits in their interaction with students, improvements in the quality of their own teaching, and in the quality of student work.

However, it is important to note that deeper, sustained changes across schools required longer periods of time, skilful leadership, and the careful building of collegial cultures. In some cases, the schools taking on formative assessment were at the "tipping point" – that is, they were ready to take on formative assessment quite quickly and to see significant benefits, including high value-added, and overall gains in achievement. In several of the cases, teachers were participating in special projects and innovations, and thus benefited from extra resources and support.

There is the danger that the effect of special projects will wear off over time, and that teachers will be unable to sustain changes. However, there are at least three reasons to expect that formative assessment, when applied systematically, will have longer staying power within schools. First, when schools develop cultures of evaluation and regularly refer to data regarding the impact of teaching practices, they are more likely not only to sustain innovations, but also to take them further. Second, while schools in the case studies may have benefited from special attention and extra resources during the initial implementation phases of a pilot project, they are also developing their facility to innovate, and are preparing the ground for further change. Third, as demonstrated in Chapter 2, countries that have a strong mix of policies promoting the practice of formative assessment can use multiple strategies to support school level change.

The case study schools' experiences show that deep and sustained changes entail focused and strategic efforts within schools. Spreading formative assessment on a broader basis will require strong policy leadership and significant investments in capacity-building and opportunities to innovate. The next chapter suggests how policy can better ensure wider and deeper practice of formative assessment.

References

Airasian, P.W. and L.M. Abrams (2003), "Classroom Student Evaluation" in T. Kellaghan and D.L. Stufflebeam (eds.), *International Handbook of Educational Evaluation*, Kluwer Academic Publishers, Dordrecht, Netherlands, pp. 533-548.

Elley, W.B. and I.D. Livingstone (1972), *External Examinations and Internal Assessments. Alternative Plans for Reform*, New Zealand Council for Educational Research, Wellington, New Zealand.

Harlen, W. (ed.) (1994), *Enhancing Quality in Assessment*, Chapman, London.

Kellaghan, T. and V. Greaney (1992), *Using Examinations to Improve Education: A Study in Fourteen African Countries*, World Bank, Washington, DC.

Kellaghan, T. and G. Madaus (2003), "External (Public) Examinations", in T. Kellaghan and D.L. Stufflebeam (eds.), *International Handbook of Educational Evaluation*, Kluwer Academic Publishers, Dordrecht, Netherlands.

OECD (2004), *Innovation in the Knowledge Economy: Implications for Education and Learning,* OECD, Paris.

Pennycuick, D. (1990), "The Introduction of Continuous Assessment Systems at Secondary Level in Developing Countries" in P. Broadfoot, R. Murphy and H. Torrance (eds.), *Changing Educational Assessment. International Perspectives and Trends,* Routledge, London, pp. 106-118.

Rist, R.C. (1977), "On Understanding the Process of Schooling: The Contribution of Labelling Theory" in J. Karabel and A.H. Halsey (eds.), *Power and Ideology in Education*, Oxford University Press, New York.

Wiliam, D. *et al.* (2003), "Teachers Developing Assessment for Learning: Impact on Student Achievement", *Assessment in Education: Principles, Policy and Practice,* CARFAX, Oxfordshire.

Chapter 6
Policy Implications

> Policy can do more to encourage and facilitate wider practice of formative assessment. Building on findings of the "What Works" case studies and international literature, the chapter proposes policy principles to encourage wider, deeper and more sustained practice of formative assessment.

This study set out to examine promising practices in formative assessment across several OECD countries. The case studies and international literature reviews informing this analysis show that formative assessment is much more than a set of best practices; teachers using formative assessment change the culture of their classrooms.

Each of the countries participating in this study, as discussed in Chapter 2, has policies to promote the wider practice of formative assessment. Yet, policy can do more to encourage and facilitate wider practice of formative assessment. This chapter outlines policy principles of formative assessment to promote wider, deeper and more sustained practice. The policy principles, which are explored at greater length in the following pages, are to:

1. Keep the focus on teaching and learning.
2. Align summative and formative assessment approaches.
3. Ensure that data gathered at classroom, school and system levels are linked and are used formatively.
4. Invest in training and support for formative assessment.
5. Encourage innovation.
6. Build stronger bridges between research, policy and practice.

The aim of these principles is to ensure that the schools included in this study are no longer considered exceptional, but are representative of common practice.

POLICY PRINCIPLE 1: KEEP THE FOCUS ON TEACHING AND LEARNING

At the policy level, a strong focus on teaching and learning means that policy leaders and officials send consistent messages about the importance of quality teaching and student assessment, of adapting teaching to meet a diversity of student needs, and of promoting students' skills for "learning to learn". This does not mean that policy should provide detailed guidance on what is to happen in classrooms – far from it. Rather, policy focused on teaching and learning should recognise complexity, be concerned with the *process* of learning, and look to a broad range of indicators and outcome measures to better understand how well schools and teachers are performing.

A strong focus on teaching and learning at the policy level is essential to each of the remaining principles.

Figure 6.1. Coordinating the elements of formative assessment

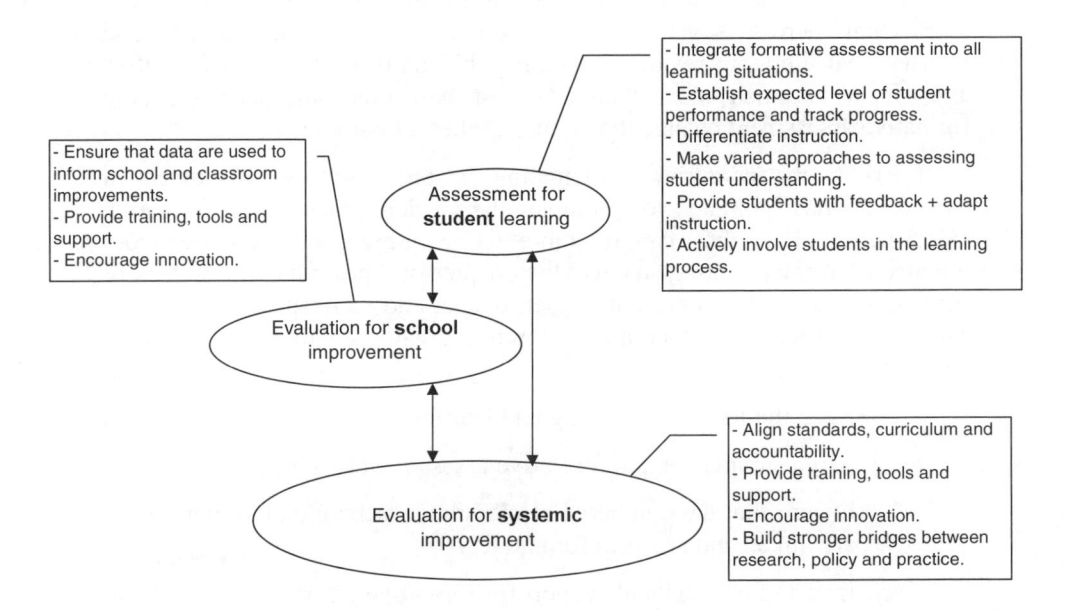

- Ensure that data are used to inform school and classroom improvements.
- Provide training, tools and support.
- Encourage innovation.

Assessment for student learning
- Integrate formative assessment into all learning situations.
- Establish expected level of student performance and track progress.
- Differentiate instruction.
- Make varied approaches to assessing student understanding.
- Provide students with feedback + adapt instruction.
- Actively involve students in the learning process.

Evaluation for school improvement

Evaluation for systemic improvement
- Align standards, curriculum and accountability.
- Provide training, tools and support.
- Encourage innovation.
- Build stronger bridges between research, policy and practice.

Keep the focus on teaching and learning

Note: Education stakeholders can use information to shape improvements at every level of the system. Teachers use formative assessment to improve teaching and learning. Policy and school leaders can also support teaching and learning through encouragement of innovation, investments in training and ongoing professional development, and the development of tools to support formative assessment. Policy can also help to build stronger bridges between research, policy and practice.

Source: Authors.

POLICY PRINCIPLE 2: ALIGN SUMMATIVE AND FORMATIVE ASSESSMENT APPROACHES

Data gathered in both summative and formative processes are vital to understanding whether individual schools – and systems – are meeting goals for high-achievement, high equity, and lifelong learning. Yet, as noted throughout this study, misalignment of standards, curriculum and accountability approaches present major barriers to the effective practice of formative assessment.

In addressing tensions between tests used for school accountability, and classroom-based formative assessments, policy officials will need to consider the need for multiple measures of student progress to ensure stronger validity and reliability of measures. Multiple measures of student progress lessen the pressure on teachers and students to perform well on a single, high-visibility test, and help to avoid well-known socio-economic, gender and cultural biases of large-scale tests.

Tests and other measures of student progress also need to be well-designed. Tests that stress recall or recognition of factual information, as opposed to critical thinking and analytical abilities, exacerbate the tendency for teachers to engage in "drill and kill" exercises (Kellaghan and Madaus, 2003).

Improving alignment of summative and formative assessment

At the most basic level, alignment means that education stakeholders ensure that policies do not compete with each other. At a more sophisticated level, the elements of formative and summative assessment reinforce each other. Well-designed standardised tests, inspection systems or school-based evaluations can measure students' ability to reason and apply knowledge to new situations. Information on student performance gathered through more sophisticated approaches to assessment and evaluation can help shape strategies at the systemic, school and classroom levels.

The first and possibly most important step in addressing these challenges is to ensure that standardised tests measure students' reasoning skills, their understanding of key concepts, and ability to develop strategies for addressing problems. Policy may also encourage the development of measurements for other important aspects of education, such as student motivation, or ability to work well in teams – an important skill for lifelong learning.

Second, teachers will likely need to be convinced that using formative assessment will lead to equal or better student performance. Policy leaders and officials may need to make a concerted effort to share the results of studies that show the positive impact of using formative assessment if they are to convince teachers that summative and formative assessments are not inherently at odds.

As noted previously, several of the case study schools achieved good or outstanding results on external examinations, have received outstanding reviews from inspectorates, or have done particularly well when results are viewed in terms of "value-added". Teachers in these schools were perhaps unusual in their willingness to take risks and to use innovative teaching methods, but their example may be useful to other teachers integrating formative assessment into their practice.

Finally, and perhaps most importantly, policy can ensure that school and teacher performance are judged not only on the results of tests or school inspections, but on a wider range of measures, such as student motivation, ability to work in groups, and so on. Policy officials, school leaders and teachers will have much richer sets of data on which to base their strategies for improvement.

POLICY PRINCIPLE 3: ENSURE THAT DATA GATHERED AT CLASSROOM, SCHOOL AND SYSTEM LEVELS ARE LINKED AND ARE USED FORMATIVELY, TO SHAPE IMPROVEMENTS AT EVERY LEVEL OF THE SYSTEM

Assessments and evaluations on student and school performance are of little consequence if the data are not used. At the school level, this means strengthening evaluation cultures. At the policy level, this means better linking assessment and evaluation at the classroom, school and system levels.

Strengthening evaluation cultures in schools

Schools that have strong evaluation capabilities are able to identify patterns and trends in school performance, and to develop a sophisticated understanding of the school and the viewpoints of various stakeholders. It is important to note, however, that there are also several potential barriers to effective school-based evaluation:

- School leaders and teachers often lack training in the art of data gathering and analysis (which involve different skills than those used in classroom assessment). A lack of understanding regarding the purposes and uses of evaluation may lead to unevenness in data gathering, poor use of evidence, or the development of unsupported conclusions (Monsen, 2002; Simmons, 2002).

- Evaluation tools may be more suited to needs of policy makers who have introduced them than they are to schools and teachers, who have needs for different types of information (Lander and Ekholm, 1998).

- External pressure on schools to conduct self-evaluation can take away schools' intrinsic motivation and feelings of control over the process of evaluation, or may even be seen as bureaucratic interference and a challenge to their professionalism (Monsen, 2002).

- School-based evaluation may face competition from new initiatives, obligations and time commitments. Teachers often complain that school-based evaluation is time consuming and does not relate to their classroom obligations (although it should be noted that teachers are willing to spend the time needed to gather information on pupil learning). School leaders and teachers may also have a tendency to see evaluation as a discrete project with a beginning and an end, rather than as an ongoing commitment (Monsen, 2002).

Several OECD countries support school-based evaluation either as the primary or only form of school-level evaluation, or as a complement to external testing, inspections and evaluation. Policy can take important steps to strengthening evaluation cultures in schools by addressing barriers and better linking assessment and evaluation at systemic, school and classroom levels.

School leaders and teachers are likely to need training in order to use data addressing concerns of school management. When schools are able to make useful connections between what's happening in classrooms and at the school level, school staff are better able to understand the implication of data for the classroom, as well as longer-term strategic concerns facing schools.

The practice of classroom-based formative assessment can help teachers to develop greater facility with data analysis. With training and experience, teachers and school leaders are better able to complement external evaluation with knowledge of local conditions and contextual issues, and by improving interpretation and usefulness of external findings (Glassman and Nevo, 1988). In turn, local evaluators may very likely be more receptive to using external data for school improvement if local conditions are recognised. Certainly, as communities become more diverse, it is important that evaluations consider the viewpoints and values of communities in the interpretation of data (Nevo, 2002).

Linking classroom, school and systemic assessment and evaluation

Policies that link a range of well-aligned and thoughtfully developed assessments at the classroom, school and system levels will provide stakeholders with a better idea as to whether and to what extent they are achieving objectives. Policy and school leaders and teachers will have a sound basis on which to make improvements, and will broaden teaching as well as policy repertoires.

Formative assessment, when applied at each level of the system, means that all education stakeholders are using assessment for learning. Policy often ignores classroom level variables, to its detriment. As Reynolds (1998) points out, the greatest variations in student learning occur not among schools, but within schools, among subject departments and individual teachers. This implies that it is more important to focus on classroom variables than on school variables. Policy has much to learn by looking "inside the black box" of classroom practice.

POLICY PRINCIPLE 4: INVEST IN TRAINING AND SUPPORT FOR FORMATIVE ASSESSMENT

Policy can support school leaders and teachers in improving teaching and formative assessment through investments in effective teacher training and ongoing professional development and extra support for pilot programmes to test new ideas and approaches to formative assessment. Policy can also support the development of guidelines, and tools such as rubrics and exemplars, to aid the assessment process.

Invest in effective teacher training and ongoing professional development

Teacher training and professional development are key strategies for improving teaching and bringing change to schools. In the majority of OECD countries, national education ministries or departments have influence over the curriculum for initial teacher training, and standards for teacher certification. Policy officials in these countries have an ideal opportunity to provide teacher trainees with the knowledge and skills necessary for student assessment, and the ability to respond to identified student learning needs with a broad repertoire of approaches and techniques. Effective training in formative assessment requires more than adjustments to the teacher training curriculum, however. When possible, policy should encourage the practice of formative assessment in schools of education, as well. University professors should model formative assessment techniques in their own teaching, and sponsoring schools should provide student teachers with opportunities to test the methods they are learning about during student teaching.

Teachers already in the workforce also need opportunities to participate in professional development programmes and to test out new ideas and methods. Effective professional development can be expensive, however. Policy officials may need to analyse the impact of investments in different schools with an eye toward developing effective and cost-efficient professional development strategies in the future. Policy can provide guidance to individual schools as to how professional development funds (often a combination of national and school level investments) are best spent.

In addition to training in formative assessment, teachers and school leaders can benefit from training in the use of data generated at the school and system levels, and in the use of research data (addressed in more detail below).

Develop appropriate tools to encourage formative assessment

Teachers need ways to translate abstract ideas – such as child-centred learning – into concrete practice. Vague or purely conceptual programmes are unlikely to get far or to last very long – particularly since teachers are busy with ongoing pressures and demands on their time. Teachers benefit from having access to exemplars and tools that help them to incorporate information gathered during the teaching process into their practice. Several of the national governments in the case study countries, as discussed in Chapter 2, provide tools, such as rubrics and forms to track student progress, exemplars, and guidelines to help teachers examine the substance of their lessons.

POLICY PRINCIPLE 5: ENCOURAGE INNOVATION

Many teachers may need explicit "permission to innovate". Teachers are often wary of developing or implementing new approaches and techniques to use with their students for fear of failure (including poor results on external tests or school inspections, upset parents, or other bad results). This is not unreasonable given teachers' frequent experience with the "implementation dip" (that is, student results go down before they improve) (Fullan, 2001).

Giving teachers permission to innovate means that policy and school leaders alike actively encourage teachers to take risks and to try new things (albeit, disciplined by careful attention to evidence of effectiveness) and have a level of tolerance for anticipated implementation dips. Policy and school leaders can encourage innovation on an everyday basis (not solely on centrally sponsored projects) by fostering and encouraging confident teachers, and encouraging peer support and cooperation with researchers.

Policy can also encourage innovation through support for pilot projects, although it should also ensure that pilot projects are not scaled up until their impact has been fully evaluated and the implementation challenges are well understood. Several of the schools included in this study have participated in pilot or other special projects before deciding to adopt formative assessment teaching methods. Their participation in these projects helped to prepare the ground for further change, and created a culture of risk-taking and interest in new and different ways of doing things. As participants in special projects, teachers have also, in many cases, received additional professional development opportunities, and occasionally, have benefited from additional resources. While, as noted in Chapter 5, there is the danger that the energy for special projects will disappear over time, schools that develop cultures of evaluation and regularly refer to data are more likely to sustain those approaches that work.

POLICY PRINCIPLE 6: BUILD STRONGER BRIDGES BETWEEN RESEARCH, POLICY AND PRACTICE

Policy can encourage the building of stronger bridges between research, practice and policy by: investing in training for research literacy for practitioners, as well as policy officials; developing "best-practice" databases and centres to catalogue and disseminate the results of research; and, investing in support for further research. Formative assessment may be particularly conducive to building stronger links among these stakeholders – as researchers may also participate in the formative feedback loop.

In several of the case studies, teachers partnered with university-based researchers to strengthen teaching methods. Working in partnership with trained researchers, teachers in several of the case study schools have developed rigorous analyses of the impact of approaches to assessment, and adaptation of teaching. But schools with these strong connections were the exception rather than the rule. Ideally, policy will encourage and support the development of more university-school partnerships. At the very least, policy can strengthen the capacity of practitioners to draw upon research findings, and of researchers to develop more "user-inspired" research (that is, research that takes user-needs and the demands of the teaching and learning process into account) (OECD, 2002). School leaders and teachers can also build their research literacy and skills in gathering evidence.

Most countries place some emphasis on identifying and sharing best-practice. It is important to ensure that practices included meet carefully-chosen criteria for quality teaching and student assessment, discuss the conditions under which practices are most effective and useful to teachers, and present information in a way that is useful to teachers. Some countries also disseminate videos of best practice to ensure that teachers have a real opportunity to see what innovations look like in practice.

Investments in further research

While there is evidence that formative assessment methods have a significant impact on student learning, there is a need for further research. Future research may address:

- **The impact of formative assessment on general student achievement.** While there is convincing evidence that formative assessment is indeed highly effective in raising levels of student achievement (see Black and Wiliam, 1998; Natriello, 1987; Crooks, 1988), the research should be extended and strengthened. Further research in this area may include both quantitative and qualitative studies of formative methods, drawing upon a breadth of international educational experiences.

- **The relative impact of formative assessment methods for underachieving students.** Several studies show that formative assessment methods have an even stronger impact for underachieving students. Selected studies focus on teaching which stresses the importance of effort over ability, or of task-centred feedback (as opposed to ego-involving feedback). These studies show relatively stronger improvements for previously underachieving students. Further research in this area may have significant implications for teachers working with larger groups of underachieving students or in "failing" schools.

- **Effective formative approaches for students based on gender, ethnicity, socio-economic status, or age.** As noted earlier in this study, there is a need for more refined knowledge of what works for students in different socio-economic or demographic groups. Research in this area may explore the differential impact of methods on diverse learners. For example, research may explore the circumstances under which different students thrive on competition, or in more co-operative situations. Research may also explore the extent to which principles of teaching that work well for a defined group, such as the Maori Mainstream Programme (*Te Kotahitanga*) included in this study, transfer to other groups of students. Studies in this area may prove extremely important to addressing long-term challenges of closing equity gaps in student achievement.

- **Connections between students' emotions and learning.** The connections between positive emotions and improved learning are a major theme of neuro-scientific research on learning. This research, along with work in the area of educational psychology, can inform studies on the impact of different formative methods on student emotions, motivation, self-perceptions and achievement.

- **The expansion of teacher repertoires to meet identified student needs.** As noted earlier, if teaching is limited, the quality of student assessment will also be limited. Teachers need a healthy repertoire of approaches to setting up learning situations and responding to student learning needs. Teachers and researchers may form a healthy partnership for research in this area. Formative assessment requires greater transparency in teaching and learning, and is also quite iterative. The approach is ideal for researchers who want to explore the process of teaching and learning in normal classroom settings. Teachers using formative assessment may also draw upon research to further build their repertoires.

- **The challenges of deepening and broadening practice of effective formative assessment approaches and techniques.** This study has asserted that formative assessment methods are more than a passing fad. Still, there are important challenges to deepening and broadening practice of effective formative assessment methods and techniques. Researchers should pay careful attention to the success of various dissemination and implementation strategies. Policy, in the formative spirit, can draw upon this knowledge to adapt and improve strategies and deepen impact.

References

Black P. and D. William (1998), "Assessment and Classroom Learning", *Assessment in Education: Principles, Policy and Practice,* CARFAX, Oxfordshire, Vol. 5, No. 1, pp. 7-74.

Crooks, T.J. (1988), "The Impact of Classroom Evaluation Practices on Students", *Review of Educational Research,* 58, pp. 438-481.

Edwards, T. and G. Whitty (1994), "Education: Opportunity, Equality and Efficiency" in A. Glyn and D. Milibrand (eds.), *Paying for Inequality,* Rivers Oram Press, London, pp. 44-64.

Fullan, M.G. (2001), *The New Meaning of Educational Change*, Third Edition Teachers College Press, Teachers College, Columbia University, NY.

Gipps, C. et al. (1995), *Intuition or Evidence? Teachers and National Assessment of Seven Year Olds*, Open University Press, Buckingham, England.

Gipps, C. and G. Stobart (2003), "Alternative Assessment" in T. Kellaghan and D.L. Stufflebeam (eds.), *International Handbook of Educational Evaluation*, Kluwer Academic Publishers, Dordrecht, Netherlands.

Glassman, N.S. and D. Nevo (1988), *Evaluation in Decision Making: The Case of School Administration*, Kluwer, Boston, MA.

Hargreaves, A. (1989), "The Crisis of Motivation in Assessment" in A. Hargreaves and D. Reynolds (eds.), *Educational Policies: Controversies and Critiques,* Falmer Press, New York, pp. 41-63.

Kellaghan, T. and G. Madaus (2003), "External (Public) Examinations" in T. Kellaghan and D.L. Stufflebeam (eds.), *International Handbook of Educational Evaluation*, Kluwer Academic Publishers, Dordrecht, Netherlands.

Lander, R. and M. Ekholm (1998), "School Evaluation and Improvement: A Scandinavian View" in A. Hargreaves, A. Lieberman, M. Fullan and D. Hopkins (eds.), *International Handbook of Educational Change*, Kluwer Academic Publishers, Dordrecht, Netherlands, pp. 1119-1134.

Monsen, L.I. (2002), "School-based Evaluation in Norway: Why is it so Difficult to Convince Teachers of its Usefulness?" in D. Nevo, *School-based Evaluation: An International Perspective,* JAI Press, Oxford, pp. 73-88.

Natriello, G. (1987), "The Impact of Evaluation Process on Students", *Educational Psychologist,* 22, pp. 155-175.

Nevo, D. (ed.) (2002), *School-Based Evaluation: An International Perspective*, JAI Press, Oxford.

OECD (2002), "Educational Research and Development in England: Examiners' Report", OECD, Paris.

Reynolds, D. (1998), "World Class' School Improvement: An Analysis of the Implications of Recent International School Effectiveness and School Improvement Research for Improvement Practice", in A. Hargreaves, A. Lieberman, M. Fullan and D. Hopkins (eds.), *International Handbook of Educational Change,* Kluwer Academic Publishers, Dordrecht, Netherlands.

Simmons, H. (2002), "School Self-evaluation in a Democracy" in D. Nevo, *School-based Evaluation: An International Perspective,* JAI Press, Oxford, pp. 17-34.

Willis, P. (1977), *Learning to Labor: How Working Class Kids Get Working Class Jobs*, Columbia University Press, New York.

Part II
The Case Studies

Part II
Case studies

Canada: Encouraging the Use of Summative Data for Formative Purposes

by

Anne Sliwka, University of Mannheim
Marian Fushell, Department of Education, Newfoundland and Labrador
Martine Gauthier, Direction de la recherche, statistiques et indicateurs, ministère de l'Éducation du Québec
Rick Johnson, Assessment for Learning Unit, Saskatchewan Learning

OVERVIEW

In Canada's federal system, provincial and territorial governments hold exclusive responsibility for setting education policy. The Council of Ministers of Education, Canada, however, plays an important role in monitoring educational achievement across the provinces and territories. All provinces and territories participate in a pan-Canadian programme to assess student achievement in mathematics, reading, writing, and science on a four-year cycle. Results of the tests are shared with the provinces and territories, along with analysis by language. In most provinces and territories, summative assessment data are used to inform decision making on several levels: the level of the individual student, the school, and the system.

New curricula developed at the regional or provincial levels emphasise the individual learning process and make room for individualised feedback and the development of "learning to learn" skills (that is, "metacognition"). Current curriculum guidelines articulate learning goals and standards. For each learning outcome, suggested teaching and assessment strategies are included. For example, each student is requested, with the help of portfolios and learning logbooks, to set learning aims for him or herself, to observe, to document and to reflect upon the learning process. Such documents are used as a basis for individualised communication between students, teachers and parents about both the learning process and result. Elements of self- and peer-assessment are also built into lessons to encourage and develop student metacognition.

HIGHLIGHTS FROM THE CASE STUDIES

The case studies include exemplary schools in three Canadian provinces: Saskatchewan, Québec and Newfoundland and Labrador. A broad range of formative assessment practices are visible in classrooms.

The PROTIC programme in Québec is notable for many reasons, including the use of ICT, with emphasis on shared platforms to facilitate group work. But the programme's defining feature, in many ways, is its focus on developing students' cognitive, metacognitive and social skills. Students learn gradually how to master their own learning process.

The Sacred Heart School in Saskatchewan has developed a number of innovative approaches to teaching and assessment – including the development of mixed level groups, emphasis on providing students with choices as to what they will work on, and most recently, the creation of online electronic portfolios that both parents and teachers use to provide students with specific and timely feedback. These changes would not have been possible, however, had the principal and teachers not first made efforts to ensure that the school was a safer and more nurturing place. Sometimes, teachers and school leaders have been able to address both learning and behaviour goals through innovative teaching methods.

Xavier School in Deer Lake, Newfoundland and Labrador has improved significantly in the past several years, largely because of its commitment to developing instruction that is informed by analysis of test data. The school's emphasis on criterion-referenced, rather than norm-referenced assessment (that is, students are assessed against a standard, rather than in reference to their peer's performance) has also been important to promoting the school's ethos of equality and inclusion. Several teachers at the school note that greater attention to assessment has also led them to develop broader teaching repertoires.

Although a significant group of teachers across the case studies still feel pulled in different directions as they try to bridge the demands of combining standardised, summative testing and formative assessment, a strong evaluation culture is developing across the provinces and territories. It is widely agreed in the Canadian education community that both forms of assessment are two sides of the same coin.

CASE STUDY 1: LES COMPAGNONS-DE-CARTIER, STE-FOY

In Ste-Foy, as in other affluent upper middle class suburbs in Québec, public schools compete with a number of private schools. In the mid-1990s that competition posed serious challenges to the public school system. The *Commission scolaire des Découvreurs* decided then to take a proactive stand to convince parents that public education provided a serious and suitable alternative to the private system. In order to find out more about how and why parents chose schools for their children, the committee conducted a parent survey. A surprisingly large number of parents expressed an interest in technology-based instruction aimed at the development of complex skills. Some educational counsellors participating to the committee subsequently worked with the headteacher of Les Compagnons-de-Cartier school to develop an educational programme for a public school. While parents stressed the development of technological and higher-level skills and were concerned about how information technology could be used to promote higher-level thinking skills, teachers saw the need to improve co-operative group work and formative feedback. The committee also called for improved instruction in English and a second foreign language.

Out of these different visions for the future of education the basic concept for PROTIC programme was born. The ambitious aims of PROTIC required teachers with special skills both in pedagogy and in technology. Whereas most teachers in Québec are recruited within a school board and are then assigned to schools, teaching positions in PROTIC are announced publicly and teachers are recruited by the school itself. To make this possible, the school board needed to sign a special agreement with the local teacher union.

Initially, PROTIC was to be open for the best and brightest students but "the best students in our traditional system are not the best for PROTIC", according to a teacher in the programme. The school assesses student applicants and spends a full day talking to and observing them. The admissions panel screens for students who are intrinsically motivated to participate in this type of programme, who read and work a lot, and who possess the appropriate social skills to work in the PROTIC programme. Two out of three applicants are then selected.

The school has produced a flyer about PROTIC which is available to parents and students interested in the programme but most of the interest is raised through word of mouth.

Teaching and assessment at the school

PROTIC pedagogy

Teaching in PROTIC is always organised around interdisciplinary projects. One of the methods used is collaborative group exploration. Thirty-one students in grade 8, for example, are currently exploring whether the conflict between Israel and Palestine is an ecological conflict about scarce water resources or a religious conflict. The teacher in charge of the project teaches geography, religious education and French. The project lasts for approximately six months. In the first stage of the project, all groups research the issue of access to water in the Middle East. In the second stage, students look into the different religions, Islam, Judaism and Christianity, and their role in the conflict.

Students, in groups of four around a table explore one sub-question of their overall research topic. Each student has a laptop computer. The students use Knowledge Forum shared software to store and structure information, and to communicate about their work inside and beyond the classroom. The Internet, learning software, multi-media encyclopaedias as well as books provide the students with multiple sources of information. One group researches water purification in Israel and Québec from a comparative perspective, another group looks at irrigation systems and the role of water in Israeli agriculture. In the second stage the groups will examine the different religious groups and their perspective on the conflict. They will then present their results to each other and enter into a dialogue based on and about the different perspectives.

The teacher plans to simulate a debate between students representing the Israeli and Palestinian points of view in the classroom. In this way, students can apply their newly gained knowledge as they argue their case. Towards the end of the project, students will be looking at the role other international powers and institutions, particularly the United Nations, can play in resolving the conflict. Just before the school year ends in June, all students provide their contributions to a common website, including texts written by the students in French, pictures and charts, maps and graphics. Every PROTIC project concludes with the development and design of a common product, a book or a website.

All classes in the PROTIC programme use information and communication technology (ICT) in range of ways. Whereas language arts projects use IT mainly for research, word processing and publishing, the projects in mathematics and science make use of computers for analysing data gained in scientific experiments.

The atmosphere in classrooms is more like that in a newsroom or a company office. There is a lot of talking, but in general, a high-level of discipline. Some students are working independently, doing research on the Internet or writing. Some students work in groups, comparing and exchanging information. Most students stay at their table but some walk around, go to other tables and ask for advice. The teacher walks around the room, spends time with individual students and groups of students, looks at their work, asks questions for clarification, and provides feedback about the quality of written material. There is very little direct instruction during the lesson. During one of the lessons observed, one of the students asked the teacher what exactly "Extrême-Orient" meant. The teacher then asked the entire class for attention and passed the student's question on to the class.

Another student responded by giving the right explanation to everyone else in the class. Fifteen minutes before the end of each 75-minute period students in their groups exchange the knowledge they gained in that lesson, discuss open questions and plan how to proceed.

Communication continues after class. All students take their laptop computers home where they have access to their common platform on the Internet. "We often send each other e-mails about our work late in the evening", one student explains. According to the teachers, written communication by means of IT forces students to be as precise as possible in their contributions to a shared work process. Whenever a student uses language that is too vague, students from the peer group or one of the teachers respond through Knowledge Forum, asking for a more precise definition or better evidence. "It forces our students to work professionally", explains a teacher.

High levels of student autonomy

In the beginning of each project, students identify their individual learning aims within the framework provided. "When you actually write down those aims for yourself, it becomes much easier to make progress", says one student. Every nine days students reflect on their learning individually. They write about their own learning, their team learning and the achievement of personal and programme learning targets in reports. This is a core part of formative assessment in PROTIC: the written reports provide a record that students can use to make future choices and to analyse ways in which they might do things differently. They are managing their own learning processes.

Positive interdependence structures the group work: in a maths assignment, for example, groups are composed of students with five different levels of expertise. In order for the group to reach a higher level of expertise each one of the group's members needs to pass a test. "We always make sure to help and support each other in our learning", one student explains. To improve work, students give each other feedback on their teamwork skills, using a list of criteria provided by the teachers. "That helps us to solve the problems we have in our teams among ourselves", says a student. Each student makes approximately 20 presentations per year in front of the whole class and students comment on each other's presentation on the basis of criteria provided by the teacher.

Students also keep a learning portfolio, a folder in which they keep important pieces of their own work. In the first two years the portfolio is kept on paper. Starting with the third year students keep an electronic portfolio. Teachers and parents have access to the electronic portfolios and can comment on the work electronically. Teachers regularly go through the electronic portfolios and comment on the quality of the work, the strengths and the points that need further development. Many of the parents also take an interest in their children's portfolios.

After each 9-day learning cycle students set aims for themselves and define strategies for how those aims are to be achieved in the next learning cycle. Four times a year students receive their report cards, so-called bulletins. Three of those report cards are purely formative and contain comments on the student's work in several different areas. Only the fourth report card of the year is summative and contains pass/fail information. Trans-curricular skills such as self-organisation, use of technology, teamwork, communication skills and social skills are part of the report card. "I always look at my report card and decide for myself, yes, those are the areas I want to work on over the next months. The criteria really help you to see what you can do to improve."

Initially, most students found it difficult to deal with the level of autonomy expected of them after having been guided and directed much more in their previous schools. After a number of projects, however, it becomes much easier for them to plan their own learning. "You understand that you are responsible, you are in charge. You begin to see how much time you need to invest in a particular task for it to turn out well."

The students visibly enjoy being part of the PROTIC programme. "Compared to my old school there is a lot more pride here about our work: not about grades but about the results of what we do in the projects", explains a 13-year old girl who has recently left a private school to join PROTIC.

One shared language about learning and teaching

In separate interviews with students and with teachers, it becomes very clear that they all share a common language about teaching and learning. Even young students use words like "metacognition", "self-evaluation", "self-regulation" and "peer-assessment" to describe their own learning. The students seem to have a genuine knowledge and understanding of learning processes. It is obvious that teachers in PROTIC talk to their students about the dynamics of learning. "When we decided to come and teach in PROTIC", explains one of the first teachers to join the programme, "... we wanted our students to become experts about learning just like they are developing expertise in the other areas we work on here".

The role of teachers

Teaching in PROTIC is quite different from what the teachers learnt during their teacher education at university. It is only recently that the Université de Laval is taking a strong interest in the role of a teacher in a learning environment like PROTIC. "To be a teacher in PROTIC you have to accept that you are no longer in control of everything that's happening in the classroom. We are not the only source of knowledge any more." The teachers agree that their role in PROTIC is sometimes different from the traditional understanding of a teacher in Québec.

Teachers have access to Knowledge Forum, the electronic platform students use to store and exchange their work, at any time. The platform allows teachers to respond to individual students and groups of students electronically. "I primarily use questioning as a teaching strategy", one teacher explains. "I always try to make my students aware of potential improvements to their work by asking them questions." Students describe their teachers as being very flexible. "They played an important role in the first two years teaching us about methodology of working and learning. Now that we have become much more autonomous, our teachers interfere very little." Another student explained that "[t]he role of the teachers is to respond to our questions and to keep the discipline in the classroom". Teachers let students work on their own most of the time, but also spend half an hour or more with individual students when they need help. Given the high level of learner autonomy in the classroom this seems to be enough contact with the teacher. Students do not feel left on their own.

Creating conditions

Most of the teachers who initially applied and were selected to teach in PROTIC had been unhappy about a lack of opportunities for experimentation and professional growth in the system, and decided to join PROTIC because of the professional learning opportunities it offered.

The teachers share offices located in between the two PROTIC classrooms and work together several times a day, often very informally. They frequently spend an entire day planning new multidisciplinary projects together. They are proud of their ethos of collaboration. "The fun thing is that you can really keep learning here as a teacher, developing new projects, trying out new things, experimenting."

In recent years PROTIC students have been getting excellent results on the ministerial tests. Teachers and administrators see this as a clear proof that the PROTIC model works. The PROTIC pedagogy has had considerable impact on the instructional practices of other teachers, professionals or head members of the school Les Compagnons-de-Cartier, but so far it has had very little impact on the four other secondary schools in the area of the *Commission scolaire des Découvreurs*. Most of the school's visitors come from universities or from other district school boards in Québec and Canada. "We don't go out to proselytise but our doors are wide open to those who are interested", explain the PROTIC teachers. Because of PROTIC's clear focus on the development of transcurricular and metacognitive skills – both aspects emphasised at PROTIC and in the current provincial curriculum reforms – public interest in the programme is likely to increase.

Since 2002 PROTIC has become almost self-sufficient and requires very little support and assistance from the *Commission scolaire des Découvreurs*. This is also a result of the teachers' desire for a greater degree of autonomy. PROTIC now has very close relations to the neighbouring university of Laval and gets many teachers trainees for internships, some of them from as far away as France. Starting in the fall of 2004, a primary school feeding into Les Compagnons-de-Cartier is teaching according to the PROTIC programme so that students will have the opportunity to learn in projects and teams across their entire student biography.

CASE STUDY 2: SACRED HEART COMMUNITY SCHOOL, REGINA

Saskatchewan Learning considers Sacred Heart Community School in Regina an exemplary community school, both for the range of good pedagogical practices in the school as well as for the school's unique culture and ethos. The school is part of the Regina Catholic School Division, which is in charge of 29 schools with about 10 500 students. Catholic schools in Regina are publicly-funded and follow the provincial curriculum and other Ministry-level regulations.

Sacred Heart Community School is an inner-city school with approximately 450 students from pre-kindergarten to grade 8. The majority of students are of Aboriginal ancestry. Most of them live in poverty. Student mobility is high because parents often move within the city or back and forth between a reserve outside the city and the inner city.

Teaching and assessment at the school

First steps: addressing bullying and vandalism

The school's change story started when the new principal, an experienced female teacher and administrator who came to the school in 1995, made it a priority to take action against the high level of aggression and vandalism in the school. The first change she introduced to the school was the complete reorganisation of recess time. After each break there had been a long line of students in front of her office, sent there because of disciplinary issues. One boy, a victim of bullying, admitted to her that the thing he feared most in the school was recess time. Working in close collaboration with teachers, the new principal decided to completely restructure the school break. Recognising that students needed a break she replaced recess time with two breaks of 20 minutes each, with the class either in the gym or outside playing sports and different kinds of games the children enjoyed. The number of disciplinary incidents dropped immediately and that gave everyone in the school the courage to initiate and support further changes in the area of discipline.

One of the next moves was to address the high level of vandalism in the school. The principal talked to students about it in a special assembly and made them aware that the school's scarce resources could be spent on school trips and books for children instead of paying for the damage created by vandalism. She promised the students to provide them with the money to have an ice-cream party and go on a school trip if vandalism could be significantly reduced. As had been the case with restructuring recess time, the second innovation was a success. When vandalism dropped to almost zero, she invited the District Superintendent into the school to congratulate the children and to hand them the cheque with the extra money for the school. Vandalism and violence in Sacred Heart Community School have remained low since that time.

Split grades

Early in the history of its change process the school had a grade 5 class that was highly energetic with little discipline for learning, resulting in a high teacher turnover for that class during the one year. Principal and staff decided they needed an innovation that would harness their students' energy and "put it to more positive use". The following year, when the students entered grade 6, they put the class together with younger students so that the grade 6 students could act as mentors and leaders for the younger grade 2 students. Again, the change was successful. The two teachers who took on the task of "team-teaching" the class later won an award for one of the most innovative educational projects of the year in Canada.

The unique split grades have since been expanded to include the entire school. The split grades give each of the older students the opportunity to act as responsible leaders and to mentor younger children. Teachers try to create a culture of mutual support in the classroom. Now all of the school's classes are made up of students of two different age groups. Older students in lower secondary provide individual feedback and support to the younger primary school students.

School like a good home

The school's Catholic values are reflected in its core idea that every child deserves "to be treated like the Christ child". This strong value statement is part of the school's mission statement and is openly shared with the children in the school. Children refer to it when they talk about the way they are being treated by teachers and by other students in the school.

Aware of the deprived and often unstable conditions in many of the students' homes, the staff decided to turn the school into a place as safe and nurturing "as a good home" to provide the emotional stability necessary for learning. Now, students have access to the school at any time of the day. There is a warm breakfast for all students in the morning before the first lesson starts. Later, students get a snack and a warm lunch.

Parents are welcome to come into the school at any time. Many of them have had very negative experiences in their own school days, so Sacred Heart Community School tries to be as welcoming and open as possible. Every year there is a spring tea, where parents come in and are served tea by students and teachers. Parents are also invited to join field trips and to watch sports activities. Once every year there is a teacher-parent conference. Students present their work and their portfolios to their parents and teachers. Together teachers, parents and student discuss what the student needs to focus on in his or her own learning and how parents can support learning and development. During these meetings teachers encourage parents to help their children with homework and to take an interest in their child's portfolio.

Meeting individual learning needs

Sacred Heart Community School has developed different methods to meet the individual learning needs of students. Teaching assistants are available to provide individual student support inside the classroom. Computer programmes as well as library books are clearly marked with regard to their level of difficulty so that students themselves can look for the resources that best meet their individual learning needs. When a particular topic is being studied among mixed ability students, teachers choose different books for students of different ability level. In one case, for example, seven books about animals were being used when a class was studying animal behaviour. In the split grades, teachers often use two or more different coloured worksheets, with colours indicating the level of difficulty. Students can choose which sheet to work with according to their motivation and ability level.

From grade 3 onwards, students diagnosed with severe learning disabilities get extra support. They are referred to the teaching assistance team and are put on a Personal Programme Plan (PPP) to get the individual support they need. Whereas 2% of all Saskatchewan students are currently on PPPs, 10% of students in Sacred Heart Community School get extra support. Teachers observe a correlation between learning difficulties and the high poverty rate in the area. Some of the children from poorer families are more likely to have learning difficulties because of emotional, nutritional or other problems in their homes.

Classrooms are well-equipped with books for young readers and computers funded through local and provincial taxes. In each classroom there are shelves with a large number of books for the respective age-groups and each one of the classrooms is equipped with four networked computers connected to high-speed Internet. Students and teachers have access to the Internet and use it in the classroom. In the morning assembly, for example, the school principal frequently sets up a quiz such as, "How many taste buds are on a human tongue?". When they enter their classrooms for the first lesson, they go onto the Internet and research the answer.

A key part of the school's philosophy is to provide students with choices for their own learning. This is seen as part of the school's formative assessment strategy because it enables individual students to pursue their own interests and learning needs. Whenever a student is finished with a task in the classroom he or she is free to work on one of the computers with a range of ICT learning resources, or to get one of the books from the bookshelves in the classroom or from the student library and sit in the back of the classroom's comfortable reading chairs to read.

Brain-based learning in a resource-rich school

In recent years, the teachers have taken part in a lot of training activities in brain-based learning and multiple intelligence teaching. Even the children now speak the language of multiple intelligences. They talk about being "picture smart" (visual-spatial intelligence), "word-smart" (verbal intelligence) or "number-smart" (mathematical intelligence). It is part of the school's philosophy that each child discovers those things he or she can do really well. In the classroom teachers encourage children to use their strengths to learn those things that are a bit more difficult for them. In their portfolios children talk about their intelligences. "The teachers help us recognise what we are really good at", one student explains. Another student, an 11-year-old girl, reports that the teachers "asked me and two other students to write a book about Saskatchewan because we are good at writing". The books written by students are laminated and kept on the shelves of the school library. Students are proud of their own work and are happy to share their books on subjects such as starfish or dinosaurs.

Learning portfolios for every child

A pilot scheme in 2002/2003 with all grade 3 and grade 5 students convinced the staff of the effectiveness of electronic portfolios. Starting in September 2004 each child in the Sacred Heart School will be documenting his or her own learning on an ongoing basis with the help of such an electronic portfolio. Portfolios will primarily serve as a basis for formative feedback and student self-assessment. Through the portfolios, students will be able to track their own progress in writing, in reading and in other areas.

Students keep exemplary pieces of their own writing, document their projects, scan in hand-written texts and art work and even record their own reading in their portfolio under different headings. Teachers invite students to share their progress with other students and the teachers provide guidance to the students on how to assess their own work. In the near future, students will have benchmarks for portfolios, related to the proficiency targets developed in the school. A team of experts in the school is currently creating templates for every grade level. A teacher new to the school has developed user-friendly portfolio software allowing students to do as much work on their portfolios on their own as they possibly can. In the past year, the school has been very pleased with the way older students mentored younger ones in keeping their portfolios updated, saving and spell-checking their work. In the electronic portfolios, learning is documented under the following headlines: the Academic Self, the Social Self, the Artistic Self, the Problem-Solving Self and the Catholic Self. For the students keeping a personal learning portfolio seems to be a genuinely exciting project.

Report cards for formative assessment

Three times a year, students get report cards. The school has already made considerable changes over the past years to fit report cards to its pedagogy. Now, formative comments are a key part of any report card, along with marks. Nevertheless, most teachers in the school feel that they need to go one step further and change the approach to report cards completely. The teachers feel that it would make so much more sense to have rubrics on the report card, so that parents can see how they can help their child learn.

The teachers believe that there should also be a section on cross-disciplinary skills on the report cards. This would provide students, parents and teachers with information on a student's broader cross-curricular skills such as working in teams, communicating, and so on. In the meantime, the

Catholic school division has noticed that Sacred Heart School is ahead of its time. Teachers from the school have been nominated for a committee that will be developing new report cards for all schools in the Regina Catholic School Division. The school's open and non-bureaucratic mindset with regards to experimentation is now providing a successful model for other schools in the school division.

Creating conditions

When the school's previous principal took over eight years ago, the school was known throughout the city for its low achievement level, violence and vandalism. Few teachers wanted to work there and that was reflected in high teacher mobility. "Neither teachers nor students wanted to come here", according to the School Board's Superintendent. Today, the Superintendent notes, Sacred Heart leads in many areas. In terms of teacher collaboration, student assessment and early literacy strategies the school is even considered an example of best practice by Canadian standards.

The catalyst for changes in approaches to teaching and assessment at Sacred Heart came from unrelated initiatives developed to address bullying and vandalism. Success with these initial efforts led to enthusiasm for further change. "You notice", one teacher says, "that there is no end to innovation. You can't just change a little. Once you've made a change and you notice it works, you have to keep growing and changing". Since then, the school has made a number of bold changes in organisational and teaching approaches, as well as in the involvement of parents. Today, the school stakeholders share a philosophy that every child and every staff member can and does grow in a school organised as a professional learning community.

CASE STUDY 3: XAVIER SCHOOL, DEER LAKE

Xavier School, located in a small town in western Newfoundland, has 288 students (in 2001/2002) in grades 7 to 9. The school had received comparatively bad results when provincial testing first started, but results have significantly improved over the past years. The school has made a commitment to the development of instruction based on an analysis of test data and to building a strong professional learning community among teachers and members of the administration.

In 1993, the province introduced a tri-annual testing programme. Since 2001, the province has tested students in language arts and mathematics on an annual basis. The Department of Education advocates that the results of provincial tests be explicitly linked to school development. In some school districts, schools are required to respond to the test data by completing a written analysis of how the school will use the test data to improve the quality of instruction and which specific targets the school sets for itself as a result of the data analysis.

There are no rewards or sanctions for over- or under-performing schools and the data are not compared or ranked with data from other schools. The Department of Education's and the school districts' philosophy is to work with the principal and the teachers of a school to build on the strengths and to address deficiencies identified in the data. Individual schools are encouraged to view their progress over time.

Since 2001, schools in Newfoundland and Labrador have been developing action plans based on the provincial test results. School boards manage the planning process. Each school board brings principals together for two days. Consultants from the Department of Education review all test results with the district programme staff and school principals. Through this review and subsequent discussions, principals identify learning needs and incorporate them into their school development plan. The consultants are then available to help plan and implement teacher professional development programmes for schools that have identified teacher training as part of their action plan.

Teaching and assessment at the school

A range of assessment methods

Coinciding with a greater provincial and school-level focus on the importance of analysing test data, the teaching staff at the Xavier School have developed a stronger professional interest in formative assessment for learning. The analysis of data has made teachers aware of whole classroom as well as individual student learning needs.

In 2001, the school introduced school-designed mathematics tests at all grade levels tied directly to curriculum outcomes. The tests are used at mid-year and at year end as a complement to the provincial criterion-referenced tests (CRTs). These and other tests are being kept in a test bank to which each teacher has access. Now, test data are seen as informing teaching practice: "How well have I as a teacher done in teaching certain concepts?"

Student learning has become the focus of teachers' attention. "We are carefully monitoring and observing learning processes like we have never done before. Much greater attention is being paid to the quality of the individual learning experience." The systematic use of data to change practice at the classroom level and in the work with individual students shows a strong commitment to formative assessment.

Teachers also now make more use of reflective journal writing, rubrics, and portfolios than they did five years ago. The language arts teacher, for example, describes how she uses formative assessment in her classes. For example, she helps students to select appropriate reading texts and to determine writing activities. Students have a high level of choice, as the teacher believes that students must be accountable for their own learning. She monitors individual student tasks, and the type and amount of work that students do. To determine if the students understand what it is they are reading, each student must write a summary on the text and his or her thoughts on it.

In their response journal for reading in language arts, grade 9 students keep track of what they have read, why they chose a particular book, how they liked it, who their favourite character was and whether they would recommend the book to another student. Every week the language arts teacher takes her time to read the journals and comment on student writing. Her written response is based on a rubric. She also holds individual conferences with students. She sees evidence that close monitoring and immediate feedback show positive results. One student, for example, had stopped his reading of any book after about twenty pages. The teacher entered into a written dialogue with him and found out that the books he had chosen to read had been far too demanding for him. When she decided to suggest books to him rather than letting him select his own reading she observed his sudden pride in being able to finish and report on an entire book. "Constant interaction on a one-to-one basis, continuous observation and commenting, that's what makes students learn", she says.

A mathematics teacher describes his professional role in guiding student learning: "I get different pieces of information about a student, from the after-school tutor or the special needs teacher, for example". He sees it as one of his core tasks to draw all the information together, to make sense of it, to come up with a coherent strategy suited to that individual and to communicate that strategy to all of the adults helping that student learn.

The mathematics teacher notes that he and the students work through incorrect responses to problems. The teacher prompts the students to think about previous skills they have learnt that might help them solve the problem, to consider the different mistakes students have made and look for commonalities or trends among their problem-solving approaches. Through questioning, the teacher is able to help the students not only to determine the correct solution, but also to recognise and identify errors in their work.

The use of portfolios and rubrics for student self- and peer-assessment

Most students in Xavier School keep a portfolio of their own best work. In grade 9 language arts, for example, students are given 26 broad assignments to complete for their portfolios. Students move at their own pace to complete the assignments. To edit and improve their own writing, students make use of the criteria in the language arts rubric that was developed as part of the provincial assessment programme. The same rubric is used for peer- and self-evaluation. "I grade your paper with a rubric, you do it and then we talk about how our assessments match", she explains her approach to the students. This format gets teacher and student talking to each other about learning.

Tutoring and scaffolding for improved learning

A culture of peer tutoring is clearly visible in the school. Students work in pairs and support each other in English, in mathematics and in science lessons. Sometimes they can choose who to work with. In a mathematics class as well as in an English class, the teachers pair students deliberately, making sure that a student who is strong in the particular subject helps another student who is not as strong.

In a science lesson about temperature, grade 8 students get into groups of four to conduct an experiment. They measure temperatures of different materials in the room and discuss why the surfaces of certain materials are always colder than others. The teacher walks around the class to provide extra help to some of the groups. By prompting and scaffolding (providing individual students with hints that enable them to reach the next level) she helps the students in the groups find an answer to the research question.

In a grade 9 English class, students are working on their independent research piece for their portfolio. Those who have almost completed their written assignment are given a checklist for peer editing. The teacher puts them together in groups of two. Taking turns, the students read each others' research pieces and together they then use the checklist and the rubric to improve the quality of each other's written text with regard to expression, structure, grammar and spelling. Most students visibly enjoy working with rubrics: "You can see what you did wrong and how you can fix it. It also makes it a lot easier to set aims for yourself".

Inclusion and integration

In all Canadian provinces, students with severe learning disabilities are legally entitled to extra help inside and beyond the classroom. Students with disabilities seem to be well integrated in the Xavier School in Newfoundland. During a mathematics lesson, a special needs teacher in Xavier's school in charge of 13 students comes into the classroom to provide the additional support that one particular student needs for his mathematics learning. In addition, there is after-school tutoring for students who have problems getting their homework done without extra help.

The school's philosophy that every adolescent is different and everyone can learn has greatly contributed to an ethos of equity and inclusion. It obviously works for the students. This principle and practice of dealing positively with difference makes it okay for students with learning disabilities to have a special tutor come in.

Two lower secondary students, whose learning disabilities are too severe to allow them to be integrated into the regular class, work with a special needs teacher in a separate room. Whenever there is a birthday in the school those two students together with their teachers bake cupcakes for the birthday children. They deliver those cupcakes to the birthday child's classroom and congratulate the student whose birthday it is. It gives them a task in the school's daily life and makes them part of the wider school community. The principal says that they are fully integrated and well respected by all other students.

Creating conditions

Before 1999, Xavier School was in a very different condition. At the end of the 1998-99 school year, Xavier students had very low achievement scores in mathematics and science. There was little to no co-operation among teachers. "All seemed to be doing their own thing", describes the principal who took over the school in September 1999. The school building was in state of neglect. The staff room was old and poorly kept, corridors were in a terrible shape with ceiling and floor tiles missing throughout. In the school library books were scattered all over. Staff meetings were confrontational, and the school council (an association of parents, the principal, and a teacher representative that provides support to the school and provides a forum for parents to be involved in the education of their children) was not working well. The new principal was put into office with the clear mandate to turn the school around.

The new principal introduced a number of initiatives in an effort to change the climate of the school. Some of them were physical and meant to improve the school's outside appearance. The staff room was renovated, refurbished and enlarged and the school bought new furniture for the offices. The expectation for new staff members was that they would work toward increasing student achievement and building a collaborative culture in the staff room and in the school as a whole. School committees were formed to work on staff development, technology, finance, student supervision and the development of a school handbook.

Today, Xavier School in Deer Lake has a clear focus on meeting the particular needs of adolescents. This philosophy is based on a shared conviction that adolescents need support to balance their social and emotional life in order to concentrate on learning. There is a strong team ethos to achieve this aim. Teachers share information about each student's emotional, social and academic developmental needs. "Everyone here wants children to do well", the teachers report. Compared to other schools that some of the teachers have worked in previously, staff in Xavier's perceive this school as more welcoming and much more receptive to sharing of ideas and resources. "In dealing with adolescents, when there is no team spirit among the teachers, you sink", one teacher explains. A few years ago, teachers in the school worked in complete isolation, now they set aside half an hour of shared planning time almost every day. All of them now consider knowledge about how students learn and achieve to be their most important asset. "Five years ago we were doing a lot of nice projects in the school but we didn't take any interest in academic achievement", reports a teacher.

A clear mandate from the Department of Education and the local school district to let attainment data drive the process of school development also helped to change the school's culture. Initially, the staff resisted discussing achievement data or letting that data guide the development of a "school growth plan". By the beginning of 2000, however, the culture of the school had begun to change. For the first time, on the occasion of midterm reports, staff identified those students who were failing core subject areas. Their discussions centred on what could be done for these students. They subsequently decided to inform the parents of every student who was failing in order to try to build support for getting the students on track. Teachers also created a system of parent volunteers for individual tutoring. The school undertook a range of measures to motivate students for learning, one of them being the introduction of an annual awards night to honour exemplary achievement.

The school's greatest gains have been in academic achievement. Now teachers place a much greater emphasis on curriculum outcomes and pay more attention to the weakest students. Analysing assessment data has become the focus of professional training during what are called "school growth days". Since 2000, the staff have developed a two-year School Growth Plan, aligning the plan with professional development activities. Regular staff meetings are used for a sharing of good teaching practices.

Staff members of Xavier School report that they are using a lot of synergies they were hardly aware of five years ago. "All of us had three times as much work when we were working in isolation." Most of the teachers now also know each other better on a social basis, and meet with each other outside the school. Those friendships have contributed to the school's strong team ethos developed in recent years. A culture of recognition now permeates the school. The school administration acknowledges teachers' creativity and efforts. Teachers put activity sheets and other didactical material they use in their lessons into each others' mailboxes and discuss strategies they use to teach particular content with colleagues teaching the same or similar subjects.

Both students and teachers notice that most of the school's change has taken place with regard to the understanding of what "success" actually means. A few years ago, teachers in Xavier School asked "Who is our top student?". Now, each student is judged individually on a criterion-referenced basis rather than a norm-referenced basis. "Teachers notice how much effort you have put in, how you have improved based on where you were before", reports a student.

Parent involvement in the school has also improved over the past years. A parent representative reports: "You can come into the school and the staff room any time and are welcomed". The new emphasis on formative assessment has contributed to an improved understanding of learning among parents. The parent representative points out how much she and other parents like to read the comments that are now frequently written onto students' work. "They inform our own behaviour as parents. We can better help our children learn, because knowing the rubric we know what is considered good quality."

Denmark: Building on a Tradition of Democracy and Dialogue in Schools

by
John Townshend, education consultant
Lejf Moos and Poul Skov, Danish University of Education

OVERVIEW

In Denmark, primary and lower secondary phases of schooling are provided within the *Folkeskole*. The *Folkeskole* is to educate students for their role as autonomous, informed citizens. Open dialogue and exchange between and among students and teachers are considered essential to education, and reinforce the Danish model of democracy.

Parents pay a particularly strong role in Danish schools. They hold the majority of seats on school boards, as well as the chair. In schools, parents are involved, along with the child and teacher, in setting individual learning goals. Parents' rights and responsibilities are also spelled out in national legislation.

There have been several important changes to the education system in recent years. The Education Act of 1993 introduced the idea of "central knowledge and proficiency areas" to be taught in all Danish schools (although municipalities still approve curriculum proposed by school boards). Subsequent amendments have defined the knowledge and proficiency areas more precisely (2001), required schools to publish the results of average grades and leaving examination results for ninth graders on their web sites (2002). A 2003 Act introduced an "outcome-based" curriculum framework, defining competencies to be achieved by students at different levels (attainment targets).

There have also been several efforts to raise standards in Danish schools through special initiatives, starting in 1987 and continuing through the present. In 1999, the Danish Evaluation Institute (EVA) was established to carry out evaluations of teaching and learning throughout the education system. In spite of these many initiatives, EVA reports that there is a confusion about evaluation methods and tools that are appropriate for continuous evaluation in classrooms.

A recent OECD task force also noted the absence of a "strong tradition of healthy school self-appraisal", or of monitoring at the municipal or national levels. The task force called for the introduction of an evaluation culture in Danish schools, and reinforced the importance of the Ministry's recent emphasis on establishing central standards to better gauge students' progress and to provide accurate feedback to students about how well they are doing.

HIGHLIGHTS FROM THE CASE STUDIES

The Statens Pædagogiske Forsøgscenter (SPF), based in Copenhagen, was established to develop teaching innovations, and share the results of their work with schools across Denmark. Much of the work is centred on the importance of dialogue, verbal and written feedback, and active student (and parent) involvement in setting learning goals and evaluating work. There is also a strong emphasis on teacher teamwork, ongoing professional development, as well as institutional evaluation.

The Snejbjerg School in Herning has placed great emphasis on formative assessment techniques in its school and classroom planning. True to Denmark's strong democratic tradition in education, the school has established a transparent learning environment. Teachers, parents, and students engage in dialogue about their expectations of teachers, the school, and each other – for academic, social and emotional aspects of education. Teachers and students agree that this emphasis on dialogue and transparency of expectations makes this school different from many others in the area.

CASE STUDY 1: THE NATIONAL INNOVATIVE CENTRE FOR GENERAL EDUCATION (STATENS PÆDAGOGISKE FORSØGSCENTER – SPF)

Statens Pædagogiske Forsøgscenter (SPF) is a state pedagogical centre based in Copenhagen. It consists of an experimental school and a Youth Town. The SPF is intended to be innovative and developmental, but in a way that whatever is developed in this school can serve as an inspiration to other Danish *folkeskoler*. The purpose of SPF is to:

- Develop ideas for teaching the older grades of the *folkeskole*.
- Test the ideas in practice.
- Assess and disseminate the results of this work.
- Bridge the gaps between the *folkeskole*, the upper secondary schools, trade and industry, and society at large.
- Develop international collaboration.
- Participate in educational development.

The students of the experimental school start in the 8th grade and can continue for two or three years to 9th or 10th grade before they move on to higher secondary education, work, or other vocational courses. At the Youth Town, based at the same site, students from a lot of schools in greater Copenhagen are introduced to aspects of economic and professional life as well as aspects of democratic citizenship by means of courses conducted by teaching staff and visiting professionals.

The 144 students (48 at each year level) are taught all the Danish subjects required by law. As innovation is integral to teaching methods, all teaching goals are described in the annual project descriptions both for the specific subjects and as an overall plan for the three years of each student's tenure at the school.

Teaching and assessment at the school

Mixed groups

The students sometimes work in mixed groups where 8th, 9th and 10th graders are together. This is part of a whole school initiative called Moving toward a Project Oriented School. Mixed level classes are considered useful in furthering students' social development. However, for social and administrative purposes, students are put into classes of 24 or "core groups" of roughly 16 each which remain relatively stable throughout their three years at the school.

The school promotes varied teaching and assessment methods. The teachers use Howard Gardner's theories of multiple intelligences to diagnose children's varied learning styles, develop project-oriented approaches to teaching, and use portfolios to track learning and assessment. They often work in teams to develop and assess new teaching approaches and sometimes also work in teams in the classroom.

Development of verbal competencies

Students must feel self-confident in class if they are to dare to show what they are able to do. Activities to facilitate this in this school are: reading and telling stories, writing stories, logbook, diary, listening to music, interviewing other people, inviting guest teachers. Humour and fun are developed through play, games, video production, role plays, etc.

Verbal competencies are considered important for many reasons. One reason is that goals are set and feedback is given orally in the day-to-day classes, in study groups and individually. Goal-setting and oral feedback are also the focus of more formal student-parent-school conversations. SPF does not give more weight to tests and grading than is prescribed by regulations. Instead, the school stresses the importance of setting explicit goals and providing feedback in various forms. Great effort is put into displaying products of many kinds – writings and artwork, scientific models and other products in the portfolio and the logbook. Verbal communication is by far the most important means for gathering information about students' own goals, assessments, reflections and feelings and about the teachers' goals and assessment. Oral, rather than written, assessment is preferred because it is quick and flexible and permits students to initiate or respond to teachers. In this way it is possible to detect and correct misunderstandings and ambiguities on a timely basis.

One teacher, for example notes that she varies the forms of instruction, the ways in which desks are placed, and the material used according to the theme of the lesson. Sometimes she provides whole class instruction, sometimes students work in small groups, and sometimes they work individually. Project work is the most common working method. Regardless of theme and working method, she assembles the cohort at the beginning of the module and in the few minutes before ending it. At the beginning of the module, she wants to know what students are going to do in the next 90 or more minutes and how they are going to do it. At the end of the module, she wants to reflect with them on what they actually did, what they learnt and what they want to take up next time.

Over the course of the module she sometimes stops student activities in order to reflect on the work: How does what they have discovered or learnt fit the intentions of the module? Can the students utilise the model or concept presented to them as a learning tool? For example, the teacher has introduced a narrator-model as a means of analysing and interpreting short stories and she has asked the class to try to present what they have learnt in a short story and on a video. Often students get involved in different ways to interpret models.

Assessment through dialogue

Most often teachers communicate the results of assessments orally to students. Through questionnaires, qualitative interviews, and quick expressions of opinion, teachers evaluate the signs of progress. Teachers explain their assessments, and how the results influence further planning. The results of classroom assessments are sometimes posted to parents.

It is obvious that teachers at the school are considering how to balance verbal exchanges with students with more robust and written assessment. Teachers assess whether the intentions and the goals were achieved to a degree that is desirable and acceptable. Students are graded two or three times per year in each subject.

Student interviews

As in most Danish schools, there are student interviews several times per year. The student's progress is discussed and – in dialogue between teacher and student – new learning goals are set. Teachers use different assessment forms for the student interviews. Teams of teachers have developed these forms and they focus on whatever the team finds important at any particular time. There are questions on subject matter outcomes, objectives for learning, attitude toward the work, and social competencies. Sometimes the assessment is designed in collaboration between teachers and students.

Teachers often develop oral or written items for feedback on teaching procedures. Often the questions are about what the students have learnt and whether their objectives were achieved. Students also indicate where there is a need for further teaching.

Integration of formative assessment into all teaching and learning

SPF describes the concepts and practices of formative assessment that are integrated in the processes of learning as including:

- The student profile, which at SPF includes a record of student learning goals and assessments of progress.
- The logbook, which tracks each student's learning process.
- The portfolio, which is a compilation of student work and a record of learning outcomes.
- The student core groups.
- The student-parents-school conversations.

The student profile

Students in 8th grade are new to the school and unknown to the teachers. Therefore there is a need for students to reflect on their expectations of the work at this school and at the same time a need for teachers to get to know the students as well as possible. At the beginning of the school year students are introduced to basic learning theory/learning styles concepts, and among these to Howard Gardner's concept of multiple intelligences. Using these concepts, students write a profile that is both a self-description in relation to the multiple intelligences and a description of their expectations and goals for learning for the next two years in this school. The profile is a basis for a conversation between student, his/her parents and teachers in the autumn term.

One teacher described how students were introduced to Howard Gardner's theories of multiple intelligences, and were asked to fill in a questionnaire where all eight intelligences were represented and to mark all the expressions that applied to them. They were now getting a clearer picture of their own intelligence profile, and ended up making a circle divided in eight pieces, where they put all statements about themselves in the right area of the circle to visualise the profile. When students become aware of being "body smart" or "number smart" or any of the other ways of being smart, they also learn something about their own learning style. Do they prefer to work alone or in groups, to have details or an overall view, to look at or to listen, to move about or to sit quietly? The same group of 8th grade students had a topic in English called "How do I learn new words?". They were given a certain number of new words and different approaches to learning them. All approaches represented the different intelligences, and after they had all tried all approaches and activities, they were asked what method they had enjoyed the most and what had worked best for them. Linguistic students prefer to use the words in a text, make flashcards and construct games. Logical/mathematical students make systematic wordlists, look for similarities or compare them with other meanings or make up ways of testing. Spatial students like to combine word and picture, to use mind maps, colours and varied layout and writing in order to visualise the words. Musical students like to use the words in rhymes, music or rap, to say the words out loud both seeing and hearing the words. The interpersonal students prefer to do the activities in groups while the intrapersonal prefer to work alone.

The more conscious they become of their own preferred learning methods the more efficiently they learn and remember new words.

The logbook

The logbook is intended to facilitate and support students in their reflection on the goals and areas where they need to make effort for learning. It also gives more students the opportunity to be heard. Teachers may enter into written dialogue with students and discuss teaching and the outcomes. In this work teachers can strengthen the effort to develop students' writing as a springboard for more active participation in oral discussions.

Teachers collaborate with students on what parts of the work they are going to assess. Sometimes students complain about the number of assessment sheets and assessment deliberations. Therefore it is very important to stress the intentions and the use of the assessments. Every half-year – at school-parents meetings – teachers formulate new goals for the next semester. They try to find goals that can be written in the logbook.

Portfolios

Portfolios are a basis for student-parent-teacher conversations – sharing reflections and setting new targets and goals in collaboration with parents and teachers. Parents get, when working with students' portfolio, a better, more concrete background for entering into dialogue with teachers and their children. They can see for themselves some of the outcomes of students' learning and in what ways they themselves can support and encourage their children's education.

Core groups

The students' core groups are intended as forums for reflection. Students help and support peers as they reflect on goals, effort, and outcomes. They help each other to choose what material should go into the portfolio. For example, in an introduction to enquiry-based and project-oriented learning, 8th grade students were given a certain number of lessons to define something that puzzled them and then to come up with an answer by doing independent research. They were asked to present their answers orally to the rest of the group. The core group then engaged in many levels of formative assessment. The students gave each other oral feedback after each presentation and also wrote their opinions in their logbooks. They were asked to comment both on the content and presentation, based on written criteria for content and presentation methods (as well as what was important in the process) they had received at the beginning of the project.

Student-parent-school conversations

In each class there are two student-parent-school conversations every year. The basis for the conversation may change: the portfolio exhibition, the student profile. In one class students were asked to prepare the conversation by considering:

- In which areas of strength did you grow?
- How did you challenge your weaker fields?
- How do you assess your relations to class?
- What plans do you have for next year?

Students were invited to answer these questions in their preferred medium, for example with a cartoon, a cue for a conversation, a poem expressing his or her thoughts and feelings, or a mind map providing an overview.

Creating conditions

SPF's unique mission, to develop and disseminate innovative teaching methods to schools throughout Denmark, requires teachers to be up-to-date with advances in the learning sciences and school development. Formative assessment in the classroom – and secondary levels of formative assessment for school development – serves as a tool for teachers to evaluate the usefulness of the methods they are developing.

Formative assessment has also helped to create conditions for ongoing change. While school leaders felt that it was difficult to point to specific effects arising from the use of formative assessment, they describe the main effect as being a cultural change: students are more competent at seeking and handling information, and at reflecting on their own learning, their potential, and the effect of their actions. Many students are more socially confident. Both teachers and students were more than usually aware of learning goals. Some teachers felt that the stronger focus on goal-setting and on the feedback loop (that is, setting learning goals, assessing student progress and providing feedback, and revision of goals) was rewarding but time-consuming.

There is a strong emphasis on professional development and co-operative work. Teachers at SPF plan and implement in-service courses (a few hours each) for schools and teachers throughout the country, publish articles on their experiences in school development journals, and also participate in school development processes in other schools.

Teachers feel that sometimes it can be a problem to be both the agent and the subject when evaluating and analysing an ongoing process, and that it is sometimes very hard to formulate precise goals that are assessable. In the teams, teachers discuss how to interpret the results and how to be more objective than subjective (because "one sees what one wants to see"). Teachers say they are on a continuous pursuit for better and more secure methods.

Some students also were critical of too much discussion and reflection. In general, though, students were very positive about their educational experience and quite clear that this school was different from others they had known or heard of. They focused on two aspects: better relations with teachers resulting from different approaches to teaching; and formative assessment procedures. They felt that instead of getting "just grades" they now were involved in a process with teachers during which they got to know the teachers better and learnt why they had not got as high a grade as they might have wanted or expected.

There were some secondary levels of formative assessment as teachers used experiences and data from previous lessons to plan future lessons but this was greater in some subjects (Danish, humanities) than in others. Students found the various assessment processes (logbooks, etc.) stimulating and felt that formative assessment involved more commitment from teachers. Students were less positive about the portfolios. One said that the portfolio added nothing that his parents did not already know about his work.

The parents' representative confirmed that the aspects selected by the pupils were the essential differences in this school's approach. She described how her own son's logbook had improved over three years from single sentence factual statements ("Today we had maths") to quite sophisticated analyses of what teachers want compared with what he had done. She had also seen improvements in his approach to problem solving. She confirmed that the school's emphasis on social and personal development worked and that her son and other pupils she knew had grown in self-esteem since they had been at the school.

Those pupils interviewed were articulate and very positive about the school's innovative approaches to assessment. They were very able students, chosen for the interview partly because of their ability to communicate impressively well in English. The parents' representative and at least one of the teachers interviewed were convinced that these approaches were working well for good students but wondered whether they would work as well for all. Where there was reference – by parents, teachers and pupils – to achievement in subjects, they tended to be implicitly (and in a few cases explicitly) critical of innovative approaches to team-teaching and cross-year or cross-subject groupings. One ambitious cross-year team-teaching project had been progressively cut back from an original 17 weeks to four weeks this year and two weeks next year as a result of this kind of reaction. Innovative approaches to teaching and formative assessment within subjects tended to be seen more positively.

CASE STUDY 2: SNEJBJERG SKOLE

Snejbjerg Skole is part of the educational system in Herning, a town of about 55 000 in Jutland. The school is situated in a prosperous village-suburb. After the sixth class, all pupils are transferred from Engbjerg Skole to Snejbjerg Skole where they follow the curriculum for grades 7, 8 and 9. Seventy per cent of students at Snejbjerg Skole enrol in grade 10 (which is optional) at another school, which is attended by all 10th graders in the municipality.

The head of the Snejbjerg School had been involved with a European project on Evaluating Quality in Education six years prior to coming to the school. Her one-year tenure with the project coincided with changes in the role of school heads as defined by the Danish Ministry of Education. She used formative assessment as part of a strategy for change.

There is a strong emphasis in the school on the professional development of teachers and on spreading good practice by example. Some of the principles guiding the school's approach are:

- Students are always informed of the purpose of the evaluation before commencement.
- As a minimum, the evaluations are made public to the people involved before further publication.
- Results from formative assessment are only used for the agreed purposes.

During the last decade, the school has been involved in several school development projects, in which evaluations have formed part of the process of development actively. Generally, the management is very open about collecting and using the evaluations in the organisation.

Teaching and assessment at the school

Cooperation between the school and the parents

The board of parents takes part in developing an interview paper to be used in the parents' consultation evening. It contains questions such as: How do you assess your own work (commitments, outcome)? What is the social climate in your grade? What will you do differently in the next period of time? Often, evaluations involve conversation based on a questionnaire. The evaluations may also be based on tests, including Danish and mathematics. In a few classes, the school has started using portfolio for evaluation.

Expectation meetings

The school holds expectation meetings for all students except those beginning 7th grade. Students set out expectations for academic progress, and also set out their social objectives for the year. The social objectives focus primarily on the need to show respect for each other, that teachers will not berate students for any reason, that students will not bully one another, that students will take responsibility for themselves and their classmates, and so on.

The adults involved also set out expectations of each other (parents and teachers alike). At the Snejbjerg school, parents have set out their expectations as including: good and energetic teachers, who are aware of differences between children, are professionally competent, and who keep dialogue going between all participants (students, parents and teachers, and others). In turn, teachers communicate their expectations of parents: that parents help create the best conditions for their children's learning, and so on.

Parents expect each other to be supportive and open, to ensure that children are well-prepared for school, to show interest in the child's education, to take responsibility, and so on. At meetings held later in the year parents are to evaluate their expectations: "have our expectations been fulfilled and do we live up to our roles as parents?". These expectation meetings create a concrete and constructive starting point for school-parent collaboration.

Evaluation of a subject course

In the light of the objectives set, the teachers evaluate subject courses. The participation of the pupils takes place in different ways. The objectives are set collaboratively within the context of the curriculum, binding goals, etc. The evaluation is a part of the planning of the activities that strengthen the social community at school level. This means that students and teachers agree in advance (via intermediate aims) what points they will pay attention to during evaluation. Teachers and students may always discuss the course and learning objectives relative to new and possibly unintended results.

The evaluation takes place through group conversations, or between teacher and student, and joint conclusions are reached.

Assessment in teacher teams

The teachers evaluate the subject courses in teams. The evaluations are part of the written minutes from the meeting. Assessment in teacher teams is advantageous in that teachers can assess the work of individual pupils across a range of subjects. If a pupil is making better progress in Danish than in mathematics, this approach permits a reflection on why this is so and what different approaches might be used in mathematics. As pupils react differently in different instruction situations, teachers will find it natural to compare these different approaches to instruction. In this way teaching, as well as pupils' progress, is assessed. The key question is: What approach best facilitates the learning of individual pupils?

Stakeholders at the school see the formulation of these expectations as an important part of the process of formative assessment in the school.

Creating conditions

Snejbjerg has established an organisation that focuses on learning and on all round personal development of the individual pupil. The head of the school has had an important role in this. The development of the school is regarded as something concerning the whole school. Evaluation is essential to development, and parents participate actively in this evaluation. Teachers confirmed the importance of professional development in implementing the changes.

The school head and teachers are convinced that the new approaches based on formative assessment are working although some of the teachers said that this relies on a much greater workload for teachers. Both the students and the parents interviewed focused on students' self-esteem and social development as the main differences between this school and others. Objective evidence of success is difficult to pin down. The municipality publishes and compares the results of its schools but teachers and school leaders agree that the results reflect school intakes (*e.g.* the proportion of non-Danish speaking students) as much or more than school performance. There is no attempt to assess "value-added" to the students' learning over the year.

England: Implementing Formative Assessment in a High Stakes Environment

by
Janet Looney, OECD
Dylan Wiliam, King's College, London

OVERVIEW

England introduced radical changes to its education system with the Education Reform Act (ERA) of 1988. Under the Act, the government:

- Introduced a national curriculum and standards for compulsory schooling.

- Provided schools with a limited amount of autonomy (including control over the managerial and financial decisions, and decisions regarding pedagogical approach).

- Encouraged quality through market-style competition, allowing students to apply for admission to any school, in most cases guaranteeing admission, subject to available space.

- Required pupils to sit tests at the ages of 7, 11, 14 and 16, measuring achievement in relation to the curriculum. Subsequently, media initiated the practice of publishing results of tests in "league tables" as an indicator of individual school quality.

Formative assessment was not new to the British national education agenda when these reforms were introduced. In the 1970s and 1980s, a number of research projects had explored the ways in which assessments might support learning. Such interest in the use of assessment to support learning was given added impetus by the recommendation of the Committee of Inquiry into the Teaching of Mathematics in Schools (1982) that a system of "graded tests" be developed for students in secondary schools whose level of achievement was below that certificated in the current school-leaving examinations. Similar systems had been used to improve motivation and achievement in modern foreign languages for many years (Harrison, 1982).

In 1987, when the government announced its intention to introduce a national curriculum for all students of compulsory school age (ages 5 to 16), it was made clear that the national assessments at the ages of 7, 11, 14 and

16 (the end of each "key stage") would combine the judgements of teachers with externally-set assessments (DES, 1987). The National Curriculum Task Group on Assessment and Teaching (NCTGAT) asked to make recommendations about the structure for reporting the results of these assessments. They concluded that while ongoing, formative assessments could be aggregated to serve a summative function, in general it was not possible to disaggregate the results of summative assessments to serve learning purposes or identify specific learning needs. NCTGAT's first report therefore recommended that formative assessments should provide the foundation of national curriculum assessment for key stages 1, 2 and 3 (NCTGAT, 1988). There followed a vigorous debate about how the results from external assessments and those from teachers' judgments could be reconciled, but this debate obscured the fact that the teachers' assessments were summative rather than formative, albeit based on different sources of data than the external tests.

Efforts to incorporate formative assessment into the national curriculum were further complicated in the first five years following the introduction of the national curriculum by ongoing revisions to the new curriculum and national tests, and four changes of Secretary of State in five years. The central education agencies did little to promote the use of formative assessment in classrooms either through leadership on the issue, or through the provision of financial resources or teaching materials for teachers to enable them to devote more time to incorporating new teaching methods.

In the early 1990s, a group of education researchers and other professionals formed the Policy Task Group on Assessment, under the umbrella of the British Educational Research Association. The policy task group set up the Assessment Reform Group (ARG) with funding from the Nuffield Foundation. The ARG commissioned Paul Black and Dylan Wiliam of King's College to conduct a review of the research on formative assessment (also with the support of the Nuffield Foundation). The review, "Assessment and Classroom Learning" (Black and Wiliam, 1998), drew upon 681 English-language articles relevant to formative assessment, including a number of controlled experiments. Their synthesis of the evidence showed significant gains in student learning in classrooms using formative assessment.

While the Black and Wiliam article received attention among researchers and at the national educational policy level, the authors also wrote a short booklet, entitled *Inside the Black Box* (Black *et al.*, 2002), aimed at teachers and policy makers, which described the research and drew out some of the policy implications of the research. This booklet has sold over 30 000 copies since its publication, and Black and Wiliam have given over 400 talks about their work in the last five years, addressing over 20 000 teachers directly.

Funding from the Nuffield Foundation supported Black and Wiliam in working intensively with 24 secondary-school teachers (12 mathematics and 12 science teachers) in six schools in the nearby local authorities, where they knew there was both interest and organisational support for such a project. The King's-Medway-Oxfordshire Formative Assessment Project (KMOFAP) began in January 1999 by introducing teachers to the research on formative assessment through a series of three one-day workshops over a six-month period, between which, they were encouraged to try out some innovations in their practice, and to plan the innovations they wanted to implement with one class in the following school year beginning in September 1999 (for further details of the project see Black and Wiliam in Part III of this study). Lord Williams's School, featured here, participated in the KMOFAP study. Seven Kings High School, also included in this case study, developed partnerships with researchers at the University of Cambridge and King's College through the Learning How to Learn Project (based at the University of Cambridge), and through a replication of the KMOFAP project in the local authority of Redbridge. The other two schools in this case study, Brighton Hill Community College and The Clere School, were part of another replication of the KMOFAP work undertaken by King's College London team in Hampshire.

The KMOFAP, Learning How to Learn and Hampshire stories are important not only because of what teachers and researchers have achieved in these schools, but also because national level policy makers have paid close attention to these projects – as well as other research by Black and Wiliam and ARG – to learn more about what works. The experiences of schools included in this case study hold implications for national strategies to scale-up with the use of formative assessment across schools in the United Kingdom. In addition, Black and Wiliam have continued to make regular presentations on their research findings to teachers throughout the United Kingdom, an approach they have found to be quite effective in raising practitioner interest in formative assessment.

In 2002, the Department for Education and Skills (DfES), the Qualifications and Curriculum Authority (QCA) and the Office of Standards in Education (OFSTED) adopted the Assessment Reform Group's (ARG) interpretation of assessment for learning:

> Assessment for learning is the process of seeking and interpreting evidence for use by learners and their teachers to decide where they are in their learning, where they need to go and how best to get there.

The Assessment for Learning (AfL) project aims to provide teachers, school heads, local education authorities and other stakeholders with guidance and resources on the principles of good classroom assessment, as supported in research. The AfL campaign is perhaps the most visible national effort to promote the use of formative assessment in classrooms. Teachers are able to access a number of tools, background materials, and references on formative assessment from the DfES's *www.teachernet.gov.uk*. Teachernet materials include sample lesson plans, a case study database, an online pupil achievement tracker, links to professional development opportunities, ARG materials describing the basics of good assessment practice and a national benchmark tool to help schools answer how well they are doing as compared to other schools. In addition, DfES's The Research Informed Practice Site (TRIPS, *www.standards.dfes.gov.uk/research*) makes available summaries of recent assessment for learning research written for teacher audiences.

Changes to the Key Stage 3 (KS3) strategy for students in grades 7-9 (ages 11 to 14) have also been an important part of the Ministry strategy for reforming teaching and learning in lower secondary schools. According to the DfES, the KS3 strategy, "... helps schools to improve standards by focusing on teaching and learning. It offers continuing professional development for subject teachers and school managers, plus consultancy, guidance and teaching materials" and encourages "engaging and well-paced lessons".[1] Several strands of the revised KS3 strategy were piloted between April 2000 and March 2002, and were introduced to schools on a national level in the 2002-03 school year.

HIGHLIGHTS FROM THE CASE STUDIES

The four case study schools partnered with researchers at the King's Formative Assessment Programme in projects developed following publication of Black and Wiliam's 1998 literature review on "Assessment and Classroom Learning". Black, Wiliam and other King's College researchers involved in the project (Lee, Harrison and Marshall) worked directly with teachers to develop and incorporate formative assessment methods into their daily classroom practice, and to measure the impact of the new teaching approaches by tracking the performance of their students with students in comparable classes at the same school (Black and Wiliam, 2003).

Each participating school identified four to five teachers for the project – usually department heads who would be in a position to influence practice throughout their departments. Many of the teachers found that by

---

[1] "Funding to Double over Next Two Years as Drive to Boost Standards in Secondary Schools Gains Pace – Blunkett", 23 March 2001, News Centre, *www.dfes.gov.uk*

making little changes they could get some very convincing results from students. In the schools visited, programmes quickly scaled up.

Some of the most striking features of the case study schools were:
- Focus on the process of learning as well as the content of what students were being asked to learn.
- Efforts to identify and put into practice more often those things that work well.
- Greater attention to what students retain, rather than curriculum coverage.

The research team tracked outcomes for the project, using a "local" design method that took advantage of available data to track progress. The details of their evaluation methodology are described in Black and Wiliam (2003). Researchers derived a standardised effect size for each class, with a median effect of 0.27, and mean effect size of 0.32. In practical terms, the researchers note, such improvements, "… if replicated across a whole school, … would raise the performance of a school at the 25th percentile of achievement nationally into the upper half".

This study includes four schools – one in Oxfordshire (Lord Williams's), one in East London (Seven Kings High School), and two in Hampshire (Brighton Hill and The Clere School). The experiences of these schools are described below.

CASE STUDY 1: LORD WILLIAMS'S SCHOOL

Lord Williams's School in Oxfordshire County serves 2 142 students between the ages of 11 and 19 (the school includes a 6th form, which caters to students preparing to enter university. Schools with 6th forms generally attract the best teachers in the system). There are 120 teachers at the school. Lord Williams's School is bigger than the average secondary school (Office for Standards in Education, OFSTED, 2002). It is on a split campus, with two sites more than three kilometres apart.

Four teachers from Lord Williams's joined the King's-Medway-Oxfordshire Formative Assessment Project (KMOFAP) in early 2000. Each of the teachers involved in the KMOFAP had a lead role in his or her subject-department and played a strategic role in disseminating the lessons they were learning and the new techniques that had developed through the project with others in their departments.

Teaching and assessment at the school

At the time of the case study visits, teachers at Lord Williams's School said they were doing a variety of things differently than they would have even a few months earlier. Importantly, teachers say that their lesson plans now focus on the regulation of learning (what students learn in class), as opposed to the regulation of activity (what students do in class). A teacher notes, "Rather than thinking of which article in the newspaper or which page in the text I'm going to use, I'm really thinking of which formative assessment I'm going to use, or a bit of both. ... But you've got to have the energy to do it."

Lessons are now more transparent. Teachers often set up learning objectives at the beginning of class. One teacher said, however, that she prefers not to always write up aims – instead, at end of lesson she asks, "what was the point of that lesson?". Teachers also use criteria in a more systematic way. Students are also given criteria regarding teachers' expectations for homework.

Teachers may also share exemplars with students, asking them to look at the difference between a piece of work that would merit a D grade, and one that would merit an A grade. Usually, however, the teachers do not leave the exemplars of prior work with the students for too long, for fear that the students will just mimic the good work they've seen (although that may have its value, too, teachers note).

Often, teachers will give students learning targets in science, mathematics, English and history classes. Each student will receive a different target, depending on what the teacher thinks individual students need to work on. Targets include goals such as: "use more variety in your vocabulary, use more conjunctions; check over your work more carefully" and so on.

Teachers at Lord Williams's School have given a lot of thought to their modes of questioning, for example, playing more emphasis on "why" questions so that students are forced to use their own logic to understand a concept. A teacher notes that "Sometimes you've got to start out with the difficult question first off, talk about fewer questions, in-depth. There is quite of bit caring about the answers, ... how they get the answers ...". In the science department, teachers discovered that a very good task was to uncover students' misconceptions. For example, teachers started asking students what would happen if chlorophyll stopped working, and discovered a common misconception – that all the world would be dark. Teachers have found that giving thinking time (the three second pause) has improved the quality of responses from students. Teachers also ask other class members to add to ideas discussed in class.

The Green/Amber/Red light strategy works well as a method for gauging student levels of understanding. Using this strategy, students will hold up a green card to indicate "yes I understand the concept", amber for "I think I understand, but I'm not sure", and red for "I don't understand". When students don't understand, teachers take a variety of approaches. For example, they may reinforce the concept through repetition. Sometimes they will ask a peer to explain the answer – an approach they often find has worked well. At other times, the teacher will do a bit of scaffolding with the students, helping them to the point where the new concept starts to become clear.

Students are now sometimes asked to mark their own work, or the work of their peers. However, they note, there are two issues with peer work. One is that the students have to be really well trained to do this. The other is that students have to understand the nature of the error when they are marking. Teachers often engineer the pairs, putting weak students with stronger students, depending on the task, or taking other dynamics into consideration. Peer marking takes more time, teachers note, and therefore takes time away from the curriculum. Some teachers would prefer to spend more time on content, particularly in the sciences, where the national curriculum is quite content-heavy. Many teachers have taken a closer look at the actual content they feel they most need to cover. They say the rush through curriculum is difficult. Most of the teachers interviewed for the case study said that it is more important to focus on quality than quantity in their classes. They also try to emphasise connections between lessons.

Both teachers and students say that using formative assessment is quite different than what they have been used to. For the teachers, it involves "… running around the classroom, because you're thinking, what have I taught, how do I pick this up, what do I need". "In the past", teachers say, "… it was the teacher speaking, I'm going to take you there, I'm going to see what I think you've picked up, what you haven't picked up, and I'm going to teach you. It's faster. The pace is faster. It is a much tighter regulation of learning".

These techniques have been quite useful in creating a safe environment for students to take risks and make mistakes in the classroom. The students report that "… it's okay if we give wrong answers. That's life. You learn more that way".

For teachers, an important part of the process has been making the good things they often do intuitively, more systematic. One teacher commented that "If you're aware that you're doing it, and you're aware of why you're doing it, rather than it just being a happy accident, then you're more likely to acquire it.

It's the same thing we have to do with marking. Being able to analyse the flaws is the first step pointing in the direction of solving the flaw".

Not all teachers in the school have bought in to formative assessment. Several teachers feel that they don't need to change their teaching methods, or that it's too much work. Those participating in the project observe that "You have to be quite a confident person to go into your classroom and do something completely different. If you're struggling with the class anyway, or struggling with discipline, then you're not going to put yourself in that position". A significant number of teachers in the school have been getting an increasing number of children with behavioural difficulties, and lack adequate support to work well in these circumstances. If the teacher is not in a position to manage a classroom discussion, then trying to change teaching methods isn't necessarily going to help, teachers say. These "more confident" teachers note that they still have a hard time "providing high quality" formative assessment with some of their classes.

Teachers also noted that they do not see formative assessment as a panacea, nor as a special programme. Rather, they see formative assessment as being about the nature of the relationship between the teacher and the learner. It has been helpful with other very good and important innovations they are involved in at the school.

Significant changes in the curriculum for Key Stage 3 have provided another very important push for change. The new Key Stage 3 curriculum embeds guidance on the use of formative assessment in nationally distributed materials. Teachers note that while they had to re-write curriculum to make things work with the new guidance, they already had staff well-trained in formative assessment, so the new schemes were easily adapted at the school.

Creating conditions

The current Lord Williams's head teacher joined the school in September 2000 – just as teachers and managers were talking about bringing formative assessment methods to classrooms throughout the school (the prior head teacher had initiated Lord Williams's involvement in with KMOFAP). At the beginning of his tenure, the incoming head teacher comments that he observed a strong focus on teaching and learning at the school, and was happy to support directions chosen by the faculties.

Because Lord Williams's is a big school, the head teacher comments, he has relied heavily on his management team, and on initiatives from teachers and departments. He sees the high calibre of middle management as having been very important to Lord Williams's success. Middle managers at the school have a high degree of autonomy, and teachers also "have permission to be innovative".

There are a number of indicators of a strong school culture including peer-to-peer professional development. Several key informants pointed to the fact that the school is big as being important to this culture. Because teachers often have to teach outside their own specialist areas, specialist teachers in departments develop and share valid "schemes of work" to support the non-specialist teachers. For example, two different teachers teaching an English module will follow the same sequence, using the same or similar resources. This type of sharing also happens within the humanities and science faculties. Within departments teachers are all expected to contribute to and follow the schemes of work – which also make their own work easier. Teachers have confidence in the quality of the schemes of work.

Many of the faculty do not have that much in common so teaching is the thing people at Lord Williams's talk about. According to teachers at the school, a lot of dissemination has happened informally by talking to people in the staff room. There is an atmosphere of collaboration and consistency in practices in each faculty, and between faculties, so ideas from even small-scale projects spread.

Whole school inset days (that is, time set aside for professional development and whole-school discussions) have also been quite important, as teachers will make presentations on what they've done – including the meeting where formative assessment was discussed and subsequently taken on as a whole school focus.

The initiative to focus on formative assessment across the school came shortly after the core group of teachers began working with the KMOFAP, at a September 2000 inset meeting. Several teachers had seen Black and Wiliam present their research to the whole school, had heard about what the Lord Williams's teachers involved in the KMOFAP were working on, and had been impressed by their enthusiasm as well as reports that their methods were working well with students. The timing for KMOFAP also appeared to be right: teachers at the school had been focusing on teaching and learning for several years. KMOFAP made sense to a lot of the teachers at the school, and therefore, very quickly scaled-up from a core group of four teachers to whole-school involvement.

The four teachers participating in the KMOFAP believe that the model of having a core group working with the King's College researchers has worked well. They comment that "sitting there and sharing our ideas is training. It is invaluable to hear about how other people have been experiencing the practice". However, they were surprised that they were actually "inventing" teaching methods as they went along. "What we were kind of expecting was, 'this is formative assessment, here's how you do it'. What we found is that we were kind of working it out together. That's the impression we got."

CASE STUDY 2: SEVEN KINGS HIGH SCHOOL

Seven Kings High School, in the east London Borough of Redbridge, serves 1 292 students between the ages of 11 and 19. There are 376 students in the school's comparatively large sixth form.

During the 2001-02 school year, Seven Kings High School attained notice as having the second highest level of "value-added" in the country. All students attending the school, including special education and bilingual students, were entered into the exams (75% of the students are bilingual, and 2.5% of students have statements of special educational needs). The school has "Beacon/Specialist School" status, which means that it has been identified as among the best performing in the country, and charged with sharing effective practice with other schools.

Seven Kings was part of the Learning How to Learn project of the University of Cambridge in 2002 (and involving some King's College, London researchers from the KMOFAP project, including Black, Wiliam and Marshall). The project has quickly scaled up, and teachers are now using formative assessment strategies throughout the school.

Teaching and assessment at the school

Prior to the introduction of formative assessment in classrooms, Seven Kings was already a very strong school. Teachers nevertheless have continued to seek ways to improve their practice. Some of the things that they are doing differently now are:

- Providing students with criteria for a good piece of work before they actually receive an assignment. Before, teachers would mark a piece of work, and then tell students the basis on which they had been marked.

- Making sure that students feel safe to take risks. One teacher notes that he asks students to write down their ideas, share them as a pair, and then share ideas with the whole class.

- Organising more group-work and more discussion-based activities. A science teacher says that they probably did not do as much of that in science before, but that formative assessment forces the teacher to do more questioning and to get students to talk.

- Having students mark their own and each other's work, and they have a better idea now of what they're looking for than they did before.

- Not giving students marks. One teacher noted that in the past she wouldn't write anything on student papers, or if she did, the students would just look at the grade and ignore the comments.

Teachers say that integrating formative assessment into their teaching has involved a process. They have had to think about how to prioritise what they will cover in the curriculum; using formative assessment in the classroom can take time away from the curriculum (although teachers commented that they do not see it as more time-consuming in terms of their own planning). Teachers have found that they have given more attention to what students are retaining, rather than trying to rush through the curriculum. Finally, they note that new Key Stage 3 requirements have forced them to re-think how they use assessment in their classrooms.

Teachers note several indicators of improvements resulting from using formative assessment. For example:

- Teachers feel that they get different and much better products from their students now that they share information before the students work on their assignments.

- In classroom discussions, students are more confident that they've got something to share if they've thought it out and shared with a partner first. Students are also doing a better job of presentation.

- Teachers comment that students are doing more in the classroom, and pay attention to the criteria for a good piece of work much more than they used to. Teachers also feel that, in the absence of marks, students are doing much better because they actually read the comments on what they are doing well and how they can improve their work.

- Teachers as well as the students share the language about formative assessment.

In January 2002, the Office of Standards in Education (OFSTED) highlighted several strengths at Seven Kings, reporting that:

"... Standards of attainment are high and pupils' achievements are excellent across the whole range of ability in comparison with similar schools. ... The school constantly reflects on and reviews its provision to improve it further. The full integration of pupils from different ethnic origins and groups into the school – including pupils with special educational needs, pupils with physical disabilities and those with refugee status – has produced a very harmonious community that is dedicated to high achievement. Pupils are achieving at a very high level when compared with pupils with a similar starting point". (OFSTED, p. 8)

Creating conditions

The head teacher at Seven Kings has been at the school since 1985 and has seen the school through a number of changes and experiments in teaching and learning. He notes that early in his career at Seven Kings, there was not a culture of class observation – typical of English schools at the time. Moreover, he claims, nobody believed that teachers made a difference.

The head teacher believes that the 1988 Education Reform Act, while painful, encouraged a number of positive changes in schools. The best changes, he notes, were in the ability to manage the school's own resources. The use of data, as encouraged by school reforms over the last 15 years, has also been important. In the past, he says, the culture of the school was to "let a thousand flowers bloom". No one looked at data to see if innovations were really working or not.

Over the period of his tenure, the head teacher has encouraged the development of a strong management team. The former deputy head teacher was responsible for getting the school involved with KMOFAP. The project has been important to school-wide discussion on what teaching and assessment should look like.

The head teacher and his management team have tried to ask questions, and to put things on the agenda in order to lead change. For example, they have asked teachers what their aspirations would be in two years time. They have also created expectations for high quality teaching, and have followed up by looking at student outcomes. In 1993, the head teacher established baseline standards which he expects all teachers to observe (and not just a cluster of teachers involved in an innovation). Most people want to do well, he comments, so they will try to meet the expectations set out. In turn, teachers have developed high expectations as to the type of training they will get, and the kinds of speakers they will have for the teacher inset days. The leadership and management feel they need to deliver (if they don't, they hear about it).

Other strategies for encouraging change in the school have included:

- Insisting that teachers set homework assignments at the beginning of lessons (and ensuring that the assignments are directly related to the lesson). This strategy has allowed more students to do well on assignments (in the past, underachieving students often left the classroom not knowing what they were expected to do for homework, or how to do it), thus building student confidence.

- Supporting school-based research for up to 12 staff a year. Their projects must be approved as being of benefit to the school.

- Creating opportunities for teachers to learn from each other about what types of pilots and projects they are trying in their departments. There has been a "buzz" about formative assessment, so people have wanted to get involved.

- Recruiting the best and the brightest for the school's special education programme. These teachers have pioneered many changes at the school.

- Using the school's reconstruction project – bringing the formerly split school together on to one campus – as an opportunity to encourage seemingly unrelated changes in curriculum. The head teacher recounts that he told teachers, "we're moving, so we have to think how we might address Religious Education differently in the future". The bringing together of the two campuses also created a culture change for the school.

While there are some staff offices at the school, teachers are encouraged to use the collective staff room. Teachers confirm that the school has a very "fertile culture". They hold departmental meetings about 12 times a year. In order to keep the focus on teaching and learning and not on administrative issues, staff get notes on administrative matters so that they don't have to spend time in departmental briefings. All teachers at the school participate in the AfL programme.

CASE STUDY 3: BRIGHTON HILL COMMUNITY COLLEGE

Brighton Hill Community College in Basingstoke, Hampshire serves 1 250 students between the ages of 11 and 16. There are 75 teachers at the school. According to the most recent report (1998) of English inspectorate (OFSTED), the school is popular in the area, and "substantially oversubscribed". Students are primarily from middle-class homes, with 9% of students eligible for free school meals. In 1998, approximately 23% of students were on the school's register of special educational needs (SEN). The OFSTED report noted that "[v]ery few students are from ethnic groups other than white". (OFSTED, 1998, p. 9)

Brighton Hill's head teacher agrees with a 1998 OFSTED appraisal that assessment at Brighton Hill has been and still is a weak suit. And it is perhaps for this reason that Brighton Hill signed on to the King's Formative Assessment Programme in late Spring 2002.

Teaching and assessment at the school

Teachers at Brighton Hill use common strategies in classrooms. For example:

- It is now common to share lesson objectives and criteria and standards for a good piece of work with students.
- Teachers also use the "traffic light" strategy, asking students to hold up a green, amber or red sign to indicate they understand the concept, think they understand the concept but aren't quite sure, or do not understand at all.
- Teachers commonly use the "no hands up" approach across the school, where students are called upon at random rather than calling upon those students who put their hands up first.

There is now wide use of peer-assessment across the school. Teachers note that it has taken some effort to train students in using peer-assessment. Several of the teachers commented that they initially found students to be very critical of each other. They developed the "two stars and a wish system" – where students were asked to find two things they liked in their peer's work, and something they wish that person would improve in relation to the shared objectives of the work.

Brighton Hill was not included in the original set of KMOFAP schools, but school managers were eager to be involved in the project, and asked for project leaders to consider taking on one more school. School leaders and teachers across the school have been enthusiastic about the project, and have not only scaled-up with good practices quite quickly, but have also started the process of considering what they will need to do to change the existing school culture, which has been heavily focused on student grades, to an emphasis on more frequent communication, including more specific feedback, with students and parents. The system of grade cards is under review.

Teachers say that they have had to give time to including formative assessment in their classrooms and that they have had to give up some things. But, they have developed much stronger relationships with pupils.

Creating conditions

The deputy head teacher, who has been at the school for more than 20 years, notes that the school has participated in a number of innovative projects. She comments that no two years at the school have been the same. Many of the changes resulted from the Education Reform Act of 1998, which she believes have created positive changes in schools over time. For example, the staff sit down together to discuss policy changes, the subject leaders attend briefings at the Local Education Authority and they are responsible for sharing this information with their colleagues; and, the GCSE national tests have involved a large-scale national training programme.

Teachers participating in the King's Formative Assessment Programme are already having an impact throughout the school. Thus far, they have been able to influence the teaching practices of staff through word of mouth, observations, informal discussions, and departmental discussions.

Teachers at Brighton Hill say that they are taking the formative assessment strategies on as extensions of their own personal teaching styles, selecting those "bits" that feel right for them. The English department uses Assessment for Learning strategies as a regular part of teaching practice.

More recently, Brighton Hill has also been involved in a "High Impact Teaching" programme and implementation of the national Key Stage 3 and the literacy and numeracy strategies. Key Stage 3 has also helped to focus the effort to bring formative assessment to classrooms, and has provided practical suggestions about how to teach reading and learning.

One of the biggest challenges at Brighton Hill has been to bring these various strategies together and make them coherent. School staff are also paying close attention to teacher workload, and trying to "… clear away the clutter". Formative assessment has helped them to make sense of the various innovations in the school.

In terms of ongoing professional development, every teacher is allowed five non-teaching periods per week, and soon, all teachers will reduce their teaching time from 80% to 60% (this will be accomplished by bringing on more classroom assistants). With the reduction in teaching time, 40% of teachers' time will thus be devoted to preparation of high quality teaching materials.

School leaders are also placing more emphasis on classroom observation. Everyone at Brighton Hill has a line manager and is observed two to three times a year. They are also looking at having more peer-teacher assessment in the future. Brighton Hill became a training school in September 2003. The school leadership hopes to provide professional development with observation/classrooms and video. According to the head teacher, Brighton Hill is trying to grow talent in response to teacher shortages.

CASE STUDY 4: THE CLERE SCHOOL

The Clere School, a rural school in Hampshire Country, Southeast England, has 530 students between the ages of 11 and 16 years. According to the most recent report of OFSTED (November 2000), there are an "average number of pupils with special educational needs and very few pupils from minority ethnic groups. A high proportion of pupils attend the school from a large number of dispersed communities who rely on buses to get to and from school".

OFSTED inspectors note that the previous report (1996) had been quite critical of the school, but that "[s]ince then, and particularly in September 2000, there has been a high staff turnover caused in the main by the school's effective improvement strategies". (OFSTED, p. 7) The school is now one of the schools of choice in the region.

Joining in September 2001, The Clere School is among the most recent members of the KMOFAP, but drew whole-school interest almost from the beginning of the project.

Teaching and assessment at the school

Five volunteer teachers at The Clere School have been working with researchers from King's College, including three science teachers, one drama teacher and one English teacher since early 2002. Two teachers involved in the core group are fairly new to teaching. One has just completed his first year of teaching, the other has been teaching for five years. The two note that in their teacher training, formative assessment did not receive a lot of attention. Instead, they had studied formative assessment from a political viewpoint. Nor did they receive much guidance about how to assign marks in their teacher practice – they were merely asked to mark the schemes already being used by the teacher with whom they were assigned for their practice. The practical ideas they are developing with researchers at the King's Formative Assessment Programme are thus very new to these young teachers.

The Assistant Headteacher notes that, in many ways, the project has helped to "… build on the experience of the teachers participating in the project, reinforced things we were doing instinctively and put a label on it". They clarified and categorised their teaching methods. Then, they were asked to look at the difference the variety of methods made in student learning.

Teachers are using several creative formative assessment strategies in their classrooms. For example:

- One teacher says that he uses the students' questions on tests (although students tend to ask a lot of closed questions).

- Teachers use "feed forward" methods so pupils know what objectives of each class are.

- One of the teachers mentioned that he will often ask two pupils to run the end-of-lesson plenary – to give a summary of the topic and to ask three or four questions to the rest of the pupils. This method prompts work well, he says.

- When pupils do not understand, teachers often revise with the traffic light (as do teachers at several of the schools working with researchers at the King's Formative Assessment Programme). Teachers will spend longer with the students who show more amber. The majority of the students said they are now clearer about what they need to understand. The whole school has now adopted the traffic light approach.

- Teachers are including time for more frequent student peer-assessment.

- Teachers are trying to increase time for students to answer questions. They comment that this is one of the harder things to do, as they find it is difficult not to jump in themselves during gaps in the discussion.

Teachers say that they also make efforts not to be too formulaic. They step back and think about what works with the methods (for example, they like sharing objectives because pupils tend to take control of their learning). Teachers feel they "own the methods" when they had a better understanding of the effect of what they were doing in classrooms. Teachers also comment that in the past they would have been focusing on creating opportunities for learning, rather than managing classroom activities.

Creating conditions

At the time of the case study, the school was awaiting appointment of a new head teacher. The former head teacher was proactive about promoting innovation at the school and the school's management team continued with reforms the former head teacher started, including work with the KMOFAP. The Assistant Headteacher has taken on the leadership position in the interim and is moving forward with efforts to scale-up with formative assessment throughout the school.

An important aspect of the reform and of their communication with each other, the Assistant Headteacher believes, has been the teachers' sophisticated use of data. Teachers get a data booklet which includes IQ test scores, Key Stage 2 test scores plus current performance as of their last report as a record of each student's prior achievement. Teachers look at whether there are potential problems or challenges, and create a historical plot of the student's past progress. Individual departments then set out criteria for success and also set numerical targets for what they hope students will achieve on summative assessments, and use a regression model to predict the minimum GCSE level students should be able to achieve. There is also an extraordinarily high level of information technology at the school to use data.

The school management team has also asked teachers to use data to be more strategic in their teaching. Management have put data into staff hands and asked what questions the data raise. The Assistant Headteacher notes that when teachers become skilled at interpreting data, some things leap out. Looking at the data is also a form of triangulation, so even if teachers can automatically predict performance of all their students, it helps to have their views confirmed by the data. The Assistant Headteacher likens the process to statistical process control in Total Quality Management models. School managers also follow the data to ensure that important factors are being dealt with, and that students are making progress as they should.

There is also a systematic interaction between the tutor and the senior staff (each English school has a pastoral department charged with taking care of individual students' social needs). The academic staff heads of department and head of year oversee the social welfare of the group. The pastoral team is keen to look at the progress students should make – not just limiting their view to the students' behaviour. The pastoral staff also ensure that students in need receive mentoring.

School leaders want to bring formative assessment to classrooms across the school as quickly as possible. The Assistant Headteacher has helped to prepare the ground for scaling-up the assessment through the annual cycle of school improvement planning. She asked teachers ahead of time to think about how they assess students and to identify some of the strategies they use. Prof Dylan Wiliam led a staff inset day during which teachers talked about the formative assessment strategies they use now, or could use. Teachers were asked to quantify what they said they were going to do, and how it worked out. The Assistant Headteacher then asked teachers to start with simple formative technique(s), and to discuss their efforts with other teachers.

This approach, the Assistant Headteacher explains, was intended to introduce formative assessment "not as another initiative ... [but as] ... something that could be really useful, and that was part of what they are already doing [in classrooms]". She noted that she did not want teachers to think that they should throw years of books and marks out the window. Moreover, she said, she wanted to send the message to teachers that they are already quite good, but need to be better at some things. The Assistant

Headteacher believes that motivation is what's best for teachers, commenting that "They can't make progress if they are not happy". Logistically, teachers have also been helped by having a lowered classroom load.

The Assistant Headteacher hopes to create a "buzz" about formative assessment throughout the school. She asked teachers to make presentations on what they were doing with formative assessment when all teachers are involved in developing the school improvement plan in September. With this kind of attention, it is difficult for those teachers to pretend that they are using formative assessment if they are not. The 2003/06 School Improvement Plan now includes Assessment for Learning as a Key Issue and this means all departments have a commitment and responsibility for development.

References

Black, P. and D. Wiliam (1998), "Assessment and Classroom Learning", *Assessment in Education: Principles, Policy and Practice,* CARFAX, Oxfordshire, Vol. 5, No. 1, pp. 7-74.

Black, P. and D. Wiliam (2003), "In Praise of Educational Research: Formative Assessment", *British Educational Research Journal*, Vol. 29(5), pp. 623-637.

Black, P. *et al.* (2002), *Working Inside the Black Box: Assessment for Learning in the Classroom*, Department of Education and Professional Studies, King's College, London.

Committee of Inquiry into the Teaching of Mathematics in Schools (1982), *Report: Mathematics Counts*, HMSO, London.

Department of Education and Science (DES) and Welsh Office (1987), "The National Curriculum 5–16: A Consultation Document", Department of Education and Science, London.

Harrison, A. (1982), *Review of Graded Tests*, Methuen, London.

National Curriculum Task Group on Assessment and Testing (NCTGAT) (1988), *A Report*, Department of Education and Science, London.

Finland: Emphasising Development instead of Competition and Comparison

by
Joke Voogt, University of Twente
Helena Kasurinen, Finnish National Board of Education

OVERVIEW

Finland does not have an inspectorate, and does not sponsor national examinations, except for the matriculation examination at the end of upper secondary general education. Instead, the National Board of Education tracks school quality through random sample evaluations of different subjects in each comprehensive school every third year. The results of these evaluations provide information on the quality of learning outcomes, and are utilised in ongoing development of the education system and core curricula, as well as in practical teaching work. The Act for Comprehensive Education (628/1998) encourages local and school-level self-evaluation. At the municipal level, evaluations focus on financial accountability and whether and how schools are meeting local educational and cultural objectives. The same Act and the national core curriculum for comprehensive education (1998) encourage the development of students' self-assessment skills.

The growing importance of self-evaluation at the institutional level has also resulted in attention for student self-assessment. The main idea behind school evaluation and student self-assessment is that it is more important to focus on development than to compare your school or yourself with other schools or students. The process of student self-assessment and school-evaluation is as important as the outcomes are, because they will inform further development.

The National Board of Education has formulated the main principles for student assessment in Finnish comprehensive schools:

- Assessment of study skills, working skills and behaviour should be individual, truthful and versatile.

- Feedback should support the development of self-knowledge and motivation of the pupil.

- Learning-to-learn, learning to set goals for learning, and studying and working at school have been understood to be key competencies for lifelong learning.

- Assessment is considered to be a tool to counsel and support studying and learning, and development of the pupil's self-assessment skills.

HIGHLIGHTS FROM THE CASE STUDIES

The Finnish educational system's emphasis on development instead of competition and comparison, is striking. The two case study schools, Tikkakoski and Meilhati Upper Comprehensive Schools, are clearly applying this philosophy in their approaches to teaching, learning and assessment. A focus on student self-evaluation is intended to help students to feel responsible for their own learning, and to be aware of the process of learning (not just the outcomes), and their own development. The focus on self-evaluation also reflects a more general philosophy in the Finnish educational system, that it is more important to focus on development than comparison.

CASE STUDY 1: TIKKAKOSKI UPPER COMPREHENSIVE SCHOOL

Tikkakoski Upper Comprehensive School (grades 7-9) has 278 students and 31 teachers. It is a rural school in Central Finland. Class size is generally between 15 and 20 students. The students in the school come from a variety of socio-economic backgrounds. Only a very few students are not of Finnish origin. There is little student and teacher mobility at the school. In this part of Finland, there is a healthy supply of teachers. About 40% of the students finishing comprehensive school go on to vocational schools, and about 60% go on to general upper secondary education. Only a few students go to the combined vocational/general track. Students from Tikkakoski are usually accepted to the school of their choice for further studies.

Tikkakoski upper comprehensive is a tidy, well organised school with an open atmosphere between students and teachers. The school principal knows each student by name. Teacher-student interaction is very easy. Students call their teachers' by their first names. One of the students interviewed for the case study mentioned the spirit of togetherness in the school.

Teaching and assessment at the school

Technical work and arts

In skill-oriented classes the lessons usually start with five to ten minutes of whole classroom instruction during which the teacher explains what the students should work on, and what is considered important for the lesson. For instance, during a classroom observation conducted for the case study, the art teacher explained that, in the short movie the students were to make for the lessons, the flow of the story and the camera positions were important, but, at this point, not the acting. In the technical class observed, the assignment (to make a wooden frame) was written on a large piece of paper in front of the class, along with steps necessary for completing the product. The teachers provide this kind of information to help the students to focus their effort and not to lose a lot of time on less important elements of the assignment. Depending on the assignment the students work individually or in small groups. In the technical classroom students work in their own pace in finishing a task.

The technical work teacher as well as the art teacher walked around helping students or discussing the quality of work with the students. Students were asked to take part in assessment of the quality of their work. For example, when one student had finished her product (the wooden frame), the teacher first asked her to evaluate the quality of the product, and to give herself a grade. The teacher gave the student her grade only after the student had made her own assessment. The teacher commented afterwards that this is the usual way of working. If there are differences in grading between teachers and students, they are discussed. In this way students learn to understand the criteria for a good piece of work. The technical work teacher emphasises that it is not only the quality of the product that matters, but also the learning process. Therefore he emphasises that the way students work, and the ability to reflect on that is essential for the student's development.

Academic lessons (maths, Finnish and foreign language)

In academically-oriented classes, teachers usually conduct whole-class instruction for about 10-15 minutes on central topic of the lesson. In the classes observed, students asked questions even during this lecture period. Following direct instruction, the students are given an in-class assignment. They work individually, but are allowed to discuss the assignment with peers. In a class observed for the case study, quite a few students discussed the assignment with peers, but others preferred to work alone. The teachers walked around and gave help whenever asked. The students could check their work in the student key-book. If the answer was wrong the student could ask the teacher or their peers for help. The teachers in these classes considered following students' learning processes to be more important than the students' final product.

At Tikkakoski, students are also responsible for their own learning. Students are encouraged to be both active and interactive (*i.e.*, to ask their peers for help). "Sometimes peers can better explain concepts than I can do as a teacher", one of the teachers commented. Many subjects, particularly foreign languages, promote student self-pacing.

Teachers working in different subject domains (*e.g.*, Finnish, foreign language, maths, etc.) have developed their own approaches to tracking student progress. The language teachers, for instance, told us that they do not test that much, but talk to the students frequently during the lessons. The maths teachers, on the other hand, use frequent short tests – once a week – to see what problems students have understood. Teachers try to give feedback on the tests as soon as possible – when possible, in the next class. General problems are discussed with the whole class and more specific problems are discussed with individual students, during the time that students work individually on assignments.

A few students with severe problems in a subject get extra help in separate classes. Students with less severe problems can take advantage of individual remediation instead of optional remedial courses. The organisation of the lessons (little time spent on whole classroom instruction; most of the time spent on working on assignments/exercises) and the relatively small class size, provide teachers with enough time to interact with individual students. Teachers work with students for three consecutive years, and deal with a small number of classes per term. They have a chance to know their students very well – socially, emotionally and cognitively. Students say they appreciate that their teachers are always willing to help them when they have difficulties with a subject, even before or after school hours. In all lessons observed, the students were really on task!

The examples presented above show what the teachers in Tikkakoski consider important in their teaching. They emphasise that:

- Frequent feedback is important.
- It is important to know your students and their development well.
- The organisation of the learning environment is very helpful to get to know the students better.

Teachers hope that they can communicate to the students that learning is fun through their own enthusiasm.

Organising the class schedule to better facilitate learning

Instead of courses that run throughout the school year, courses are offered in five periods of seven weeks each. Each teacher has only four or five different classes a week and a student has only three to four different teachers a week for the academic subjects. Practical subjects (technical work, arts, textile work) are taught throughout the school year. In this way, contact between students and teachers is intensified, and they get to know each other better.

To limit the workload for students, theoretical and practical/optional subjects are balanced in the timetable. Each day, all students have three or at the most four theoretical and one practical/optional subjects. Not all subjects are covered in every term (due to the course system), so there is variety in the schedule. The students say that they like this approach, and that they are able to concentrate better. Students also appreciate that they are allowed many choices for optional courses.

Teachers at Tikkakoski Upper Comprehensive School are critical of the national curriculum changes that are being introduced between 2003 and 2006. The principal of Tikkakoski thinks that the new curriculum allows less flexibility, and that there will be less room for practical subjects (such as technical work, home economics and textile work) and remediation. The new national curriculum prescribes per subject teaching hours and defines criteria for assigning "mark 8".[1]

Student self-assessment

In 1994, Tikkakoski Upper Comprehensive School participated in a pilot for the then new national curriculum. As part of this project, the school developed a self-evaluation system. The school has continued to use and develop self-evaluation since then. Self-evaluation has become even more important over time, not only at the school and teacher level, but also at the student level.

In the philosophy of the school, self-assessment implies that one is responsible for his or her own learning (the student), his or her teaching (the teacher). Teachers and students are also responsible for creating the appropriate conditions for successful teaching and learning.

Acquiring skills to learn as compared to things to learn is an important element of the approach to curriculum and assessment in Tikkakoski.

---

[1] Marks are given between 4-10: 4 =fail; 5=basic effort; 6=poor; 7=average; 8=good; 9 and 10 are excellent; in the present curriculum schools themselves decide where "mark 8" stands for.

Therefore, assessment should focus not only on student performance, but also on the development of learning-to-learn skills.[2] Tikkakoski's system of student self-assessment therefore attempts to reflect student development. The principal and the teachers do not want to limit the concept of assessment to student performance only.

Since the 2001-02 school year, the school has used a system for student self-assessment based on course reports. At the end of each seven-week period the students get a course report (the school has divided the school-year in five periods of seven weeks each). The self-assessment plays an important part in this official course report. Students determine the grade they expect in each subject, assess their study habits, their behaviour and participation during lessons and whether they have completed homework. The students use a common marking system for filling in the form. The marking system makes it easier for students, teachers and parents to interpret the form. After having filled in their own mark, the students receive a mark from the teacher. If there is a difference of two points or more, a discussion between student and teacher takes place. For the majority of the students their own grade and their teacher's grade match pretty well. The course report also includes previous assessments, enabling the student to follow his or her development. According to the principal most students seem to be able to estimate quite well how they have developed. Frequent feedback during lessons is likely helpful here, as well. If the course report shows that a student is failing in a subject he or she is responsible for initiating discussion with the teacher, and seeking additional help.

Self-evaluation form for students in Tikkakoski

Subject	Course grade	Study habits	Learning development	Student's grade
Mother tongue				
Maths				
Etc.				

Since the 2002-03 school year, parents, students and the home teacher make an extensive evaluation of the student's development at least once a

---

[2] The term formative assessment is not used so much in Tikkakoski although in practice it is considered an essential evaluation method to inform teachers and students. Formative assessment may consist of hard data, but more often and more importantly of "tacit knowledge", *i.e.* knowledge that both the teacher and student obtain through discussion, reflection and experience. Self-evaluation has an important role in the formative assessment system used.

year. One (very active and concerned) parent noted this evaluation system has helped her daughter to take on responsibility for her learning. For the parent, it is a reason to talk with her child about her progress. She very much appreciates that parents get informed about the progress of their children five times per year, which is much more than the usual case of a brief talk with the home teacher twice a year. This parent was surprised at how realistically her child could grade herself. The students interviewed also said that they appreciated the frequency of the course reports, because they could then easily follow their own development.

Creating conditions

According to the school principal, who started nine years ago, it is important to build a school culture that is a learning environment for all that are part of it (students and teachers). Within this culture there is a lot of attention for the individual learner. The school culture is made explicit to students, parents and teachers, so that everyone is aware of their freedom and responsibilities. At Tikkakoski, not only cognitive knowledge and skills are important, but also "growing up" and learning-to-learn skills.

The principal emphasises that the organisation of the curriculum and the assessment system are important to the school culture.

The principal has a clear vision on how the school should develop and how this can happen. His principles for leadership of the school can be summarised as follows:

- Communication between all involved in the school (teachers and students) is crucial.
- Decisions are made together.
- Change occurs in small steps.
- Solutions for problems need to be simple and logical.
- Barriers are sometimes resources.

There is a lot of formal (*e.g.* in the teacher teams) and informal communication among teachers and between teachers and students in the school.

Teachers and other personnel are part of a team. There are four subject matter teams, one team is responsible for student care and one for support services. All teams meet once a week. Each team appoints a team leader who discusses the plans with the principal. Team leaders rotate every other year, so that every teacher gets his or her turn. The teams are an important component of the school organisation. Co-operation between teachers (particularly those teaching different subjects) is encouraged, but not forced. Sometimes there are multi-disciplinary projects. Teachers working in the various subject areas talk about their teaching, but again they are not forced to do so.

Social cohesion is seen as an important condition for learning in Tikkakoski. Therefore students are part of a fixed group of not more than 20 students. These groups are together for about 20 of the total 30 weekly lessons. The groups stay together for three years and during this time they have the same teacher for each specific subject. This approach strengthens the relationship between students and teachers, and also between students. Both teachers and students appreciate this approach. Information gathered in student interviews and school evaluations make it clear that students like to go to school and that they are motivated.

Because of the fact that groups stay together for three consecutive years, there is a lot of attention to forming stable groups when students enter the school in grade 7. Teachers, parents and students from grade 6 are consulted. Based on these consultations socio-grams are built. The social worker and the student counsellor make a proposal for composition of the grade 7 groups. The proposal is discussed with the principal and the class and subject teachers. The purpose of this process is to form groups that will help the learning of the individual student. Group composition is not based on performance level.

The school strategy appears to be quite effective. In Spring 2003, all students in the final grade were accepted for further studies. Eighty-six per cent received a place in their first choice option. In addition, national tests consistently show that the school's results are above the average and that there are very few poor performers at the school. Comparison with neighbouring upper comprehensive schools has shown that Tikkakoski's assessment scales are at the average – students do not get their grades too easily or with too much difficulty.

CASE STUDY 2: MEILAHTI UPPER COMPREHENSIVE SCHOOL

Meilahti Upper Comprehensive School (grades 7-10) has 383 students and 48 teachers. The school is located in the centre of Helsinki and specialises in visual arts. About 10% of the students are not of Finnish origin. Most of these students come from Russia and Somalia. There is little student and teacher mobility.

There are several special classes in Meilahti: visual arts (since 1988), music (since 1999), mathematics and science (since 1999), sports (since

1999) and a Swedish immersion class. Since 2000, the school has supported one class with mentally handicapped children. After grade 9, 60% of students from Meilahti go to senior high, and the remaining 40% go to vocational school. Only a few students (17 in school year 2002-03) stay in the 10th grade. These are the most challenging students, because they tend not to be motivated to study and often have very poor study habits.

Teaching and assessment at the school

A range of approaches to integrating formative assessment into everyday practice

The teaching strategies practiced at Meilahti Upper Comprehensive School vary. Some teachers use self- and peer-assessment in their lessons, others don't. Some teachers use small group work, but other teachers prefer whole classroom instruction. The way teachers are teaching depends on what they feel comfortable with, and is part of each teacher's individual routine. The teachers are not often challenged to experiment with new approaches. Below are some examples of teaching strategies used by different teachers:

- The Finnish-language teacher (who is also the vice-principal) provides quite a bit of time for student self- and peer evaluation during lessons. For instance when the students write stories the teacher asks the students to read and evaluate each others' stories using guidelines provided. The teacher also gives comments to the students. During oral presentations (required of each at least once during the school year), all students have to fill in a feedback form about the presentation.

- The Finnish language teacher also tries to communicate with each pupil at least once during the lesson. Either during whole class discussion, during self-study time, or at the end of the lesson. During the case study observation the teacher asked questions about a text. Several (although not all) of the students were quite involved in the class and reacted spontaneously. However, not all students seemed involved in the activity.

- The mathematics teacher uses a learning diary, where students note whether they did their homework. In this way she tries to make students feel responsible for their learning process. During the case study classroom observation the teacher checked the learning diary. One student had filled in that he had not done his homework, but that did not result in any follow-up. During her maths lessons, the teacher prefers whole class instruction. According to this teacher, maths is not usually appropriate for group work. However, in chemistry and physics lessons she prefers to have students work in small groups.

- The art teacher uses a portfolio for visual arts classes. In the portfolio the students write about their work and about the process of creating a particular piece of art. One of the two teachers asks the students to give themselves a mark before she gives a mark. Both art teachers discuss students' work with them often. They also encourage students to discuss each other's work. Sometimes work is discussed in the whole class. According to the teachers this is an important part of their lessons and it is important for the development of students' personalities. The criteria for a good piece of art are based on guidelines which are defined in the school syllabus and national curriculum guidelines. The teachers explain to the students what criteria and skills are central when they discuss a particular piece of art.

- The music and drama teacher co-operate often. These teachers use a lot of feedback strategies in their work. The music teacher explained that: "Students should learn how to give feedback to each other, because you need to be very careful about that. You need to create an atmosphere where students judge each other. Students also need to give grounds for their feedback. It should be critical but positive". There are no grades for music or drama.

- The drama teacher, who is also a Finnish language teacher, pays a lot of attention to the written comments she gives on the students' writing. It is her experience that the students ask for such comments.

- The foreign language teacher observes that she gives too much instruction, because the subject requires it. "In Foreign Language we have this burden on grammar, I can't let that go. This forces me to give them instruction. I could not be very creative. I try to give them options in the assignments they make for homework. They can choose then for themselves."

- The physical education teacher gives the student clear goals, so they know what is expected of them. He considers team-work an important goal of physical education. In his lessons it is important that the students get along well, and that they work together as a group. "When there are problems I stop the game and talk about it."

- The use of tests differs per teacher and subject. But the teachers all say that tests are important. Teachers say that pupils want to show what they know, and that tests help pupils to focus on what they have to do. The teachers say that students "... always compare themselves with the others. Tests motivate them. Then they make an effort". Teachers create their own tests. According to the teachers, the tests that are part of the textbook are not always useful. The teachers emphasise that it is important to give the students feedback (they do that in the form of a written mark), and to discuss the mistakes.

The students interviewed were somewhat critical of the school. According to the students, the teachers should pay more attention to student motivation. They say that student attitudes improve when the teacher is excited about the subject. Some teachers are enthusiastic, but others not. According to the students, not many teachers inform the students at the start of a course what they will do and what is expected from them. Most teachers in the school just start teaching. One of the students said that there is too much attention to learning through listening and watching instead of learning by doing. The students also expect teachers to be somewhat stricter toward students with behavioural problems. They say that it is sometimes very noisy in classrooms, and that students with behavioural problems are not always punished for their misbehaviour, while children without behavioural problems are punished when they have a bad day.

Assessment

The term formative assessment is not known (and so not used) at this school. Teachers at Meilhati emphasise student self-assessment and the development process of the individual student. The development process is viewed not only from the perspective of academic skills, but also in terms of students' behaviour and attitude toward learning.

Student self-assessment

The school introduced an assessment of study habits in 1995, and the current system for self-assessment has been in place since 1999. The national curriculum also requires schools to focus on the development process of individual students, and that has been an important incentive for Meilahti to elaborate their own system. The current approach to self-assessment was developed by one of the Meilhati teachers, and implemented after discussion in the teacher meeting. The self-evaluation system is not much related with ongoing assessment during lessons.

Students are assessed four times a year. They get marks in the domains of knowledge, study habits and participation from each course teacher. In addition, teachers record absenteeism and tardiness. Usually teachers discuss the marks with individual students. The school has a formal description as to what each mark means in the three domains. These descriptions are discussed at the teacher meeting, so there is a shared understanding among teachers of what the marks mean.

During a course, the students and teachers fill in a small questionnaire about their study habits. In grade 7 the questionnaire is about their study habits and well-being in school and class, in grade 8, it is about their study habits and their behaviour, and in grade 9 it is about their study habits and their attitude toward learning. An example of the questionnaire for grade 7 is presented below.

Self-evaluation of student habits after the first period in grade 7

During this autumn my most important goal is:
_____

I achieved my goal: well __ pretty well __ badly __
These issues influenced _____

I	
Work actively during lessons	
Make my home-work	
Remember to take books and all I need with me	
Follow good habits	
Be in time in lessons	
Attend regularly lessons	

G= good M= moderate T= trying and practice needed

Teacher comments:
_____

Marks:
_____

Something else:
_____

Teacher signature
Parents' comments:
_____

Parent's signature

In the beginning the assessment was text-based, but teachers found that this was too much work. Now "marks" are given through a letter system: G (good), M (moderate), and T (trying and practice needed). According to the teachers, students are realistic in their self-assessment. The assessments are shared with the parents, who can comment on them. Self-assessment is thus a basis for discussion about the student's development between the home teacher, student and, when necessary, the parents.

Home teachers hold primary responsibility for administration of the forms, and for communicating results to parents. According to the teachers the forms provide the students with a lot of information they think important for the students. They believe that helps the students to know how they are developing. One of the teachers said that the forms are a way to give feedback to the quieter students. Usually the noisy students get feedback on their behaviour, but the others, hardly ever. In the beginning the students did not take the process very seriously, but now everyone is used to filling out the forms. It is not so clear, however, how the information from the forms influences teaching practices.

The several teachers interviewed had different reactions to the forms. One of the Finnish teachers uses the form as a basis for discussion with the students about their progress, because most of the students are interested in their grades. The foreign language teacher, on the other hand, does not find the assessment system very informative. The physical education teacher says that the questions are not relevant to his teaching.

The students differ in their opinions about the assessment system. Some of them think that the assessment forms are useful, but the scale should be more detailed. Other students think that they are useless. The feedback of the teacher is useful, but not so much that they have to fill it in the form. According to the parents, the assessment forms are informative, particularly when the child does not tell the parents much about school. It is easier to follow the child's grades as well as study habits with the assessment forms. Parents noted that students, particularly girls, tend to be self-critical.

Creating conditions

Meilhati has long been recognised for the way it takes care of students. The teachers are interested in the development of children. Parents appreciate that children with difficulties are welcome at the school. Not all Finnish schools provide such possibilities. The principal, who has been at the school for three years, sees her main role as preserving the good reputation of the school by creating a good atmosphere for teachers and students.

According to the teachers the school has an open atmosphere. One of the teachers expressed it as follows: "We feel good to be here. There is a good positive atmosphere. The pupils are interested in learning, they succeed, they develop and that makes you happy". The students also mention an easy relationship with their teachers. They appreciate that each student gets equal attention, which they did not always experience in elementary school, because they said, in elementary school only the more talented got a lot of attention.

Teachers meet as a group every week. During a recent meeting, teachers agreed that the main goal of the school is "learning" and that social goals are secondary. Among other things, teachers discussed students with behavioural or learning problems. Teachers teaching the same subjects share information about what they do in lessons informally. However, only a few teachers teaching different subjects (for instance the music and the drama teacher) co-operate.

Teachers can take professional development courses if they wish, as long as the resources allow. However, there are no special incentives to participate in professional development activities. Currently, due to budget cuts from the Helsinki Board of Education, it is more difficult to find financial resources for professional development.

Classes have no more than 20 students, often fewer. The school expects that class size will be bigger next year, because of the budget cuts of the Helsinki Board of Education. Each class has a home teacher who stays with the class through the ninth grade. Groups stay together, although teachers may change (except for the home teacher). All teachers appreciate the fact that a home teacher stays with a class during the whole school period, because the home teacher can get to know the student very well. "You see their development, in behaviour and in learning", according to one of the teachers. Also the contact with the parents is much easier, because teachers know them for a long period of time.

The parents interviewed said that the school has a good reputation. They appreciate that the school is not only selecting the most ambitious children, but taking a variety of children.[3] Contact between the parents and the children's home teacher is good. When there are any problems with children, either at home or in school, the parents or the home teacher easily contact each other (often through e-mail).

---

[3] Finnish schools do not have a selection system for comprehensive education. Usually students are going to the most nearby school. In schools like Meilahti which are specialised in certain subjects students can be selected, but only for the specialised classes.

Italy: A System in Transition[*]

by
Janet Looney, OECD
Cosimo Laneve, University of Bari
Maria Teresa Moscato, University of Bologna

OVERVIEW

The 1962 unification of the lower secondary schools, and the extension of compulsory schooling through the age of 14 are perhaps the most significant innovations of Italian school policy in the post-World War II period. Work, including apprenticeship, was made illegal for children under the age of 15. Between 1962 and the early 1980s upper secondary school attendance tripled as an indirect consequence of the law, as well as the post-War baby boom in Italy.

Yet, the development of a single path for lower secondary school students has long been viewed as incomplete: while more students have had access to higher levels of education, schools have not provided the support necessary for students to succeed. Secondary schools have become a kind of "passing channel" between compulsory school and university. The rate of school failure also increased after 1962.

In 1976, several Italian scholars succeeded in calling attention to the need for better assessment instruments as a way to fight school failure and to strengthen pedagogy, calling attention to positive empirical results (see for example, Calonghi, 1976; Vertecchi, 1976). These researchers share a common conception of the school as a promoter of democracy and participation, and therefore advocated the development of assessment systems that avoid the selection and early exclusion of students, particularly students from the lower socio-economic classes. In 1977, the Italian parliament authorised legislation for the creation of a national "valuation form" as a way of tracking individual student progress and addressing school failure.

The valuation form was a key catalyst in influencing changes at the case study schools explored below. Nevertheless, Ministry officials note that teaching remains fairly traditional in the majority of schools, reporting that

---

[*] Thanks to Marcella Deluca of the OECD for her contribution to the development of this report.

"Active didactics, group work, *cooperative learning* are forms that are beginning to be more frequent in nursery and primary school, while they are still rare experiences in the secondary school ...". (MIUR, 2003, p. 109).

The Italian parliament authorised a series of major reforms to the school system between 1997 and 2003. As a result of these reforms, the Ministry of Instruction and University Research (MIUR) is now in the process of developing new standards, tests, and systems for school and teacher evaluation. MIUR is also developing approaches to help teachers better tailor learning to meet the needs of an increasingly diverse student body.

Reforms authorised in March 2003 incorporate the principle of *personalizzazione* (personalisation) as a way to reinforce formative assessment in more Italian classrooms at the lower secondary level, as well as differentiation of curricular content and tasks to address learning and cultural differences and special educational needs. The bill emphasises the *laboratorio didattico* (learning laboratory) as a way to tailor teaching methods and to provide students with the chance to integrate learning from different classes. The bill also introduces the position of tutor/co-ordinator for each class. The co-ordinator is to be responsible for gathering data from students, talking with families, and lining up resources for students. This new role, which will be filled by individuals with teaching qualifications, may prove an important resource for helping create the conditions amenable to greater use of formative assessment teaching methods in more Italian classrooms.

HIGHLIGHTS FROM THE CASE STUDIES

Between 1985 and 1995, the Michelangelo School was among a small number of schools selected by the Italian Ministry of Education to participate in a project to revise the national valuation form, which had been in use since 1977. Several of the teachers who participated in the demonstration project recall that the experience of working on this project helped to shape a strong working relationship among them. In 1995, the current valuation form became a part of regular practice in Italian schools. Teachers at Bari have continued to discuss and revise their approaches to assessment since then. The school provides core classes as required by the national curriculum, and also has several optional classes.

At the Testoni Fioravanti School, the valuation form helps to shape teaching and student assessment, as at the Michelango School. The school is also distinguished by the learning paths, developed following authorisation of a 1996 law allowing schools to increase teaching from thirty to thirty-three hours per week, and creating greater curriculum flexibility. The three paths include: advanced studies in math and science; advanced studies in language; and, recuperation – or remediation – activities. Currently 55% of the students in the school are enrolled in advanced, or empowerment, classes. The school is thus able to provide curricula that are partially but nevertheless significantly differentiated and tailored to student interests and needs. Seventy per cent of the students follow at least one additional activity during the afternoon.

CASE STUDY 1: THE MICHELANGELO SCHOOL

La scuola media statale Michelangelo, located in the City of Bari in southern Italy, is attended by children from high and middle-income families. There are 684 students at the school, and 26 students in each class (this is the legal limit for class size in Italy). The school is highly rated in the area and attracts students not only from the city, but also from nearby local government areas.

The school provides core classes as required by the national curriculum, and also has several optional classes where students can pursue particular interests more deeply, such as journalism, health education, music, animation-dramatisation, chemistry; and so on. In Italy, students stay together as a class for the three years that they are in the lower secondary school. Incoming students are placed in heterogeneous groupings, so that each class includes students of varied abilities, personalities, and backgrounds. Students with disabilities are integrated into core classes (a common practice in Italy since the 1980s), and also have additional special education classes. There is a support teacher if there are students with disabilities in the core class.

Teaching and assessment at the school

Diagnostic assessment

Students are assessed when they first enter the Michelangelo School. Assessment tests are used to gauge students' abilities, acquired knowledge, and learning styles. Teachers use this information to shape their initial lesson plans, and to make sure that they have the right kinds of resources on hand to satisfy the variety of learning needs in the class.

Using assessment data to enhance the learning process

Interactions involved in the formative evaluation process are carried out with care. For example, if a student has difficulties in expressing an idea or an opinion verbally, the student is invited to represent it in the way that he or she prefers. In subsequent exercises, the student may be asked to go through a similar process, but to think about that image and express himself verbally.

Teachers comment that they are more concerned about enhancing the students' learning process than they are about the result. They feel it is essential to have some kind of instrument to gather information about how each student is learning. For example, several of the teachers have developed personalised booklets on each student's progress. In this way, they can get to know each student better and also can pass on a portrait of the student to other teachers.

Teachers also keep graphs and tables tracking students' acquisition of knowledge, ability to comprehend, analyse, synthesise, and use various ways of expressing themselves. They can compare their assessments of how students are doing with other teachers during the class council discussions. The discussions among teachers and the use of tracking tools also help to ensure that they are treating students equitably.

Using assessment data to modify the teaching and learning process

Between 1985 and 1995, the Michelangelo School was among a small number of schools selected by the Italian Ministry of Education to participate in a project to revise the national valuation form, which had been in use since 1977. Several of the teachers who participated in the demonstration project are still at the school. They recall that the experience of working on this project helped to shape a strong group relationship among them. In 1995, the current valuation form became a part of regular practice in Italian schools. Teachers at Bari have continued to discuss and revise their approaches to assessment as a group.

Teachers recount that they had varied experiences in using formative assessment when they first started using these methods. One teacher commented that she started in a very difficult school, and needed to adjust her teaching methods to better meet the students' needs. "It depends on who you have in front of you, basically", she says.

Teachers comment that they've always talked about assessment among themselves and with students in a transparent way. If they give a student a bad assessment, they will discuss why they have made that decision and the student is asked to reflect on why they did not perform as well hoped. The student is then given an opportunity to revise the work. (Note that in Italy, students do not receive official marks until they are in upper secondary school. Instead, they receive qualitative marks as part of a more formal assessment every three to four months.)

Teachers claim that formative assessment has changed their approach to teaching. First, they "lose" the leadership of the class, and become participants in discussions with the students. They may activate classroom discussion with techniques such as brainstorming, games, simulation, and other activities, and by engaging students in a way that encourages spontaneous responses and creates a positive classroom climate. In this way, the teachers can also learn more about individual students' personalities and draw them into co-operative construction of knowledge.

Because there are not yet any nationally-defined learning standards, the class council develops objectives and standards for the whole school, and teaching approaches that will help reach these goals. Teachers at the school have a policy of making the standards and evaluation criteria, and how they relate to the learning objectives, as clear as possible to students before they start a new assignment. Students receive feedback on their performance in relation to learning objectives. This practice is followed throughout the school, so students are quite used to this process. Teachers tend to follow a similar format for classes – beginning with a starter activity, discussion of lesson objectives, and sharing of criteria for good work.

Teachers also work hard to tailor interventions to meet the needs of the individual students. They draw from a variety of learning theories as they develop their teaching plans. However, the teachers say that they do not assume that the teaching methods are appropriate until they have seen that the methods and theories actually make an impact on student learning.

Feedback and adaptation

Teachers at this school say that they plan feedback activities so that they can create the time and space for interaction, better diagnose students' learning needs, and shape feedback. Formative assessments are intended to assist students in the ongoing learning process and at the end of learning paths, to review and revise, to reinforce what they have learnt, to help students apply previous learning in new situations, and to deepen and enrich their knowledge. Teachers at the Michelangelo School make formative assessments of student performance according to criteria they have set based on their own research, and in departmental work groups. Teachers note that they are always revising and refreshing the criteria they use in order to refine their techniques and to keep their work fresh.

As a part of their regular practice, teachers also have developed the habit of asking students open-ended questions so that they can make better informal assessments of students' understanding, and encourage students to develop the skills of self-evaluation and self-correction. By helping students to diagnose the initial source of a misunderstanding, they guide them toward the habit of self-correction.

The teachers review homework with students, correcting mistakes and guiding students toward the practice of self-correction, reflection on the work process, review of sources. They also give students the opportunity to revise homework. Teachers use test results formatively, determining what interventions would be appropriate to meet students' learning needs.

Teachers have developed a variety of models for helping students to learn new concepts. These models may be textual, descriptive, analytical, or rhetorical. Teacher and students will discuss the model thoroughly before students start to work on their own. Students say that they do not study in a linear way – instead, they progress through concepts through the use of models. Students often develop conceptual maps in order to see where a subject fits into a larger scheme. At the beginning of a new unit, they are likely to brainstorm about what they already know about a particular subject, and how it relates to other subjects they have studied.

Summative evaluations

Schools are required to evaluate students with reference to the Ministerial schemes and objectives in each of the disciplinary branches. The summative, or "global" evaluation occurs only after the "intermediate" process of teaching and learning. Teachers use oral and written tests and graphics (*e.g.*, technical or artistic drawings, histograms, ideograms, aerogrammes, diagrams, conceptual maps to verify the acquisition of a system of interrelated body of knowledge through various modalities). Students receive both "structural and semi-structural" written results every three to four months. They are assessed according not only to what they have learnt but also their ability to integrate and use the learning more broadly.

Gradual and cyclical learning paths

At the Michelangelo School, subjects are organised as triennial "paths". In other words, the curriculum is developed for the full three years. At each level, students will cover particular subjects (fairly briefly) – developing specific knowledge, concepts and abilities as appropriate for their age and prior knowledge and abilities. In the second and third years, teachers will re-address subjects, covering them in greater depth and breadth – building new data, concepts, abilities, skills and information. This "gradual" approach to learning allows students to cover subjects from their most simple to most complex level – for example, moving from consideration of the space around them (the school, the street) to the abstract concept of infinity. In a literature class, students may move from study of the fable in the first year, to (sometimes autonomous) study of novels, poetry, or epics by the third year.

Aiming toward student autonomy

Teachers observe that using formative assessment in their classrooms takes more time, but they also emphasise that by the students' third year, they recuperate much of this time. By year three, students are expected to have developed a relatively high level of autonomy, the ability to "learn to learn", and to make decisions for their own development. This is the teachers' ultimate goal in using formative assessment.

The students provided evidence that they are indeed learning to be autonomous. As one year three student reported, if she does not understand a new concept, she often tries to relate it to another subject, to understand the context better, and its relation to other ideas. In other words, she develops her own learning scheme. Ultimately, this student told us, "it is up to us to learn". This sentiment was widely echoed across the classroom.

Teachers note that several of their students have come to visit the school after they have moved on to upper secondary school. The students tell their former teachers that the learning and assessment techniques they developed at the Michelangelo School have made them better students and provided them with an advantage in secondary school. They miss the type of interaction they had with their teachers at the Michelangelo School – finding their classes in upper secondary school to be very traditional.

Time to get to know students

Having the same class for three years means that the teachers have more opportunities to get to know their students, find out what works for them, and tailor their teaching more carefully. As teachers note, "We know (our students) very well". However, they also note that they "… don't think they have sure and absolute recipes" and are "humbly aware in every moment of the complexity in working with human subjects whose answers are not always foreseeable". Teachers at the school try to be creative, flexible, and self-critical in their work. Teachers engage in ongoing action research, and construction and updating of a variety of teaching tools according to experiences and new needs.

Teachers teach classes in teams. Team teaching means that there are opportunities for some teachers to pay more individual attention to students who need more help. Support teachers have the time and training to help adjust to the needs of the individual students.

Creating an environment where students feel safe to take risks

Teachers note that they are careful to stress students' positive qualities, not to discuss personal problems within the classroom, and, in their interaction with parents, to deal only with the problems and potential capacities of their own children. They also comment that they hope to instil a certain resiliency in students that will help them in areas where they are not as strong.

The students themselves say they feel safe to make mistakes in the classroom – this is just part of the learning process. The students comment that it is important that their teachers are kind, noting that this sometimes helps them to develop a greater interest in a subject than they might have in a stricter environment. More important, however, they say, is the teacher's knowledge of the subject and ability to explain things to student and to understand the learner's perspective.

Creating conditions

Italian school heads tend to fill more of an administrative role than an instructional leadership role. Nevertheless, teachers and observers of this school attribute the school's success, in large part, to a series of strong school heads over the past 12 years (there have been three school heads in 12 years). The recent school heads have also fostered an environment that has helped to maintain the school's focus on integrated learning and multi-faceted assessment. The current school head started a year ago. He notes that at his previous school, one of his strategies had been "… to provide serenity during work, meaning to try and facilitate work". He sees himself as a group leader, but not as a boss. The teachers make the decisions, he says, and he puts his energy into supporting those decisions that he also sees as priorities.

Teachers' careful analysis of what is going on in classrooms, along with emphasis on teaching theory, has helped them to modify teaching methods. As a group, teachers have analysed issues related to the quality and quantity of feedback, levels of attention they give to individual students, student motivation, how to make group activities work (*e.g.*, whether homogeneous groups work better), and the role of tutoring. The teachers have been trained in cognitive psychology, and this has been very helpful for doing interactive lessons.

Teachers at the school participate in action research. They are always in contact with the University of Bari – for their own research and professional development, during student-teacher internships at the school, and with support teachers who complete apprenticeship hours at the school. The teachers say that their relationship with the university has been quite fruitful. They have been able to test the validity of various didactic innovations in history and science. However, as the university-based expert notes, professors of education are not taught how to teach – so they are learning along the way, as well, about some of the more practical aspects of teaching and learning.

Parents are regularly welcomed to the school. The school has a weekly "receiving hour" when parents can come to the school to meet with teachers. Once every four months, teachers schedule individual meetings with parents. There is also a schedule to talk with the school leader. Parents can schedule meetings with the teacher or the school head. Parents note that the teachers and school head are always very available. Many of the parents at this school are quite involved, and make time to talk with teachers about how their children are doing in the classes, how they mature, their relationships, respect for rules, and school and class project plans.

CASE STUDY 2: THE TESTONI FIORAVANTI UNIFIED SCHOOL

The Scuola media unificata Testoni Fioravanti serves students in the area of Bolognina within the city of Bologna. The area was revitalised in the 1960s, attracting new residents from the regional hinterland and from the south of Italy. Residents in this area are socially diverse. The area, which was formerly the regional residential nucleus for blue-collar workers and farmers, has also recently attracted a middle class base – modifying the character of the area. At the beginning of the 1990s, the area became the home for a large community of Chinese, as well as Maghrabine, Romanian, Indian and Pakistani immigrants (the composition of this immigration follows the general wave in Italy). The school has developed programmes to meet the needs of the local population, including specific initiatives for immigrant children and their parents.

According to school administrators, following completion of lower secondary school, approximately: 30% of the students go on to *Liceo* (high school); 30% go on to an *Istituto Tecnico* (technical institutes – 5 year schools that may be followed by further university-level study over two years); and 30% choose to got to *Istituti Professionali* (vocational training – 5 year terminal degrees).

Teaching and assessment at the school

Adaptation of the national valuation form

The teachers at this school first developed a "whole-school" approach to change in 1980, following introduction of the national valuation system. In response to the new national forms, teachers worked together to develop a valuation instrument that would meet their own needs within the school.

The valuation form ranks student performance in subject areas as "optimum, distinct, good, sufficient, or insufficient". Teachers also track each student's overall level of maturation, including their ability to respect rules, to establish good relationships with peers and teachers, and to engage in learning and to contribute to the class. Teachers also follow the development of students' autonomy (including their ability to organise themselves and develop good work habits), attention in class, ability to comprehend and analyse information, and to make links between subject areas.

Diagnostic and ongoing assessment

Welcoming of new students is very caring and individualised. In December and January, before enrolment for the next school year, parents can attend an assembly with the head of the school and with teachers who will explain the school's plan of formative offer (POF). The incoming students who are in the last year of primary school in the territorial area are also invited in this lower secondary school before and after enrolment to learn about the organisation of the school. Usually teachers hold individual meetings with the parents of each incoming student starting in February of the year that precedes the beginning of the new school year. Families have the opportunity to decide whether they are comfortable with their choice of school.

Teachers in the lower secondary school and primary schools have developed a grid to prepare for transition of students. The school also administers some disciplinary/subject area entrance tests following the school's POF. The entrance tests help teachers to evaluate the starting point of the students as they enter the school. The grid is a descriptive instrument and includes indicators on the child's situation. The teachers usually use this grid to guide their discussions with parents. It includes information about the student's prior scholastic success, attitudes, aspirations, and habits. This information helps teachers to form classes that are heterogeneous in terms of abilities and student personalities, and also helps the pupils to choose the optional curriculum activities they prefer.

The teachers find that formative assessments help them to tailor learning to an increasingly diverse set of students (diverse with regard to knowledge and competencies, cultural and ethnic identities, and other subjective variables). The teachers also aim to help students develop self-assessment skills over their three years at the school – including their ability to evaluate their learning progress, and to understand if and why they make mistakes.

Teachers track student progress from the initial diagnostic test through the exit exam, and they believe that a higher percentage of children at the school are attaining well than in the past. In addition, a very low percentage of students repeat classes (repeating classes is not preferred in the Italian system – the worst that a school can do is to fail children).

Heterogeneous classes

The school has developed a special commission to place incoming students in one of four levels (A, B, C or D). Members of the commission put together all the information that they have gathered on each student. They use this information to distribute students in new first classes. The classes include a similar mix of students with various competencies, levels of attainment, and behaviour problems. The commission also takes into account where possible, the specific requests the student and his/her family may make in regard to class placement.

Creating a safe environment for learning

Teachers at the school believe that assessment needs to support all students psychologically. Teachers believe that assessment can create many problems, particularly with respect to the more fragile and less self-confident students. They see the system of daily assessment as supporting the individual identity of these children and helping to increase their self-confidence.

Summative tests occur only after a period of ongoing formative assessment

Teaching staff also plan periodic tests to verify student progress, as a part of formal assessment, and to inform parents about how well their children are doing in school. The teachers make clear that the summative assessments occur periodically and only after daily formative assessments are carried out. These summative tests are anticipated and students are prepared so that they do not get nervous about having to take a test.

Encouraging student autonomy

Teachers emphasise that the assessment process – facilitated by the national form and the grid that the school has developed to better adapt valuation to the needs of the school and students – tends to encourage student self-assessment. The teachers observe that students over the course of their three years at the school, start to adopt the methods the teachers have been modelling in classes (such as restating what students have said, helping students to think about subjects in a new way, and analysing performances with the students). The formative process also stimulates student engagement and responsibility for their work.

Partially differentiated paths

In 1996, the school introduced a new, experimental curriculum. The curriculum takes advantage of a national law that allows schools to increase teaching from 30 to 33 hours per week, and creates some flexibility for teachers within that time period. Teachers at the Testoni Fioravanti School chose to develop three partially differentiated paths for students. The three paths include: advanced studies in math and science; advanced studies in language; and, recuperation activities. Currently, 55% of the students in the school are enrolled in advanced, or empowerment, classes.

At the Testoni Fioravanti School, the three extra hours are mandatory for all students. Initially, the extra courses were offered to only some students at the school, but the options were then extended to students throughout the school in order to avoid "ghettoization" of classes. Students attend the extra classes six mornings a week, and one afternoon. School hours are distributed over six mornings of five hours plus one afternoon of three hours – for a total of 33 hours each week. Students may also participate in additional extra-curricular activities, such as art, music, information technology, gymnastics, or more academically oriented programmes, such as German or Latin for two hours a week (only available to 3rd year students at the school). The school is effectively able to provide curricula that are partially but nevertheless significantly differentiated and tailored to student interests and needs. Seventy per cent of the students follow at least one additional activity during the afternoon.

Teachers have continued to revise the innovative curriculum according to general observations of results in the school. Teachers new to the school have also introduced modifications to the programme, and have taken ownership. There is no summative assessment in the optional laboratories – only formative assessment.

Creating conditions

The current school head has been at the Testoni Fioravanti School for three years. She has charge of the lower secondary school and beginning in Autumn 2003, two primary schools. While the school head describes her work as primarily administrative, teachers note that she is also the recognised leader of the school. She backs the teachers and mediates occasional differences and clashes among teachers. While she is centred on the institutional tasks of the school, she is also respectful of people – teachers, parents and students. The school head has a management team (selected by the school head) to support her in her various functions. The teachers recognise that the school head should be able to choose her own collaborators.

Teachers describe the school as having a positive climate that emphasises respect for the different backgrounds and approaches of teachers on the staff. They also note that the introduction of the national valuation form, as well as subsequent modifications to the form, their participation in training and refresher courses, and the work they have done as a group to develop a shared language and a shared understanding of the elements most important to formative assessment have contributed to the collegial culture of the school.

Teachers are able to continue professional development through training and refresher courses and sabbaticals (important for professional development, and the personal maturation of each of these teachers).

The Testoni Fioravanti School measures its performance primarily through an annual parent survey. The survey asks whether: parents are happy with the availability of teachers, staff and the school head; parents believe that their children have established good personal relationships with their peers and adults in the school; their children appear to be engaged in their classes and are satisfied with the empowerment classes; and parents are engaged with the child's learning (such as, whether parents regularly check the child's school diary). Parents' satisfaction indices, as measured by the annual survey sent out by the school, are high. Eighty-nine per cent of parents express support for the school's "didactic offer". There is also a high rate of parent participation and engagement in council meetings.

References

Calonghi, L. (1976), *Valutazione*, La Scuola, Brescia.

Ministry of Instruction and University Research (MIUR) (2003), "Attracting, Developing and Retaining Effective Teachers", Country Background Report on Italy, OECD, Paris, *www.oecd.org/dataoecd/54/7/17997702.pdf*

Vertecchi, B. (1976), *Valutazione formative*, Loescher, Torino.

New Zealand: Embedding Formative Assessment in Multiple Policy Initiatives

by
Janet Looney, OECD
Jenny Poskitt, Massey University

OVERVIEW

In the mid-1980s, the New Zealand Labour government undertook a number of radical reforms, moving both public and private sectors toward a model of greater market competition. In the public sector, the government pushed for a reduction in the role of the central government and greater autonomy at the local level, with a focus on achievement of specified outcomes. The 1989 Education Act, framed by a series of task force recommendations, followed this model. The Act provided schools with greater autonomy, creating Boards of Trustees with representatives drawn from the local community; required Boards to create individual school charters setting out school aims and objectives to be achieved within the National Education Guidelines; and gave schools control over funds distributed by the national government. The Education Review Office (ERO) was created as an independent review and audit agency, to focus both on financial management and hold schools accountable for meeting the aims of their charters.

Bi-culturalism and education

Aotearoa/New Zealand is a bi-cultural nation. The Treaty of Waitangi (1840), which established British sovereignty over New Zealand, also created a partnership between the Crown (as represented by the New Zealand Government) and the indigenous Maori population (see *www.kmike.com/country/nzdemog.htm*). Over the last thirty years, the Maori community has claimed an increasingly important role in shaping the New Zealand policy agenda and approach to bi-culturalism.

In education, the Treaty has served as the legal and philosophical basis for the creation of culturally appropriate programmes "for Maori and by Maori, aimed at improving Maori student outcomes over the last decade". Maori have argued that efforts to address and redress the dominant-subordinate pattern of relationships that had emerged between European (or

Pakeha) and Maori populations is a necessary first step in addressing multi-culturalism in New Zealand (Bishop and Glynn, 1999).

Addressing disparities in student achievement

The Ministry of Education notes that "[t]here are significant disparities in achievement evident throughout New Zealand's schools in terms of acquisitions of core literacies, participation in school, attainment of qualifications and progress on to tertiary education …". (Ministry of Education, 2002) In part, the Ministry attempts to address disparities through the decile system. Decile ratings are based on the Targeted Funding for Educational Achievement (TEFA) indicator – which is intended to identify those schools with students from the lowest socioeconomic communities. The 10 subdivisions (deciles 1-10) each include 10% of schools. Deciles 1-3 comprise the "low decile group". Lower decile schools receive additional funding (Ministry of Education, 2000).

Various Maori learning programmes appear to be having a positive impact as well. According to the Education Review Office, those schools that "… are responding best to ethnic diversity do so through acknowledgement and support of cultural differences". (Ministry of Education, 2000). However, Maori and Pacific Island student achievement still lags behind achievement of other students.

Formative assessment in New Zealand education

In New Zealand, formative assessment is not presented as a separate, high-profile national policy initiative, but is embedded in multiple national policies [including guidance in the curriculum framework, and the National Administration Guidelines (NAGS)] and examination requirements [the NCEA (National Certificate Examination Award)], as well as several nationally-sponsored professional development and innovation initiatives.

One particular national professional development programme is "Assess to Learn" (formerly known as "Assessment for Better Learning"), in which facilitators work closely with selected primary and secondary schools to develop their policies and procedures in assessment. Facilitators work intensively with each school for a two- to three-year period, increasing teacher knowledge of assessment and working with them in classrooms to link together pedagogy and assessment practice. The results of this professional development programme are evident in the two colleges involved in this study.

HIGHLIGHTS FROM THE CASE STUDIES

The Maori Mainstream Programme (MMP) reviewed in the study in Waitakere College, is built on principles of Kaupapa Maori – Kaupapa Maori is based on a critical analysis of the unequal power relations within society. Within this framework, the importance of culture and relationships is paramount.

At Rosehill College in Auckland, school leaders and staff have been working to incorporate formative assessment into their regular practice since 1998. Their initial interest in formative assessment was raised as they tried to figure out how to meet National Administration Guidelines (otherwise known as the NAGs) requiring schools to monitor progress and to address learning needs of students at risk of not achieving, or not achieving. They saw formative assessment, which requires teachers to think about what exemplifies good student work at the various learning levels, as a way to achieve this goal.

Rosehill's involvement in the national "Assessment for Better Learning" professional development programme and involvement of the school's technology department in development of national curriculum exemplars have also influenced the school's adoption and adaptation of formative assessment. The school's successful involvement in these initiatives has also encouraged teachers to find new opportunities and to continually improve themselves.

CASE STUDY 1: WAITAKERE COLLEGE

Waitakere College is located in west Auckland. It is a lower-middle decile four school (with a decile ten school counting at the high-end of the socio-economic scale). Of the 1 450 students enrolled in the school, 45% are of European descent, 22% are Maori, 18% are Pacific Islander, and 15% are Asian.

Having been involved in the "Assessment for Better Learning" professional development programme, in 2001 Waitakere College was also chosen as one of 17 schools (grouped in ten pilot clusters) to participate in the Ministry-sponsored innovation programme – the Maori Mainstream Programme (MMP, *Te Kotahitanga* in the Maori language). Each of the pilot schools has identified its own needs, and has followed a slightly different model. Waitakere College has chosen to run the MMP as a segregated programme, rather than as a school-wide initiative (which some schools participating in the project are doing).

Waitakere's principal and deputy principal responsible for professional development are particularly interested in developing a strategy to bring the teaching approach and philosophy of MMP to scale throughout the school.

Teaching and assessment at the school

The Maori Mainstream Programme encourages teachers to understand their own cultural preconceptions and to create environments where children can safely bring "who they are" into the learning situation.

Maori education scholars Bishop and Glynn note:

> ...[T]he introduction of techniques (such as cooperative learning) in isolation from other pedagogical values, beliefs and practices may not be as effective for Maori children's learning as once thought; a simple group-individual dichotomy is not enough – the cultural context is paramount. Such a context helps students 'make sense' of learning interactions by allowing them to bring their own sense-making processes to bear. Teachers need to create safe classroom learning environments in which a range of discourses and learning strategies occur. (Bishop and Glynn, 1999, pp. 157-158)

Bishop and Glynn have each played important roles in the development of the MMP nationally including scoping of the project and provision of training. Various informants spoke about the MMP as being "… all about relationships between teachers and students". MMP is based on cooperative learning, proverbs and karakia (prayer). Changes within the classrooms – and in the regulation of learning, and the manner in which students receive feedback – reflect this careful attention to relationships.

Deep changes in teacher's perception of their own role in relation to students

According to Bishop and Glynn, teachers need to develop an understanding of their own "preconceptions, goals, aspirations and cultural preferences" and to "… be prepared to listen to others in such a way that their previous experiences and assumptions do not close them off from the full meaning of the student's description of their experience". (Bishop and Glynn, 1999)

Teachers in the Maori Mainstream Programme acknowledge that sharing power with students "needs an attitude change" and that while it is nice to get away from the front of the classroom, teaching in a co-operative mode involves more risk-taking.

A focus on helping students to feel safe in the classroom

Closely related to the changes in power relationships between teachers and students are efforts to help students feel safe within the classroom. The idea behind the Maori Mainstream Programme is that Maori (and other) students feel safe when they can "... bring what they know and who they are into the learning relationship ... where culture counts". (Bishop and Glynn, 1999)

The Maori Mainstream Programme emphasises group work, co-construction of knowledge, and peer solidarity (students in a focus group commented that they felt like they were brothers and sisters growing up together). As one teacher noted, "You are often told as new teachers to be tough and keep it quiet. Individuals in their seats and to have quiet classrooms, but in this programme you can have noisy engaged learning and it is not a discipline problem". Other teachers reinforced this point of view. Indeed, Waitakere has been known as a strict school – so noisy learning in the MMP classrooms get noticed. But, the MMP teachers say, they have fewer discipline problems than do other teachers, who follow the stricter approach to teaching. The cooperative learning opportunities have also helped students' social skills and they are learning to resolve conflict, take different roles, and develop acceptance of others. Students say that they are much happier in the MMP classes. They find that they relate to their teachers better. But in non-Maori Mainstream Programme classes, they are not as happy.

Maori Mainstream Programme teachers have also placed great emphasis on providing students with positive reinforcement. The MMP teachers say that, in general, they have seen students become more and more positive and supportive of each other. In the long run, however, it will be important for teachers to discover whether students in the MMP respond differently to task-oriented or ego-oriented praise, and if, as they build confidence and grow used to working in classes using formative assessment, their responses to different forms of feedback change.

Active, problem-based and holistic learning

Maori Mainstream teachers use a number of formative assessment techniques. These include the use of feed-forward (what students will be learning that day, week, term – and why); scaffolding (providing students with as little information as they appear to need, so they have opportunity to get the answer on their own when possible); and, feedback (use of exemplars and helping students close the gap between their current performance and the desired standard). Group work is also favoured.

Teachers said that their ultimate goal was to facilitate learning, rather than to lecture students. By using feed-forward and feedback techniques, they are able to engage students in reflective thinking and problem-solving. Teachers also try to reach students who may have different learning styles. For example, one teacher noted that she may provide six tasks from which students can choose. She has students doing task work a majority of the time, enabling her to wander around and work with students one on one.

Conversations with students are also different. Teachers told us that they generally try to base their conversation around open-ended questions, providing positive feedback, and scaffolding of questions ("can you think about what might happen if you do such and such?"). Teachers are conscious of the need to be flexible and to try to use different approaches to explaining a concept, or encouraging students who do understand a concept to explain the concept to their fellow students.

The teachers said that they have a great deal of freedom with the MMP to take risks. "So long as objectives are covered ..." one teacher noted, "... you can teach what you like here. We have relative freedom to teach units we like and set the timing of the units".

Early evidence of impact

While it is too early to judge the long-term impact of the MMP on student learning, there are indicators that the programme has helped to raise achievement since 2001. The evidence includes:

- Increased student retention. In the past, the school has tended to "lose" students in years 11 and 12, but this is no longer happening as much.

- Increased average student attendance. The average student attendance across the school "houses" is 83 to 90 half days. The MMP students are attending school an average of 87½ days on average.

- Teachers spend more time on learning, and less on addressing behavioural problems.

- Ninety per cent of MMP students are earning credit toward the National Certificate Examination Award.

- Students in the case study interview reported that they are doing better in the Maori Mainstream Programme than in the non-Maori classes (although ultimately, a more positive indicator would be that students were achieving better in all classes).

Teachers mentioned a number of additional indicators that the programme is working well. For example students:

- Ask more questions and seem to feel safer asking questions.

- Are more likely to take risks (rather than not trying or giving up easily), and are more likely to ask task-related questions.

- Are making more connections between what they are learning in class and what is happening in their lives elsewhere or with what they have seen on TV.

- More readily share their ideas.

- Are happy to be doing exams (come prepared, books out, with smiling faces).

- Take responsibility for the classroom environment and for challenging unacceptable behaviour from other students.

Students also noted their satisfaction with the programme. For example, they commented that several of them had won a "brainy" competition with non-MMP students, and that they were becoming the "nerds" (noted with a smile).

Waitakere College is measuring longer-term outcomes of the programme. They are doing this by observing five students in the MMP over time. School leaders say that while there are no baseline tests for students in the MMP, they will be able to compare common assessment tests in departments to get indicators of change. Waitakere is also planning to administer a survey on student attitudes.

Creating conditions

The Maori Mainstream Programme requires a deep personal and professional investment from teachers. The twelve teachers participating in the MMP at Waitakere have various motivations for the personal investment they have made. Some say they wanted to participate in the programme because it is consistent with their own philosophy and vision for teaching. Others were recruited by school leadership, who wanted to ensure teacher involvement across departments. The participating teachers say that they have benefited from the intensive professional development included in the programme.

Teachers note that they "… have had some astounding professional development monthly meetings in the Maori Mainstream Programme". For instance, the Ministry of Education sponsored a four-day intensive cultural immersion programme for teachers participating in MMP innovation grants across New Zealand early in the school year, and a three-day programme in the second year of the programme. The Maori Mainstream teachers had a chance to hear feedback from Maori parents and students, and to explore their own cultural and professional attitudes toward teaching as well as culture and power relationships between teachers and students in the classroom. The Ministry has sponsored five additional conferences on a range of topics for MMP teachers and for principals and deputy principals.

Teachers say that they have also benefited from the increased contact, consultation and support they have had with each other. They attend training as a group, and take opportunities to observe each other. They have also shared what they are learning with other teachers in the school who are not participating in the MMP.

Teachers in the MMP say that they have had to make real changes to their professional practice – which has required "… more head-space" and more energy and input, but has also been rewarding. They are also committed to the idea that teachers can make a difference in learning outcomes (as one teacher noted, teachers have abdicated too much responsibility based on the belief that socio-economic levels are the primary determinant of student success). The school has also freed the MMP teachers from many requirements. They are thus able to devote more of the necessary thought to learning to teach in new ways.

The half-time, on-site facilitator has been vital to the MMP. According to the MMP teachers at Waitakere, the facilitator's mix of skills and passion keep the programme going. The facilitator works with experts on Maori education at the University of Waikato, brings readings and relevant research to teachers involved in the MMP, shares practical ideas on how to address challenges in the classroom, observes classes and follows formative assessment practice in her own interactions with the teachers. She has enlisted the support of Resource Teachers of Learning and Behaviour (RTLBs) in advisory capacities, as consultants on delivery and content of professional development, and as co-observers in classrooms. The facilitator has also provided professional reading for teachers throughout the school, and has run wider school initiatives – such as a teacher-only-day about the Treaty of Waitangi (which establishes New Zealand as a bi-cultural country).

CASE STUDY 2: ROSEHILL COLLEGE

Students at Rosehill College are generally from families with a fairly high socio-economic level. There are many international students at the school. Because international students pay tuition, this means that Rosehill has a fairly healthy discretionary budget at its disposal: in 2001-02 school year, about NZD 900 000.

Teaching and assessment at the school

As with Waitakere College, teachers at Rosehill College have been involved in the "Assessment for Better Learning" professional development programme. The school has focused on formative assessment in classroom practice and in school-wide policies and procedures. While some teachers feel that they have always used aspects of formative assessment (*i.e.*, in maths, teachers build on previous concepts all the time in order to move forward to successive concepts), they report that they have also become more effective by changing several aspects of their practice, such as timing and specificity of feedback, scaffolding of questions, and focusing on students' learning skills.

Constant attention to providing students with performance criteria, feed forward and feedback

Teachers and school leaders at Rosehill define formative assessment as: "... basically giving kids feedback, feeding forward about how to improve their learning ... looking at a piece of ... work that a student's doing ... and giving them some information about what's good about it and some next steps to improve".

In the English department, teachers now make a regular practice of sharing the criteria they will use for assessment of students work as they begin each unit. Criteria are set up as rubrics at each level (achieved, merit, excellence) so that students know what is required. Teachers in Rosehill's Mathematics department require students to record criteria, feed forward and feedback and their learning plans on a tracking sheet. The tracking and action plan system is part of the departmental professional development focus in the 2003 school year. At present, department members are streamlining the system, and working to ensure that all teachers are using it consistently (practice was somewhat variable amongst teachers in the first year of the system).

Feed forward techniques at Rosehill commonly consist of providing a lesson preview. For example, it is common practice for teachers to write up learning goals on the board at the beginning of the class. Teachers tend to write up a flow chart or lists outlining what students will learn during the class, and how the lesson will build on previous learning.

Teachers have found that timing of the feedback is crucial. In the past, feedback had been completely unconnected to what students were working on. For example, one teacher noted, "The science department used to follow a topic for about six weeks and at the end of the six weeks they'd mark the topic and give the kids their results. However, by the time the kids got their results they were three weeks into the next topic. There was no evidence to indicate that what the students were doing in that six-week period was actually being helped along …". Teachers noted that instant feedback can often be more important than the kind of feedback that is recorded. Teachers are also more specific about what students need to do to improve their work. In the English department, for example, students get feedback from their teacher as well as from peers on those aspects they are doing well, and those on which they need to focus their attention. Teachers provide extra references, resources and materials that address aspects of learning needing attention.

Students told us that they like the feedback they get from their teachers. They are particularly interested in the specifics about what they could change about their work in order to make it better. They told us that they were much more interested in getting constructive feedback and specific comments than they are on getting praise. Students we spoke with were mixed, however, on whether they look at grades or comments first.

A focus on content and learning skills

Teachers comment that they find one of the most challenging aspects of teaching in the formative assessment mode is instilling in students the ability to find what is missing in their work, and figuring out what to do next, and then taking responsibility for following through on next steps. Teachers try to model the steps, encouraging students to be specific about what their own work shows, and then taking it a step further to improve the work. The key thing, they observe, is in focusing student attention on specifics relating to criteria (in checklist form) for a high quality piece of work. Teachers often try to approach this task by breaking it down into smaller goals: for example, working with students to write a perfect topic sentence.

In order to accomplish these goals, teachers note that they have to have well-planned lessons – part of the goal being to have time to talk to students individually during the lesson time. Teachers find that the best feedback that they are able to provide students often occurs spontaneously. Other feedback occurs when students are working on homework. One teacher noted that some of his students often send e-mail asking for feedback. The teacher will send back bullet points on issues to consider – which students seem to like and to use. Another teacher notes that he spends quite a bit of time talking with students about what they need to do next to reinforce their knowledge. They might ask students to research information in their textbook, to look at information on the Internet, or look at student exemplars.

The mathematics department tracking system is another approach to guiding students to self-sufficiency. By keeping a record of their learning, students are able to identify what they are best at, what they need to focus on, and on what aspects they need help. Students also devise their own action plan as to what to do prior to summative assessments at the end of units of work. The department is also developing a template students can use to formulate their action plans, and classroom posters to guide students in their learning (and all topics are geared toward credits for the National Certificate Examination Award [NCEA]). Students are expected to work on identified areas of need during class and homework time, and refer to resources such as Intra- and Internet sites, homework books, textbook references, teacher, peers, maths sites (such as maths-on-line; school Intranet for extra resources), and wall charts. Students record their progress on an overview sheet for the year according to criteria given out with the unit (achieved, merit, excellence).

Importance of group work

Teachers at Rosehill use groups on a regular basis to actively involve students in learning. They note, however, that sometimes there is a tension as to when to move on – when a majority of students have understood a concept, but a few are struggling and need more time to complete the work. The teachers comment that they sometimes group students differently to adjust learning for them and allow them to continue. Often, they say, the challenge is an issue of students' own time management skills.

While teachers did not mention the culture of the school as a particularly important element, it is likely to be one of the contributing factors to their success. Students noted that teachers at Rosehill are "pretty sweet with us" and that most teachers are helpful, and will answer any questions.

Early evidence of impact

School leaders and teachers provided several pieces of evidence that formative assessment is leading to positive student outcomes. They include:

- Improvement of School Certificate results (which are national benchmarks – no longer available, due to the change to NCEA).

- Student results on NCEA exams comparable to or better than student results from higher decile schools.

- Teachers' observations that they think about more variables when teaching, and are more attentive to students' learning differences.

- Students' responsiveness to feedback, and efforts to incorporate feedback into their work.

- Increased student motivation and engagement in learning.

- Data gathered (and recorded) on student tracking sheets showing how they have addressed learning gaps, and progress toward learning goals.

- Maintenance of high standards and achievement on common assessment tasks, in spite of evidence that the writing and reading abilities and attitudes of incoming students are declining (suggesting that teaching and learning programmes are helping students to close learning gaps effectively).

- Outstanding reviews from the independent Education Review Office.

School leaders have expressed their intention to analyse NCEA data over a couple of years (once such data are available) to ascertain trends in student achievement, indicate changes to teaching programmes and adjust expectations of student performance standards. The school is also in the process of developing benchmarks, and will have more data in the future. Once they have the benchmarks, they will be able to track student progress more closely.

Creating conditions

The principal of Rosehill College came to the school in 1995. His deputy principal, who has responsibility for curriculum and assessment, and chairs the Board of Studies joined Rosehill College leadership a few months later (the school has three deputy principals).

The principal and deputy principal became interested in formative assessment around 1998. Their initial interest in formative assessment was raised as they tried to figure out how to meet National Administration Guidelines (otherwise known as the NAGs) requiring schools to monitor progress and to address learning needs of students either at risk of not achieving, or not achieving. They saw formative assessment, which requires teachers to think about what exemplifies good student work at the various learning levels, as a way to achieve this goal.

As previously mentioned, Rosehill's involvement in the national "Assessment for Better Learning" professional development programme influenced the school's adoption and adaptation of formative assessment. Teachers' practice was further deepened by involvement in the development of National Curriculum Exemplars. (National Curriculum Exemplars are authentic samples of student learning generated from high quality teaching and learning experiences. Accompanying curriculum matrices demonstrate how key aspects of the learning indicate progression of learning from levels one to five of the New Zealand national curriculum.) The technology department worked with a national technology facilitator to develop units of work and capture evidence of technological development in student learning. The provision of feedback to students enabled them to progress their conceptual development, and experience the integral role of formative assessment in learning (for more information about exemplars refer to *www.tki.org.nz/r/assessment/exemplars*). The school's successful involvement in such initiatives as these has enhanced the school's own development on formative assessment.

Teacher discussions regarding standards have also served as an important form of professional development. As the principal noted, "... actually talking about it and establishing ... what is a good piece of work ... That teacher talk stuff ... it's fantastic".

The main goal of the leadership team in implementing formative assessment teaching methods has been to make sure that staff members understand where the school as a whole is trying to achieve. According to the school principal, "... we wrote the goal ... and we backed up the goal by good research, ... and it was self-evident in a way, that what we were doing ... would be helpful to students and teachers, so that got people decided". School leaders started staff discussions and provided professional reading on formative assessment (*e.g.*, Black and Wiliam's *Inside the Black Box*), invited expert speakers, and asked individual departments within the school to work on their own ideas about how to implement formative assessment within classrooms.

There is a heavy emphasis on professional development. All teachers have an hour set aside for professional development every Tuesday morning (school starts an hour later every Tuesday). School leaders believe that "... if you've got self-review and if you're talking to teachers about focusing on teaching and learning you get a school-wide approach". According to school leaders "... there're still plenty of teachers who probably won't want a bar of it, who don't care and who think we're absolutely crazy...", but they feel that they've gotten "over the hump and suddenly it's going the right way...".

While school leaders have been strategic in their approach, they believe that school culture has been perhaps the most important determinant of their success (of course, being strategic is part of the culture). The school principal observes, "... I think the school-wide thing is about culture ... and it's about leadership [and how you lead a group of a hundred professional teachers down a particular track] and so you start to think about planning. How do you get that group of people heading in the same direction?". He stresses that "there's [not] any ... sort of mechanistic way that we can demonstrate what we've done because I think with a different leadership team it might not have been the same thing".

School leaders had earlier gathered information about teaching and learning at the school, about teachers' particular frustrations, and so on, also helped the school leadership to communicate with teachers better about formative assessment. According to the school principal, "if you can grab the teachers and get their support for the process, then whatever you put in the plan becomes almost 'kindred'". The principal notes that the focus on formative assessment has evolved as part of a long-term process. As a consequence, he believes that there is quite a deep understanding of formative assessment – what it is, what it looks like, how it makes a difference.

That said, the school has been fairly successful at influencing classroom practice across the school. The Board of Studies has developed action plans for formative assessment; professional development contributes to the action plans. Teachers are also held accountable for implementation of the action plans. Each department has grappled with separate issues related to formative assessment. In the science department, teachers address discrete topic areas. Teachers devised a grid to show more complex ideas developing. Over time, teachers have focused more on providing students with comments rather than on giving marks. They have found that the comments have helped to clarify expectations for students.

The school has been fortunate in hiring in teachers who buy into the school's strategy and approach to teaching. As the school principal describes, it's "... sort of magical in a way ... So as new teachers come into the school, particularly new beginning teachers they're sort of ... [infused] with the ideas of different people". Beginning teachers are matched with more experienced teachers who assist them with planning and schemes. Some work with prepared units and other departments provide documents linked to curriculum. Teachers who are newer to Rosehill College note that the school's professional development was a real attraction in deciding to come to the college.

References

Bishop, R. and T. Glynn (1999), *Culture Counts: Changing Power Relations in Education*, The Dunmore Press, Ltd., Palmerston North, New Zealand.

Ministry of Education (2000), "Report to the Ministry of Education on the Compulsory Schools Sector in New Zealand", Education Review Office.

Ministry of Education (2002), "Briefing for the Incoming Minister of Education", 24 January.

Queensland, Australia: An Outcomes-based Curriculum
by
Judy Sebba, University of Sussex
Graham Maxwell, Queensland Studies Authority

OVERVIEW

In 1989 all Australian State and Commonwealth Ministers of Education adopted a national curriculum framework to ensure that Australia's school education, based on agreed national goals, would provide young Australians with the knowledge, skills, attitudes and values relevant to present and emerging social, cultural and economic needs in local, national and international settings. This agreement included a commitment to eight key learning areas (KLAs) for school years 1-10: English; Mathematics; Science; Health & Physical Education; Languages other than English; Studies of Society & Environment; Technology; and The Arts. Each State and Territory has developed its own way of implementing this agreement, although there is general acceptance of an outcomes approach.

In Queensland, syllabuses and support materials have been developed for each of the KLAs by the Queensland Studies Authority (QSA). Learning outcomes, defining what students should know and be able to do within each key learning area, have been expressed for different levels of performance along a developmental continuum. In Queensland, there are eight developmental levels covering years 1-10 and these levels are labelled foundation, levels 1-6, and beyond level 6. KLA core learning outcomes are considered essential for all students. There are also some cross-curriculum priorities and an emphasis on developing lifelong learners.

Development of the current syllabuses and support materials for the KLAs began in Queensland in 1996 and was completed in 2004. KLAs were developed in pairs, the first pair being Science and Health & Physical Education. Full implementation in schools of all KLAs is not expected until 2007. The roll-out of KLA syllabuses for years 1-10 in pairs of syllabuses over several years was thought to allow teachers to adapt gradually to the new style of syllabus. The disadvantage was that schools have been unable so far to develop whole-school strategies and there is an inevitable tension and confusion between the old approach and the new. These difficulties may be resolved now that all KLA syllabuses are coming on stream.

QSA principles of assessment and reporting for KLA syllabuses emphasise that assessing students is an integral part of the teaching and learning process and that opportunities should be provided for students to take responsibility for their own learning and self-monitoring.

HIGHLIGHTS FROM THE CASE STUDIES

Teachers at both Our Lady's College (OLC) and Woodridge State High School (WSHS) make extensive use of the classic elements of formative assessment, including the development of shared objectives, higher order questioning, comment marking and feedback focused on objectives for future learning, peer- and self-assessment and group and co-operative work strategies.

Some of the focus on formative assessment techniques is certainly due to implementation of the KLA strategy. As a head of department at WSHS noted, the school's review of curriculum over the past few years has resulted in a greater emphasis on investigative work and integrated studies, and teaching now involves "… more activities and less 'chalk and talk'".

Teachers at OLC regularly share pieces of student work and discuss comments they have made on them as well as the work itself. Heads of department saw this as professional behaviour for moderation purposes rather than monitoring of marking for accountability purposes. It is seen as relatively easy to do in a small school in which departments are not isolated.

Students at both schools appreciate the new approaches. Students at OLC, for example, reported that teachers give more time to those needing help, but that more advanced students are also given time and are made to think. Students interviewed also commented that not getting grades or marks has helped them to work to their own standard, and not to worry about comparing themselves to other people.

CASE STUDY 1: OUR LADY'S COLLEGE

Our Lady's College (OLC) is a non-government Archdiocesan, suburban girls' school with 360 students and 35 staff (of whom 23 are teachers), run by Brisbane Catholic Education. Its mission statement, like many Catholic schools, makes reference to the spirit of the Christian Gospel, love and justice. It also suggests that the college will encourage "skills that students can use to critique their environment and be active members who contribute to their own welfare and that of others".

The students are mainly from middle class families although fees are waived or adjusted to enable students to attend whose families have lower income. Only 1% of the students have identified special educational needs.

For nearly one-third of students, English is a second language, including Vietnamese, Chinese, Italian, Greek and Aboriginal backgrounds. There also is a substantial percentage of Pacific Islanders.

The local area population has an average income for Queensland, with higher education levels, smaller household size although slightly higher unemployment. As a Catholic school, OLC attracts a significant proportion of students from outside the immediate area. The lower secondary curriculum offers most of the Key Learning Areas along with "electives" in the performing arts, languages, home economics and business. The formative assessment approaches are better developed in the social sciences, health and physical education and less developed in mathematics and science.

Teaching and assessment at the school

Strategies which support learning

Students at OLC suggested that active lessons with plenty of variety of activities and in which teachers stick to the point, help them to learn. One student suggested that a good teacher is one that "doesn't put you to sleep" while they all agreed that copying off the board or out of books was least likely to help learning. No copying off the board was observed in lessons in the school and students were observed to be most attentive in the lessons in which activities were varied, tight timescales were given and reiterated and classroom management was tight. Two teachers were observed to use a routine of announcing "3, 2, 1" every time they wanted the whole class's attention back which seemed to be very effective even in very large groups.

Shared objectives

The students said that objectives of the lesson were shared in most lessons, often based on the feedback about what had been given as a homework task.

Strategies that support diversity/individual needs

Students reported that teachers give more time to those that need help but more advanced students are still given time and made to think. A head of department at OLC commented that given the range of abilities in the school, more use needs to be made of fast-tracking and peer tutoring to ensure that diverse needs are met.

Higher order questioning

Heads of department at OLC stated that they used open-ended questioning extensively, particularly to extend students' thinking. One of them commented that when using open-ending questioning with the whole class, she tended to target an initial question at a student with higher ability and then use the student's reply to draw in others from the class.

Observation of the same teacher confirmed her extensive use of questioning. In a year 10 lesson on globalisation, students were working on their individual assignments in the library using books, articles and the Internet to research a company they had chosen, such as Nike or McDonald's. The teacher saw about half the 25 students individually to review their progress. She asked challenging open questions encouraging them to extend and deepen their investigations and gave specific feedback on what they needed to target for improvement.

Comment marking and feedback which identifies future targets

In some subjects at the school, there is a particularly strong emphasis on giving effective feedback through comments which indicate how to improve the work. The senior managers at OLC suggested that in maths and science, work is still graded but in other subjects it is not, although some work seen in English and social studies had been graded, including constructive comments.

In social studies, drafts of assessed work receive comments indicating how to improve and the students are given time in class to undertake the revisions. The head of science suggested that this also occurred in science and that students were more likely to read the comments on these assessed drafts than on other work. One teacher reported that when grades were dropped students asked how they were doing in relation to others. Another social studies teacher mentioned that parents wanted to know their daughters' position in the class and how they were doing.

The year 8 and 9 files from one of the teachers had a sheet giving grades for each semester based on the formal assessments (two per year) building on the previous criteria-based assessment. These included items such as "factual knowledge and understanding", "research skills" and "evaluation".

Students at OLC stated that they liked grades and found them useful as they "show you what you have been doing, make you try for an A" although one student preferred the new levels as "my parents don't know whether I have been listening or not". They reported that they do read the comments and that there are always suggestions as to how the work could be improved. The sampling of marked work confirmed this with comments such as:

Good work M. Your assignment was well researched. You gave a clear explanation of the printing press and illustrated it effectively with OHTs [Overhead Transparencies] You could have given more emphasis to the effects of the introduction of the printing press.

Although occasionally, a student may have been left in some doubt about what needed to be addressed:

C, you could have done so much more with this role play.

Teachers share pieces of work and discuss comments they have made on them as well as the work itself. Heads of department saw this as professional behaviour for moderation purposes rather than monitoring of marking for accountability purposes. Teachers believe that it is relatively easy to do in a small school in which departments are not isolated.

Self- and peer-assessment

Skills in self- and peer-assessment are an important component of becoming a lifelong learner. A member of staff commented that while students at OLC had well developed targets for their future and were generally very academically competent, some started secondary school taking insufficient responsibility for their own actions. Self- and peer-assessment skills should help to address this.

Whether students were encouraged to use self- and peer-assessment appeared to be up to the teacher and, for example, is done more in social studies and health and physical education, where a proforma is sometimes used to structure their feedback, than in other subjects. One teacher emphasised the basis of trust needed for effective peer-assessment. She reported that sometimes she asks a student who has done less well in a piece of work to select another girl the student trusts and then the two students read each other's work, which enables them to see what needs to be improved. One of the lessons observed of her teaching was designed to promote trust.

In a year 9 lesson on health and physical education, 28 students were seated in pairs, in two circles back to back. One student in each pair was given a map and the other a blank piece of paper. The one with the map was asked to give instructions to her partner to enable her to reproduce the map. This well-known trust exercise was used most effectively to draw out issues about types of communication, listening and relating to others. At the end of the lesson the students were asked to complete a proforma on what they had learnt from the task, on how well they had worked with their partner, and what they might have done differently.

Students complete a self-evaluation sheet at the end of each semester. Comments tend to focus on work practices (such as, use of time, completion of homework, note-taking, working with others), rather than subject knowledge, skills or understanding. The sheet includes an item on identifying a target for improvement which is also usually focused on work practices. Written reports to parents are constructed using "electronic statement banks", so the self-evaluation sheet is also used by the teacher as an opportunity to add something more personalised. These self-evaluations then form part of the focus, alongside the formal assessed assignments, of the twice-yearly meetings between student, parent and teacher.

When the answers are given in the textbooks, students at OLC usually check them themselves. Self-evaluation sheets are completed and sent home for parents to sign that they have seen them.

Group work/cooperative learning strategies

Peer-assessment requires students to work together (as sometimes established through cooperative group work). Teachers mentioned a Queensland initiative on cooperative learning. A teacher at OLC said that she had used cooperative learning techniques in a unit of work on human rights. The students were allocated to groups of four (to ensure ability mix) and they had to decide which four human rights out of the ten in the UN declaration, were crucial. In the year 9 library-based lesson observed on this unit, all students worked individually but this may have reflected the fact that it was a library session.

The students recounted that work in the primary school had been more activity-based and that lessons in the secondary school were more text-based. The lessons observed were mixed but there were clear subject differences with health and physical education being activity-based and the social science lessons text-based. The student comments confirmed this suggesting that there was little group work in English or social studies but some in health and physical education and their optional subjects such as Japanese.

Students' aspirations

Students' aspirations seemed fairly high and students were keen to talk about them. The guidance officer confirmed that in her experience students aspirations were high. The four year 9 students interviewed all had ideas about future careers which included cartoonist, advertising, early childhood teaching and working with animals.

Creating conditions

When the outcomes-based initiative was introduced at state level, OLC had not had any discussion about the lower secondary curriculum for some time. One teacher at OLC suggested that there was lots of resentment and scepticism about the initiative because teachers were not fully consulted during the syllabus construction process. The heads of department, who in OLC were responsible for implementation of the syllabuses, considered that insufficient support had been given for implementation. Schools have expected to devise their own methods of implementation. In time, there may be sharing among schools of the most successful implementation strategies.

At State level, the new syllabuses are being developed and introduced in two key learning areas at a time. One head of department at OLC suggested that as the outcomes-based approach gets rolled out to all subjects and students become more familiar with the statements, it may be possible to drop the grades and focus more on the outcomes and the levels associated with them. But for the moment she felt that they were not meaningful to students and were therefore of limited use in providing feedback. Another suggested that some revisions to the outcomes were likely since the responsible officers in her subject areas (history and geography) were currently working in schools and realising that some of the statements needed adjusting. Furthermore, the heads of department noted that outcomes are more easily defined and observed in some subjects than in others and in English where for example, critical analysis is encouraged, the outcomes may be more difficult to judge.

One social studies teacher at OLC felt that the outcomes-based system was not as useful as the previous criteria-based system because the previous system had been working effectively in their department. The head of department made clear that the outcomes-based statements and their associated levels are too broad to show day-to-day student progress, so she had broken them down into components which were similar to the criteria that they had previously used. Furthermore, at OLC the heads of department in the Key Learning Areas that are being implemented have agreed to qualify the levels with an additional judgement about whether the outcome has been demonstrated consistently or at a very high standard.

The heads of department at OLC reported that there had been extensive staff development associated with the outcomes-based initiative but while there were so few practical examples of implementation, teachers are left to implement it in whatever ways they can. The Queensland Studies Authority (QSA) develops syllabuses for schools but has not played a major role in their implementation, including the implementation of assessment processes. The subject associations (especially in History and English) were reported to have made pedagogy and assessment a focus in the last six years, including journal articles and seminars on self-assessment and peer-assessment.

CASE STUDY 2: WOODRIDGE STATE HIGH SCHOOL

Woodridge State High School (WSHS) is a government suburban school with 820 students and around 80 staff (60 of whom are teachers) run by Education Queensland. There is a wide range of administrative and support staff, such as a school-based police officer, and nurse, providing an inter-disciplinary service. The school also has a childcare facility enabling young parents to complete their schooling. The pastoral care system in the school allocates a teacher to each student who provides support and meets each term with the student and parent to discuss progress. The mission of the school is to develop confident, enterprising, lifelong learners through a social outcomes strategy. The strategy involves integrating cognitive, emotional and behavioural areas in order to establish, maintain and develop constructive social relationships.

The area has higher unemployment than average, with lower incomes and lower educational standards but household size is average. Due to the nature of the housing in the area there is high student mobility. The student population is diverse with 46 nationalities and 14% of students whose first language is not English. WSHS is the only school in that district with a unit to support students with English language needs to enable them to transfer into mainstream classes. Support is also provided for the 41 students identified as having special educational needs with a strong emphasis on transition to work programmes.

The school has reformed the pedagogy and curriculum since 1999. An integrated curriculum is provided in year 8 covering modules such as "Ecotourism" and the outcomes and key learning areas specified in the Education Queensland guidance are linked within this module. Students and teachers negotiate the criteria and standards used to assess work. Assessment is a continuous process and there is a strong commitment to co-operative group work.

Teaching and assessment at the school

Year 8 students at WSHS thought that learning occurred most when explanations were given in full, illustrated with examples, when the teacher talks less and there is less writing and when teachers use humour and get along well with each other. This final comment may reflect the relatively unusual experience that these students have of frequent team teaching. They compared the teaching strategies very favourably to those used in other schools attended by their friends and suggested that other schools relied more heavily on worksheets and pupils received less full explanations from teachers. No copying off the board was observed at this school.

The students commented that if they don't understand something they just ask a friend or the teacher and that getting the wrong answer was not embarrassing. They also gave examples of opportunities in which a teacher had encouraged another pupil to give an explanation as an alternative to their own. If they get behind in a subject, have difficulties with a piece of homework or do not understand an area, teachers are available in the library after school to address any difficulties.

At WSHS a head of department described the review of the curriculum that had taken place over the previous few years and noted a much greater emphasis on investigative work built into the integrated studies curriculum. Teaching now involved many more activities and less "chalk and talk". A senior member of staff described the major reforms that had been going on in WSHS for the previous two years as focusing mainly on higher order questioning, multiple intelligences and thinking skills.

Strategies that support diversity/individual needs

At WSHS, the head of student support had been at the school two and a half years. When she started there were 32 students identified as needing learning support and they spent most of their time in a separate unit. Now most of them are supported in mainstream lessons. Approaches based on multiple intelligences have been used to support students with learning difficulties, for example, through a kinaesthetic session in the playground on the concept of negative numbers.

Every week there is an allocated time for year 8 and some year 9 students to reflect on their learning, working with others and experiences and to write comments about it in their learning journals. Teachers are allowed to read them but not allowed to write in them. One student had entered the following comments:

> Yesterday my group and I made different shapes of a certain size out of newspaper. I got frustrated when nobody would listen to me. But we finished a square and two rectangles.
>
> Listen. None of our group members listened to each other. We all had ideas but wouldn't explain them. Then it would all end up in a mess.

Shared objectives

The students described one teacher's practice of sharing the aim of what they are expected to achieve in the lesson. Other teachers were more likely to give out a worksheet with the aims at the top. Teachers were observed to share objectives of lessons with the students. They also held up pieces of work from someone in the class currently or from previous years as models of what good work looks like.

In the student interviews at WSHS, students reported that teachers often used an example of a piece of work such as a poem to draw attention to positive aspects but not to suggest that this is exactly what all students should do.

Higher order questioning

At WSHS, higher order questioning was evident in integrated studies lessons. Teachers were observed deliberately to ask students who were less inclined to contribute. Questioning was used extensively to check understanding and in one lesson, at the end of each activity, the students were invited to assess it on difficulty and student feedback determined whether the teacher moved on to the next activity or gave a further explanation of the previous one. Students and other staff interviewed confirmed that reflections of this type were regularly built into lessons. When students worked in small groups, the teachers rotated around the groups to get further explanations, encouraging experimentation, problem-solving and reasoning.

Not all the teachers observed made regular use of open questions but it was a strategy evident in some lessons, perhaps linked to individual teachers rather than to specific subjects.

Comment marking and feedback which identifies future targets

The students interviewed at WSHS said that teachers give them verbal feedback on written work in class which was why their exercise books appeared not to have any marks or comments in them. One produced a history work booklet which was an assessed assignment with a sheet on the front giving the outcomes-based statements marked as either beginning, working toward or achieved. In addition, the teacher had given a comment indicating what would need to be done to improve the work. The year 8 students said that grades or marks were never given and they felt that this helped them work to their own standard and not worry about comparing themselves to other people. They all claimed to read and act upon the comments and suggested that the teacher was always willing to discuss them.

At WSHS comment marking was very specific and helpful even when commenting on a very successful piece of work:

Wonderful work J! Your answers in this booklet are very creative and well written. Your Jirrbal story in particular was exceptional. Try and label your diagrams in future. Keep up the great work! Well done!

And on less successful attempts:

Good try J! The rules asked for in Q4 are to do with what happens to the North point when the maps are rotated. Have another think about it.

And written comments signed by two teachers on an oral presentation:

Good eye contact with the audience. Avoid playing with your pencil too much, at times it distracted the audience. Your information was very interesting and you focused mainly on the changes that have occurred during the last 100 years. Well done, it was fantastic. Keep up the good effort we are all very proud of you.

Self- and peer-assessment

Teachers at WSHS are trying to ensure that the pupils are aware of, and understand the outcome-based statements and can assess themselves against the standards. In the student interviews at WSHS, they described reflection time as a feature of most lessons, the use of their learning journals in which questions to be addressed included "what do you understand about… ?". They gave examples of marking each others' work and giving each other feedback on written work. One student said he only corrected other people's work and didn't write comments on it indicating how it might be improved but admitted that it might be more helpful if he did so.

At WSHS, there is a report card every term as a basis for a discussion between the student, parent and care manager. The parents interviewed confirmed the value of these discussions which last about 20 minutes each term.

One senior teacher described the emphasis in school on self- and peer-assessment claiming, "You've got to have the kids analysing their own learning and deciding what they have learnt all the way through their schooling if you want them to learn".

Group work/cooperative learning strategies

Teachers commented that far more use was made of cooperative group work than occurred at other schools in Brisbane and that students initially complained that the teachers weren't giving them the answers. The students thought that they worked in small groups in about half of most lessons. Sometimes they worked in mixed-ability groups in which the teachers seated them for the year but they reported that within class grouping arrangements varied which helped them to learn to work in teams. Some of the integrated studies lessons are taught in a combined group of two classes with two teachers and several teaching assistants. These lessons tend to involve extensive group work in which students are sometimes grouped on an ability basis and sometimes self select the groups.

Two-year 8 groups were combined for an integrated studies lesson focusing on negative numbers and the Romans. There were 35 students in total although this group is usually larger, but some students were involved in another activity elsewhere. Two subject teachers were supported by one special needs teacher and two teacher aides. Both teachers appeared to have a secure grasp of both the historical and mathematical subject knowledge. The session was introduced and the lesson objectives shared in the whole group and students then worked in the groups of four in which they were sitting. The group activities had been carefully planned using practical materials that maximised explorations of the concepts and minimised use of whole texts. Feedback from the teacher encouraged further exploration. Feedback between students tended to be at the level of whether an outcome was correct or not rather than indicating how to improve it. Students were encouraged to reflect on how effectively they had worked as a group as well as how well they had completed the task.

When interviewed, the students who had been in this lesson commented that the lesson was typical. They are often asked to reflect on the strategies they used to address the task as well as how well they worked together in their small groups. Another lesson involving group work invited students to assign specific roles of chairperson, note-taker and leader. When feeding back, they were encouraged to assess each person's contribution, the effectiveness of the roles in supporting their learning and how they might have improved it.

In the student interview, the students claimed that working in small groups helped to develop their understanding through testing out their ideas, examples and explanations on others. They suggested that disadvantages of working in groups included having to work with people you don't like, who hold you back or mess about. Overall, they felt that the advantages outweighed the disadvantages and favoured the mixed-ability groups that they usually experienced:

> I reckon it's important to have people working together at different levels, then the people at higher levels can teach the people at lower levels in their own way. In the real world you work with

different people, you don't always choose who you work with and working with other people you don't know helps you.

Students' aspirations

Students mentioned their intentions to become a teacher, two mentioned becoming a lawyer, a prison guard, a dietician, a chef or in one case, any job that earns lots of money.

The three parents interviewed felt that the school encouraged high aspirations. One had a daughter in year 9 who wants to become a social worker, one had a year 9 daughter who suffers from asthma and wants to become a policewoman and the third had a son in year 10 with motivation problems who had done work experience in a butcher and was aiming to get an apprenticeship. Two of the three had older daughters who had been through the school and all were at university. The parents felt that the school equipped them to manage themselves through university. The school's track record for students securing university places together with the quality of staff and extent of community involvement were reasons they had chosen to send their sons and daughters to this school.

Creating conditions

The school encouraged various approaches, including regular monitoring of pupil progress, for improved teacher practice and improved student learning. Teachers were given opportunities to discuss their work in teams. There was little evidence of teachers undertaking staff development in assessment for learning, although Woodridge SHS planned some in-service work for the whole school in the near future. However, statewide curriculum implementation is supported by professional development that includes elements on assessment for learning.

Changes of staff and senior management were a potential threat to long-term sustainability. There was evidence that young, innovative teachers were attracted to coming to work at WSHS, but were then more likely to be offered promotion elsewhere relatively quickly. The school had also experienced changes recently in the senior management team. However, there is evidence that changes to teaching and learning, such as the use of student self-reflection, group work and comment marking, had become sufficiently embedded and could be maintained through some staffing changes.

Scotland: Developing a Coherent System of Assessment
by
Anne Sliwka, University of Mannheim
Ernest Spencer, education consultant and University of Glasgow

OVERVIEW

The Scottish Executive Education Department (SEED) has promoted formative assessment through a number of programmes, policies, and guidelines. These include:

- National Qualifications (age 16+, typically). In the last three years, the National Qualifications have brought some new assessment requirements into schools. Principally, these involve internal summative assessment of three modules of work in each subject, on an "Achieved/Not Achieved" basis. This internal assessment is an essential part of the certification process: students cannot achieve a grade for the whole course through the external examination without passing the internal modules. Teaching and assessment support materials for National Qualifications distributed to schools include advice on formative assessment, as well as on summative assessments and means of standardising them.

- Standard Grade curriculum (age 14-16). Assessment for this programme of work includes internal summative assessment by teachers for aspects of work not susceptible to external examining. Teachers received advice in this programme, too, on formative assessment, called "Assessment as Part of Teaching".

- National Guidelines on Assessment 5–14. The guidelines encourage teachers to think systematically about assessment as an integrated part of the complex process of learning and teaching. A central feature is the promotion of the idea that most classroom assessment should be "assessment as part of teaching". Summative judgments about attainment of the 5–14 levels should be only occasional, and based on a large amount of classwork. In English language and mathematics, when it is clear that a student's classwork shows full command of the level, the teacher selects a National Test (now called National Assessments) from a

- catalogue available from the Scottish Qualifications Authority (SQA). Teachers administer a test when they consider it appropriate: there is no "test day" for all at the same time.

- National advice distributed through "Taking a Closer Look" diagnostic procedures. The materials suggest ways in which teachers can incorporate assessment naturally into day-to-day teaching. These procedures are based on the principle that a teacher can find out much more about processes of learning through discussion with a child than by using a test, no matter how well designed.

- The current Assessment is for Learning Programme (AiFL). The AiFL aims to integrate the existing approaches and policies on assessment into a more streamlined and coherent system. One important element in this plan is the ambitious concept of Personal Learning Planning (PLP). PLP is meant to be a process of interaction between teacher and student which promotes self-awareness as a learner and self-assessment of progress toward agreed individual learning aims, within the broader context of the teaching programme for the whole class or group. It is associated in the AiFL programme developing formative assessment, including "comments only" feedback from teachers and self- and peer-assessment by students. There is an element of recording achievement (in school work and elsewhere) and of next steps in learning, but the reflective and interactive process is the critical aspect of PLP. PLP transfers a crucial amount of responsibility for pursuit of agreed learning aims to the individual learner, with support from teachers and parents.

For a number of years SEED also asked schools to set "targets" for overall attainment. This system sought to ensure that schools use institutional self-evaluation to address issues of student attainment and teaching and learning action to improve it. There are, however, disadvantages of target setting and concentration on test or examination performance in the school self-evaluation, and some, perhaps many, teachers and school managers seem to regard action to develop really effective learning and teaching as separate from, or even inimical to, their need to improve results. One disadvantageous effect of target-setting does appears to have been to encourage schools to focus attention much more on the narrow 5-14 tests in English language and mathematics than on the professional judgement about classwork and the formative assessment approaches recommended in the national guidelines.

Highlights from the case studies

Forres Academy has been using co-operative learning strategies for almost ten years. Co-operative learning is a teaching strategy using highly structured small group learning activities. This work has prepared the ground well for the school's more recent focus on formative assessment in the national Assessment is for Learning programme. Co-operative learning creates room for formative assessment, freeing teachers to spend more time with individual students and groups of students – and emphasises learning on the basis of an individualised assessment of their strengths and needs. Indeed, effective co-operative learning is an essential element of formative assessment.

At John Ogilvie High School, teachers have been actively involved in implementation of the national Assessment is for Learning programme. The programme emphasises the development of students' skills for self-evaluation. Teachers have started to focus more on the development of students' learning to learn skills, and have moved away from knowledge-focused methods of teaching, concerned with covering as much curriculum as possible during the term. Teachers at the school point to impressive evidence showing the progress of individual students over the course of a few months.

Case Study 1: Forres Academy

In Forres Academy two teachers were actively implementing "Assessment is for Learning" strategies in science in the first two years of secondary education, S1/S2 (age 12-14) and in mathematics in S1 (age 12-13) and S5 (age 16-17), as part of the national project. They and other staff had already been developing similar activities in their teaching, having been very heavily involved for almost ten years in implementation of co-operative learning techniques derived from Canadian practice. This innovative teaching approach was started on the initiative of the previous headteacher, who had observed co-operative learning during a visit to Ontario and had convinced the staff of the school to try its implementation in Forres Academy.

Teaching and assessment at the school

Co-operative learning and school development

Forres Academy is actively implementing the national programme, "Assessment is for Learning". The programme is being integrated into the school's pre-existing initiative on co-operative learning.

Co-operative learning is a teaching strategy using highly structured small group learning activities. Based on research developed by Spencer Kagan, Donald Johnson, Roger Johnson, Elizabeth Cohen, Carol Rolheiser and Barrie Bennett et al.,[1] it is based on five key elements that address the shortcomings of traditional group work:

- First, *positive interdependence* connects students in such a way that their individual success depends on a joint effort – group members need each other to complete the group's task.

- Second, interaction patterns are structured so that members have to interact with one another to complete the task (and develop *positive interdependence*).

- Third, each learner in a group is *individually accountable* and group members have to support each other to meet accepted criteria.

- Fourth, *interpersonal and group skills* needed for the work are deliberately modelled and developed by the teacher and collaborative behaviour is assessed.

- Fifth, students are given time and procedures to analyse and assess group functioning and then to modify their group interaction accordingly (*group processing*).

When several teachers in the school developed an interest in co-operative learning strategies they had seen in Canada, the school brought in professional trainers from Canada and encouraged every teacher to take part in a range of training opportunities. The training opportunities linked the new teaching strategy in a fairly formal way to development planning. No teacher was formally obliged to join in the training activities or to try out co-operative learning in the classroom, but the new approach created a lot of enthusiasm about teaching and learning. This "feel-good factor", as the deputy headteacher describes it, created a pull. Teachers who were not involved in the project initially decided to join the training the second or even third time around, so that over a three-year period, a large majority of

---

[1] Slavin, R., *Cooperative Learning*, New York, 1983; Sharan, S., *Handbook of Cooperative Learning Methods*; Johnson, D.W. and Johnson, R.T., *Cooperation and Competition – Theory and Research*, Edina/Minnesota, 1989; Johnson, D.W., Johnson, R.T. and Holubec, E.J., *Circles of Learning: Cooperation in the Classroom*, Edina 1986; Kagan, S., *Cooperative Learning*, San Clemente/Calif. 1997; Cohen, E., *Designing Groupwork: Strategies for the Heterogenous Classroom*; Bennett, B., Rolheiser, C. and Stevahn, L., *Cooperative Learning: Where Heart meets Mind*, Toronto 1991.

the teachers in Forres Academy became involved in implementing the new teaching practice. Most perceived co-operative learning as a promising strategy to involve a greater number of students' actively in learning and to develop their social skills at the same time.

Practitioners and researchers in education have developed a variety of co-operative learning methods. A simple one is the Placemat Activity, in which four students in a group write down ideas individually in separate sections of a large sheet of paper during a first stage, read out loud their individual ideas and then come up with a group proposal which they write in the middle of the sheet. The Jigsaw Technique is more complex. Students research different aspects of a broad topic and then learn about the entire topic by teaching each other about its different components.

The headteacher and the teachers are convinced that formative assessment can be incorporated into a variety of teaching strategies and is part of a much larger set of teacher repertoires. Even if co-operative learning activities do not of themselves guarantee use of formative assessment, they do create opportunities for the teacher to provide individual students and groups of students with feedback and learning support.

Co-operative learning creates room for formative assessment

A deliberate use of co-operative learning strategies frees the teacher to spend more time with and provide scaffolding for individual students and groups of students with different learning needs. Scaffolding contributes to formative assessment because it provides students with advice on how to proceed with their own learning on the basis of an individualised assessment of their strengths and needs.

In an S5 (age 16-17) psychology class on anorexia nervosa, for example, students were given a newspaper article, a case study and a sheet with scientific information on theories explaining abnormal behaviour. The teacher started by asking simple questions aimed at fostering a deeper understanding of the case study and progressed to more abstract questions that linked the anorexia case to several different psychological theories on abnormal behaviour. She gave the students a very clear deadline and task. The class seemed to be quite advanced and familiar with co-operative learning; there was no need to model social skills in terms of how they should work together. The groups worked in a focused and effective manner, with every member contributing.

While the 20 students were working on the assignment in groups of four, the teacher walked around the classroom and checked their understanding of the text and the task: "What do you think of this theory?

Does it make sense to you?". She listened with great attention to each response, encouraged students to think beyond the text and added detailed expert knowledge to enhance students' personal understanding of the subject. The students visibly enjoyed the class. The atmosphere was professional, even academic. The groups respected the teacher as an expert and as somebody who was responding to their interests as she helped them to develop their own expertise. Ten minutes before the end of the period, students presented the results of their group work to each other. They listened attentively, asked questions and further discussed particular issues.

Evaluating their learning experience after the class, students pointed out how much they appreciated and valued the teacher's professionalism. Combining the use of various sources (newspaper articles, theoretical writing and case studies) with very well planned and professional classroom management (including direct instruction, co-operative learning and personalised feedback) motivated the students to work hard for the class. The students considered the way in which the teacher integrated different methods and materials to be exemplary.

Learning through teaching others: the Jigsaw Puzzle

The sixteen students of Forres S2 (age 13-14) science class were seated in rows. At the beginning of the lesson the teacher asked the class to recall the recent Elgin floods. She thus linked global warming to the students' own experience of local floods and told them they would be considering the factors affecting floods, such as global warming and climate change. She explained that they would be doing a "jigsaw puzzle" activity. They would work in four groups to research different aspects of climate change and global warming from material provided and then, in a second phase, would explain to others what they had established. She created four mixed-sex groups, each of which contained students of broadly similar levels of current attainment. She advised them to write down their responses in sentences in order to be sure they understood what they were talking about and to remember that they needed to agree about their answers. The task involved reading three to four paragraphs and agreeing upon and then writing answers to questions. Differently coloured texts were designed for the different reading ability levels represented in the four groups. The groups then worked on the tasks.

When this first part of the jigsaw activity was over, the teacher brought into play a co-operative learning strategy called "Numbered Heads Together". She allocated the numbers 1 to 4 to the students in each group and then re-grouped all 1's, 2's, 3's, 4's together. She assigned specific roles, each with a printed description, to each student in these new groups: reader, checker/encourager, recorder, resource manager. The new groups' task sheet required them to answer a range of questions about global warming, using the specialist expertise each one of the group members brought from their previous group studies. The recorders were told to record the group's findings, the checkers to check the findings and the encouragers to ensure that all members of the group contributed. The "checker" role could, in principle, have involved checking the accuracy of students' answers from the reading they had done. Such sophisticated peer-assessment could be a very significant part of assessment for learning, but to ensure that peer-assessment was indeed formative, teachers would need both to demonstrate skills for formative assessment and to reinforce them regularly.

The Jigsaw method seems to be a very good basis for both independent thinking and co-operative learning. It creates positive interdependence and makes each student accountable for his or her own learning, particularly since each is required to contribute to the new group what they have learnt in the prior group. The Jigsaw method can also be used with varying levels of complexity: with more experienced students, who are used to independent research, the tasks could involve a wider range of printed or electronic material, more time and expectation of a presentation by each member of the group during the second stage (rather than just contributing to answering questions).

Peer scaffolding and teacher feedback

A similar strategy was used for students preparing for the National Qualifications in Higher mathematics. They sat together in groups of four. The use of co-operative learning methods was not as deliberate as in the psychology and the science classes, but had similar effects. While solving mathematical problems, students could exchange ideas and discuss various ways of tackling a particular problem. "We argue in our group about the right way to do things. We use different methods, we compare the way we did it. If someone gets it wrong and the others get it right, then they explain it to that person in the group."

Only if students in the group did not know how to move ahead or if there was great controversy about the solution to a problem did they refer to their teacher. "If you have problems he will point you in the right direction. He will ask you an additional question to show you how you might be able to do it." In other words, the teacher used scaffolding techniques to respond to different learning needs. He sought to expose any conceptual misunderstandings individual students may have, and explained the mathematics taking account of those misunderstandings. Students were then able to develop new insights by exposing prior misconceptions. The teacher strongly emphasised the importance of asking the students to explain their methods of arriving at answers and solutions, even when wrong, and of using each example to explain mathematical concepts.

Feedback needs to be immediate and personalised

Most students noted that individual and immediate feedback was most useful. Feedback given to an individual student in front of an entire class was often experienced as humiliating. Delayed feedback, returned weeks after a test or essay, was of little interest to students because it did not relate to their work at that time.

The most productive kind of feedback from the student perspective was comment while doing a task, rather than later. "When a teacher gives you little hints it triggers something. That is useful."

Students see comments on exercise books as being useful, as long as they are provided soon after they have completed the work. From the student perspective, self-assessment works only if it is accompanied by teacher feedback and peer-assessment. One girl described self-assessment as a chore, and most of the other students interviewed agree with her: "Teachers need to tell me what my strengths are. I find it difficult to do that myself". Most students found self-assessment challenging but did appreciate peer-assessment.

Creating synergy between an academic task and a social skill

All of the students interviewed agreed that group work can be done extremely badly but also very well. That depends on the teacher's skill at moderating group work processes. Good use of co-operative learning in Forres Academy aimed to promote synergy between academic learning and the development of social skills.

In an S2 English class the teacher started her lesson by explaining that students would be working on an academic task and a social task. The class had recently watched "Robin Hood – Prince of Thieves" and that day they would be reflecting on the qualities and characteristics of "a hero". After explaining the academic learning goal to her class, the teacher spent an equal amount of time explaining the social task for the day, namely the use of "quiet voices" in group work. The four students in each group gave themselves a number each. The teacher referred to these numbers in assigning and explaining certain roles the students would take on during co-operative learning to manage their own group process better. Each group thus contained a leader, a noise monitor, a materials manager and a writer.

The teacher spent a good deal of time explaining the different roles and making sure that each student understood his or her responsibilities. She spoke of the importance of "social skills" for working in teams and discussed with the students the meaning of "using a quiet voice" in teamwork. Students brainstormed what the use of a quiet voice in teams "looks like" and "sounds like" and the teacher noted the ideas on the blackboard.

The groups' task was to brainstorm about the different qualities of a hero under four subheadings provided by the teacher. While they worked on the assignment, the teacher walked around the class, questioning, approving and encouraging. She spent more time with those groups who seemed to have greater problems in identifying and categorising the qualities of a hero. She prompted students to think further. When a student said a hero would be "manly", for example, she asked him to define the adjective. When he added "brave and active" as associated with "manly", she suggested that those adjectives could also be added to the description of a hero.

After the presentation of group work the lesson ended with a group activity related to the social skill "use of quiet voices". In each group the student who had acted as noise monitor was asked to grade the group's use of quiet voices on a scale from one (high) to five. At the same time the three other members were to discuss and decide on a grade for their group. Then both grades were compared and discussed. The teacher advised that the group needed to agree on strategies for improving their group work skills.

Creating conditions

Subject departments play a crucial role in disseminating good practice within Forres Academy. Weekly department meetings are partly used for sharing and discussing good practice. Teachers often share ideas across departments during the two in-service staff development days per year. In the past, joint training events on co-operative learning also brought together Forres staff with teachers from the associated primary schools, in a deliberate attempt to align teaching strategies across the entire school life of a student.

Even though enthusiasm for co-operative learning has somewhat lessened over the past years, there is an infrastructure for continuous development in place within the school. It is not the case that teachers have developed scepticism about its effectiveness, but some of the initial excitement has faded. Four teachers acting as internal coaches for co-operative learning are available to work with and provide advice and coaching to colleagues in different departments who want to integrate co-operative learning strategies into their own classroom work. There seems to be a good basis for reawakening some of the enthusiasm for the innovative approaches of co-operative learning and formative assessment.

In recent years, Moray Council has encouraged schools to develop according to their own needs and has consequently devolved quite a large amount of its budget to the schools themselves. A part of those funds was used to free the four coaches in Forres Academy from part of their teaching obligations to allow them to provide material and coaching support for other teachers in Forres and in neighbouring schools who request advice about co-operative learning methods. Sometimes the authority runs workshops where staff members from the same departments of different schools share good practice. This teacher network is seen as very useful for developing teachers' practice. In past years, Moray Council has invited the co-operative learning trainers from Canada to provide training for teachers from the various schools in the region.

CASE STUDY 2: JOHN OGILVIE HIGH SCHOOL

In John Ogilvie High School a team of social subjects teachers (History, Modern Studies and Geography) are the prime movers in the "Assessment is for Learning" developments, principally with classes in the first two years, S1/S2, (age 12-14). One of the deputy headteachers, the school's assessment co-ordinator, took up the government initiative and asked the social subjects departments to become involved in the programme, because he was aware of the interest in formative assessment of the most senior history teacher, who had been using a range of innovative teaching and assessment strategies in his classroom before the Assessment is for Learning Programme (AiFL) started. The headteacher encouraged joint development work and sharing of good practice by asking other teachers in social subjects, mathematics and English to co-operate in further developing formative assessment practice in the school under the leadership of the senior history teacher.

Teaching and assessment at the school

Toward the consistent use of formative assessment

The school has tried to make assessment practices as coherent as possible in social subjects, English and mathematics for this particular group of S1/S2 students. Staff teamwork has been a crucial factor in the successful implementation of formative assessment strategies in the project. The senior history teacher had already, before the introduction of the AiFL programme, been experimenting with new ways of assessing oral presentations using detailed evaluative comments, rather than marks. At an early stage in the project they agreed on a need for close co-operation through regular meetings to carry the initiative forward. The material they had access to initially, most of which came from England, was not entirely suited to the Scottish 5–14 requirements, and was not seen as sufficiently user-friendly.

The teachers worked together to produce more appropriate material to meet agreed goals for teaching and formative assessment. They spent considerable time discussing, selecting, simplifying and adapting different subject criteria statements suitable for the S1 presentation project and the written essays.

The fact that the initiative is primarily teacher-driven and focuses on improved learning appealed to the group of teachers in John Ogilvie High School. They attended a national conference in Edinburgh and received background information and videotapes on formative assessment practice in English schools that had been involved in the research by Dylan Wiliam and Paul Black (reported in *Inside the Black Box*).

Self- and peer-evaluation on essay writing and group presentations

The S1 history teachers decided to focus the innovation on specific aspects of the S1 syllabus, namely on oral group presentation and, later, extended essay writing. The group presentations were based on short team research assignments and were evaluated by all the other members of the class. Student teams were to research controversial historical questions like "Did the Romans create a civilised society in Britain?" or "William Wallace deserved to be executed? How far do you agree?". Students were asked to prepare and present a balanced presentation containing:

- An introduction and sufficient background information.
- Evidence to support the case for the argument.
- Evidence to support the case against the argument.
- A conclusion.

Each group member was required to find relevant information and to take part in the group presentation.

Over the course of the history programme each student was also asked to write three extended essays based on historical sources provided by the teacher and located through additional team research. Students were asked to develop a well-balanced argument based on evidence. Students had access to written criteria on which their work would be judged, as had been the case with the oral presentations.

Initially, the teachers had required teams of students to present a case related to a given historical theme in direct competition to a contrary presentation from a rival team. This competitive approach to presenting the historical evidence was later abandoned in favour of a more balanced one, where a team of students needed to present the entire case, introduction, evidence in favour of, evidence against, and conclusion.

Consistency and transparency in the use of criteria for high quality work

Working as a team, teachers deliberately aligned the criteria for extended essay writing in the social subjects with the criteria used in structuring oral group presentations. (There was also a parallel application of similar criteria in English essays.) "The group work should instil and reinforce the qualities looked for in extended writing."

Teachers determined that it was crucial that all students in the class be very familiar with the criteria for effective presentation. In order to do this, the teachers provided written statements (sometimes in the form of sticky labels for attaching to a response sheet) representing different levels of success for each important aspect of a presentation. There were three levels of possible success for each of the key aspects of a good presentation: a very successful argument, with full evidential support; a capable, but not complete argument, with some appropriate evidential support; and, an argument which needed boosting in various ways. The students had been introduced to these evaluative descriptors early in the subject programme. Before the research teams set about their tasks, the students in the class observed for the case study spent a good deal of time discussing what a good quality group presentation would look like, in terms of both content and style. As each research group presented its argument and evidence, the other students made individual judgements of the quality of the presentation in relation to the criteria and then took part in group discussion to reach a consensus about which criteria had been met.

As each research team in the class observed completed its presentation, the teacher opened class discussion, asking the class first to consider the strong and weak points of the presentations, and emphasised the need to provide evidence for their evaluation. This strategy was a means of keeping open the possibility that some students could come up with insightful critique of their colleagues' work without the help of the relatively pre-determined criteria statements (which the teacher nevertheless considered important as support for students who were not yet used to making constructive evaluative comments on one another's work). The teacher also took care to restate what each student said in this class discussion, to ensure that everyone heard the point that was made. He encouraged the class to agree or to take issue with individual students' initial statements at this stage. Only after this open-ended discussion did he invite the students, first individually, then in groups, to apply the criteria statements to the presentation they had heard. The teacher charted group views of the presentation, noting their input on a chart on the blackboard, and creating a summary.

The entire class session was videotaped and tapes were used later by the teacher team to observe and discuss classroom management and student progress stimulated by the new way of teaching and learning. The tapes were also used for formative assessment: When watching the videotape students got a chance to view themselves in action and discuss their own strengths and developmental needs with other students in the class.

To ensure coherence, teachers and classmates used the same evaluative statements to give students feedback on their work. The same basic structure and criteria statements also underpinned the three extended essays students were required to write. This allowed teachers to compare the essays and assess whether students were making progress over time. Teachers wrote fairly detailed comments on particular skills or objectives for greater attention. Students were then required to respond by writing down their own learning strategies for the future, taking into account the teacher's observation.

Another significant aspect of the social subjects work in John Ogilvie High School was the flexible use of learning and teaching time. As a key part of the programme, students spent time in the library doing the necessary research for presentations, while the rest of the class continued other classwork. This strategy was justified by the staff on the grounds that the process of learning was as valuable as the content to be covered. Students spent approximately equal time in classroom work and research/presentation activities, allowing for both direct teaching of subject content and skills and practical application of the latter in pursuit of a deeper understanding of the ideas and evidence.

More time for discussion and support in a divided class

An S1 (age 12-13) mathematics class at John Ogilvie High School worked on areas in geometry. The class was divided in half. About 14 students stayed in the classroom to work with the teacher, the other half went to the computer room to work with an individualised programme called Successmaker. The teacher divides the class frequently so that she can get students to discuss a mathematical problem in a comparatively small group and can spend more time with those students who need extra support and prompting. While dividing the class she always pays attention to creating mixed ability groups and to separating students who misbehave when together.

Thinking time instead of hands-up

The previous lesson had focussed on how to calculate the area of a rectangle. In revising, the teacher introduced the new topic: calculating the area of a triangle. She gave the class a task to think about: "How can one derive the area of a triangle from the area of a rectangle?". She then explained again that in this class students do not put their hands up, and that there will be sufficient "thinking time" for each student before the answer is discussed in the class. She made it very clear that the idea was that every student would get a chance to respond to the question. When the thinking time of about two minutes was over she asked a few students for an answer. On the basis of their answers she got the class to discuss how the area of a triangle might be derived from the area of a rectangle. On the board she gave a few examples to demonstrate how to do it, using the base and the height of the rectangle. Again, the students were given time to think for themselves, after which the class identified the formula for calculating areas of triangles: $A = 1/2 \times b \times h$.

Following the discussion, students worked in their exercise books to apply the formula just derived to a number of different examples. The teacher walked around the class and supported those who needed extra help. By asking questions and prompting she helped them to find solutions to the problem on their own. After about 15 minutes, the other half of the class returned from the computer room and the group that had been working in the classroom went to the computer room. The teacher then repeated the lesson for the other half of the class.

A range of activities in English

A mixed ability first year class in the English department worked with a variety of formative assessment strategies for the three terms. The teacher had developed an expectation that students would be given "wait time", that is, before the students were asked to respond to questions, individual students were given time to answer fully and without interruption. The students responded positively to this, as well as to the more open-ended questions that the teacher posed. All students participated, answering and listening to each other's answers carefully.

The students also experienced far more peer-assessment than previously, specifically in the areas of talk and imaginative writing. They were taped giving solo talks so that they and the class could then review their performance using agreed, shared criteria. They did similar exercises with imaginative writing, reviewing and editing each other's work. They also worked more together in groups. The students seemed to improve their listening and co-operation skills in the class over the year. They were very enthusiastic about the various assignments and learnt to work well together.

Creating conditions

Among those teachers involved in "Assessment is for Learning" programme at John Ogilvie, an emphasis on student learning, the development of student skills and the capacity to self-evaluate on the basis of transparent criteria have clearly replaced a previous orientation toward covering as much of the curriculum as possible. The teachers still express some doubts as to whether they actually manage to combine broad curriculum coverage while spending the time needed to develop students' learning strategies really well.

There is, nevertheless, a growing confidence among this group of innovative teachers that their work really improves the learning and self-monitoring skills of the students and is thus much more sustainable than traditionally knowledge-focused methods of teaching. Metacognitive skills, developed through the consistent application of criteria in commenting on students' work and having students evaluate their own work and that of their peers and set learning aims for themselves are more likely than the mere transmission of knowledge to make them confident, self-directed learners. The school does not yet have quantitative evidence of, for example, improved examination performance, but the teachers do point to impressive classwork showing the progress of individual students. Comparison of essays written at the beginning of the project with those written after several months of regular formative assessment shows notable improvements both for students who began on a comparatively low level, and for those whose skills were stronger at the start.

Observing and noting the progress and the individual students' motivation for learning gives the teachers the confidence to carry on and expand their work, despite the pressures to cover a broad curriculum. Working as a close-knit team provides the teachers with opportunities to share experiences and learn from each other. Teamwork also bolsters courage to deal with the problems and possible failures that come with any innovation, and makes it possible – and satisfying – to share and celebrate successes.

The innovative teachers felt that improved learning strategies would probably enable students to learn curriculum content more quickly. Their practice clearly shows that deliberate experimentation and continuous adjustment and modification, based on an analysis of what worked and what was problematic, are important components of professional development. Several characteristics of good teaching need to combine consistently to overcome the alleged contradiction between curriculum coverage and student-centred learning and assessment. These include clear instruction and modelling of skills and processes; students' independent and co-operative learning; well designed, appropriately challenging tasks, with helpful "scaffolding" for students; sharing of learning aims and criteria of success with students; and positive, constructive feedback on their work.

The innovative practice among the small group of teachers was, initially, quite isolated in the school. Due to its design, the school's large staff room is not used on a daily basis and most of the interaction takes place within small subject department rooms. Teachers not involved in the Assessment Project at this stage knew little about it. Some argued that they already used a number of formative assessment strategies. When the nature of the work done in social subjects was described to them, they expressed concern that such an intensive and careful use of formative assessment to facilitate the growth of individual students might impede the ability of staff to cover the required syllabus at a reasonable pace.

During the past 12 months, however, the school, through access to the in-service staff development menu provided by South Lanarkshire Council Education Authority, has taken major steps to promote formative assessment across departments, as well as to develop it further in social subjects, English and mathematics. Twenty five new members of staff in 11 departments have attended Council staff development events on formative assessment in October, 2003, February 2004 and March, 2004. Staff involved in the Pilot have also planned and led discussion groups during a staff development day in the school, giving "witness" to their work. In addition, the pilot group was invited to give a major presentation to the staff of a neighbouring secondary school. Within the school and the "cluster" of its associated primary schools, teachers who have been involved in the formative assessment project in the past year have already contributed to staff development discussions and there are plans for another similar event.

Working on the premise that real, sustained change and improvement in the quality of learning can only happen when the teacher is convinced of the value, effectiveness and credibility of the methodology, the aim is to encourage colleagues to use formative assessment strategies through exposure to good practice, support and a professional willingness to change. In addition, all subject departments have identified formative assessment within their Development Plan targets for the current session 2004-2005.

Part III
The Literature Reviews

Changing Teaching through Formative Assessment: Research and Practice
The King's-Medway-Oxfordshire Formative Assessment Project
by
Paul Black and Dylan Wiliam, King's College, London[*]

INTRODUCTION

This paper is the story of a development which started with a review of what research had to say about formative assessment. The work of this review is first described. Its results led to development work with teachers to explore how ideas taken from the research could be turned into practice. A description of this work in a second section is followed by reflections on outcomes and implications in a third section. Broader reflections on how this experience throws light on the task of turning research results into practice are set out in a fourth section.

THE RESEARCH REVIEW

The story starts with our long-standing interest in formative assessment, which led us to decide that it was essential to review the literature in order to look for evidence that improving formative assessment raises standards. It also seemed necessary to look both for evidence about whether or not present practice left room for improvement, and for guidance about how to improve formative assessment.

Our survey of the research literature involved checking through many books, through the issues of over 160 journals for a period of nine years, and studying earlier reviews of research (Crooks, 1988; Natriello, 1987). This process yielded about 580 articles or chapters to study. Out of this we have

---

[*] We would like to acknowledge the initiative of the Assessment Policy Task Group of the British Educational Research Association (now known as the Assessment Reform Group) who gave the initial impetus and support for our research review. We are grateful to the Nuffield Foundation who funded the original review, and the first phase of our project. We are also grateful to Professor Myron Atkin and his colleagues in Standford University, who secured funding from the US National Science Foundation (NSF) for the last phase. Finally, we are indebted to the Medway and Oxfordshire local education authorities, their six schools and above all to their 36 teachers who took on the central and risky task of turning our ideas into practical working knowledge.

prepared a lengthy review, which used material from 250 of these sources. The review was published (Black and Wiliam, 1998a) together with comments on our work by experts from five different countries.

A *first* section of the review surveyed the evidence. An example was a study published in 1986, which concentrated – but not exclusively – on classroom assessment work for children with mild handicaps, and surveyed a large number of formative innovations from which 23 were selected (Fuchs and Fuchs, 1986). All in this group showed quantitative evidence of learning gains by comparing data for an experimental group with similar data from a control group. Since then, many more papers have been published describing similarly rigorous quantitative experiments. Our own review reported about 20 more such studies all of which showed that innovations which include strengthening the practice of formative assessment produced significant, and often substantial, learning gains. These studies ranged over ages (from 5-year olds to university undergraduates), across several school subjects, and over several countries.

The fact that such gains had been achieved by a variety of methods which had, as a common feature, enhanced formative assessment indicated that it is this feature which accounted, at least in part, for the successes. However, it did not follow that it would be an easy matter to achieve such gains on a wide scale in normal classrooms.

A *second* section covered research into current practices of teachers. The picture that emerged was depressing. In relation to effective learning it seemed that teachers' questions and tests encouraged rote and superficial learning, even where teachers said that they wanted to develop understanding. There was also evidence of the negative impact of a focus on comparing students with one another, so emphasising competition rather than personal improvement. Furthermore, teachers' feedback to students often seemed to serve social and managerial functions, often at the expense of the learning functions. Overall it seemed that formative assessment was weak in practice and that its implementation calls for rather deep changes both in teachers' perceptions of their own role in relation to their students and in their classroom practice.

A *third* section focused on research into the involvement of students in formative assessment. Students' beliefs about the goals of learning, about the risks involved in responding in various ways, and about what learning work should be like, were all shown to affect their motivation to take action, their selection of a line of action and the nature of their commitment to it. Other research explored the different ways in which positive action could be taken, covering such topics as study methods, study skills, and peer- and self-assessment.

A *fourth* section looked at ideas that could be gleaned from the research about strategies that might be productive for teachers. One feature that emerged was the potential of the learning task, as designed by a teacher, for exploring students' learning. Another was the importance of the classroom discourse, as steered by teachers' questions and by their handling of students' responses.

A *fifth* section shifted attention to research into comprehensive systems of teaching and learning in which formative assessment played a part. One example was mastery learning programmes. In these it was notable that students were given feedback on their current achievement against some expected level of achievement (ie the 'mastery' level), that such feedback was given rapidly; and that students were given the opportunity to discuss with their peers how to remedy any weaknesses.

A *sixth* section explored in more detail the literature on feedback. A notable example was the extensive review of empirical evidence by Kluger and DeNisi (1996) which showed that feedback can have positive effects only if the feedback is formulated and used as a guide to improvement. Of equal importance was the conceptual analysis which defined feedback as "… information about the gap between the actual level and the reference level of a system parameter which is used to alter the gap in some way" (Ramaprasad, 1983) and the development of this by Sadler (1989) to emphasise that learners must understand both the "reference level" – *i.e.* the goal of their learning – and the actual level of their understanding.

Equally important was the clear message from the research on attribution theory (for example by Vispoel and Austin, 1995) that teachers must aim to inculcate in their students the idea that success is due to internal, unstable, specific factors such as effort, rather than on stable general factors such as ability (internal) or whether one is positively regarded by the teacher (external).

Overall, the features which seem to characterise many of the studies were:

- Formative work involves new ways to enhance feedback between those taught and the teacher, ways which require new modes of pedagogy and significant changes in classroom practice.

- Underlying the various approaches are assumptions about what makes for effective learning – in particular that students have to be actively involved.

- For assessment to function formatively, the results have to be used to adjust teaching and learning – so a significant aspect of any programme will be the ways in which teachers do this.

- The ways in which assessment can affect the motivation and self-esteem of students, and the benefits of engaging students in self-assessment, both deserve careful attention.

Interpreting the research

Synthesising research cannot be an objective process – it will inevitably remain subjective. The structure of the six sections outlined above did not emerge automatically: it was our chosen way to reconceptualise, to organise, and to focus the relevant literature field. Our definition of "relevance" expanded as we went along, so we had to find ways of organising a widening field of research, and to make new conceptual links in order to be able to combine the various findings into as coherent a picture as possible. This was one reason why our review generated a momentum for work in this field: it provided a new framework that would be difficult to create in any other way. Reviewing research is not merely a derivative form of scholarship.

Publicity

Although we tried to adhere closely to the traditional standards of scholarship in the social sciences when conducting and writing our review, we did not do so when exploring the policy implications in a booklet, entitled *Inside the Black Box* (Black and Wiliam, 1998b) that we published, and publicised widely, alongside the academic review. This raised a great deal of interest and created some momentum for our project and for subsequent dissemination. While the standards of evidence we adopted in conducting the review might be characterised as those of "academic rationality", the standard for *Inside the Black Box* was much closer to that of "reasonableness" advocated by Stephen Toulmin for social enquiry (Toulmin, 2001). In some respects, *Inside the Black Box* represented our opinions and prejudices as much as anything else, although we would like to think that these are supported by evidence, and are consistent with the 50 years of experience in this field that we had between us. It is also important to note that the success of *Inside the Black Box* has been as much due to its rhetorical force as to its basis in evidence. This would make many academics uneasy – for it appears to blur the line between fact and value, but as Flyvbjerg (2001) argues, social enquiry has failed precisely because it has focused on analytic rationality rather than value-rationality (see also Wiliam, 2003).

MOVING INTO ACTION

Setting up a project

The second stage of our story followed the first almost inevitably: given that our review had shown that innovations in formative assessment could raise standards of student achievement, it was natural to think about ways to help schools secure these benefits. Our own experience of teachers' professional development had taught us that the implementation of new practices in classrooms could not be a straightforward matter of setting out a recipe for teachers to follow. For one reason, given the varied nature of the innovations and the different contexts in which they had been tried, we could not assume that they could simply be "copied" to other contexts. A second reason was that, from reading the reports of the researchers, one could not describe their work at the level of detail that would be needed to formulate advice on how to replicate them. A third reason, which would have been decisive even in the absence of the first two, was our approach to the task of turning research into practice. We believed that new ideas about teaching and learning can only be made to work in particular contexts, in our case that of teachers in (initially) UK secondary schools, if teachers are able to transform them and so create new practical knowledge relevant to their task.

So we obtained funding (from the UK's Nuffield Foundation) for a two-year development project. Six schools who taught students in the age range 11 to 18 years agreed to collaborate with us: each selected two science and two mathematics teachers willing to take on the risks and extra work involved. In second year of the project we added two teachers of English, from each of same schools, and one additional mathematics and science teacher, so that in all 48 teachers were involved. They were supported by staff from their local (district) education authorities and the project was called the King's-Medway-Oxfordshire Formative Assessment Project (KMOFAP) to highlight our close collaboration with all the other partners (Black and Wiliam, 2003).

The teachers and the researchers met in a whole day meeting every five weeks, over two years. In addition, two researchers were able to visit the schools, observe the teachers in their classrooms, give them feedback, collect interview data on their perceptions, and elicit ideas about issues for discussion in the whole day meetings. The detailed reports of our findings (Black *et al.*, 2002, 2003) are based both on records of these meetings, on the observations and records of visits to classrooms by the King's team, on interviews with and writing by the teachers themselves, and on a few discussions with student groups.

Following this project, members of the King's team have responded to numerous invitations to talk to other groups: over three years they have made over 200 such contributions. These have ranged across all subjects, and across both primary and secondary phases. In addition, there has been sustained work with four groups of primary schools. The King's team has also been involved as advisers to large scale development ventures, in several local government districts in the United Kingdom, with education ministries in Scotland and in Jersey, and in a recent exploration of classroom outcomes for a government programme which aims to improve teaching and learning practices in schools.

The quantitative evidence that formative assessment does raise standards of achievement was a powerful motivator for the teachers at the start of the project. One aspect of the KMOFAP project was that the King's team worked with each teacher to collect data on the gains in test performance of the students involved in the innovation, and comparable data for similar classes who were not involved (Wiliam *et al.* 2004). The project did not introduce any tests of its own – the achievement data used were from the tests that the schools used for all students, whether or not they were involved in the project. The analysis of these data showed an overall and significant, gain in achievement outcomes. Thus the evidence from the research review can now be supplemented by evidence of enhanced performance on the UK national and on schools' own examinations.

The practices developed

These practices will be described here under four headings: oral feedback in *classroom dialogue*, feedback *through marking*, *peer- and self-assessment*, and the *formative use of summative tests*. The account given will be brief – more detailed accounts have been published elsewhere (Black *et al.*, 2003).

For *classroom dialogue* the aim was to improve the interactive feedback which is central to formative assessment. An account of wait time research (Rowe, 1974) motivated teachers to allow longer time after asking a question so that students would have time to think out responses, and so that all could be expected to become actively involved in question and answer discussions, and to make longer replies. One particular way to increase participation was to ask students to brainstorm ideas, perhaps in pairs, for two to three minutes prior to the teacher asking for contributions. Then all answers, right or wrong, had to be taken seriously, the aim being to develop thoughtful improvement rather to evoke the expected answers. A consequence of such changes was that teachers learnt more about the pre-knowledge of their students, and about any gaps and mis-conceptions in that knowledge, so that their next moves could address the learners' real needs.

As they tried to develop this approach, teachers realised that more effort had to be spent in framing questions that were worth asking, *i.e.* questions which explored issues that are critical to the development of students' understanding. They also had to focus closely on follow-up activities to formulate meaningful responses and challenges that would help students to extend their understanding.

The task of developing an interactive style of classroom dialogue required a radical change in teaching style from many teachers, one that they found challenging, not least because it felt at first as if they were losing control. Some were well over a year into the project before such change was achieved. Subsequent work with other schools has shown that it is this aspect of formative work that teachers are least likely to implement successfully.

To address *feedback through marking*, teachers were first given an account of research studies which have established that, whilst students' learning can be advanced by feedback through comments, the giving of marks or grades has a negative effect because students ignore comments when marks are also given (Butler, 1988). These results surprised and worried the teachers, because of concern about the effect of returning students' work with comments but no marks. However, potential conflicts with school policy were resolved as experience showed that the provision of comments gave both students and their parents advice on how to improve. It also set up a new focus on the learning issues rather than on trying to interpret a mark or grade. To make the most of the learning opportunity created by feedback on written work, procedures that required students to follow up comments had to be planned as part of the overall learning process.

One consequence of this change was that teachers had to think more carefully in framing comments on written work, for it was now evident that these had to identify what had been done well and what still needed improvement, and to give guidance on how to make that improvement. As the skills of formulating and using such feedback were developed, it became more clear that the quality of the tasks set for written homework or classwork was critical: such tasks, alongside oral questioning, had to be designed to encourage students to develop and express their understanding of the key features of what they had learnt.

For *peer- and self-assessment*, the starting point was Sadler's (1989) argument that self-assessment is essential to learning because students can only achieve a learning goal if they understand that goal and can assess what they need to do to reach it. Thus the criteria for evaluating any learning achievements must be made transparent to students to enable them to have a clear overview both of the aims of their work and of what it means to complete it successfully. Insofar as they do so they begin to develop an overview of that work so that they can manage and control it: in other words, they develop their capacity for meta-cognitive thinking. A notable example of the success of such work is the research of White and Frederiksen (1998).

For the development of self-assessment skills, the first and most difficult task is to get students to think of their work in terms of a set of goals. In practice, peer-assessment turned out to be an important stimulus to self-assessment. Peer-assessment is uniquely valuable because students may accept, from one another, criticisms of their work which they would not take seriously if made by their teacher. Peer work is also valuable because the interchange will be in language that students themselves would naturally use, and because students learn by taking the roles of teachers and examiners of others (Sadler, 1998). In particular, students appear to find it easier to make sense of criteria for their work in the context of other students' work than when looking at their own.

However, for such peer-group work to succeed, many students needed guidance about how to behave in groups, *e.g.* in listening to one another, taking turns, and offering affirmation together with constructive criticism about one another's work. A typical exercise would be on the marking of homework. Students were asked to label their work with "traffic lights", *i.e.* using red or amber if they were totally or partially unsure of their success, and green where they were confident. Then those who had used amber or green would work in mixed groups to appraise and help with one another's work, whilst the teacher would pay special attention to those who had chosen red.

Teachers developed three ways of making *formative use of summative tests*. One way was to ask students, in preparation for a test, to "traffic light" a list of key words or of the topics on which the test would be set, an exercise which would stimulate them to reflect on where they felt their learning was secure and where they needed to concentrate their efforts. One reason for doing this was that teachers had realised that many students had no strategy for preparing for a test by formulating a strategic appraisal of their learning.

A second way was to mark one another's test papers in peer groups, in the way outlined above for the marking of homework. This could be particularly challenging when they were expected to invent their own marking rubric, for to do this they had to think about the purpose of a question and about the criteria of quality to apply to responses. After peer marking, teachers could reserve their time for discussion of the questions that give particular difficulty.

A further idea was introduced from research studies (Foos *et al.*, 1994; King, 1992) which have shown that students trained to prepare for examinations by generating and then answering their own questions out-performed comparable groups who prepared in conventional ways. Preparation of test questions calls for, and so develops, an overview of the topic.

The teachers' work on summative assessments challenged our expectations that, for the context in which they worked, formative and summative assessments are so different in their purpose that they have to be kept apart. The finding that emerged was quite different – that summative tests should be, and should be seen to be, a positive part of the learning process. If they could be actively involved in the test process, students might see that they can be beneficiaries rather than victims of testing, because tests can help them improve their learning. However, this synergy could not be achieved in the case of high-stakes test set and marked externally.

REFLECTIONS ON THE OUTCOME

It was clear that the new ideas that had emerged between the teachers and ourselves involved far more than the mere addition of a few tactical tricks. Some reflection was needed to tease out more fundamental issues that seemed to be raised.

A focus on learning

One of the most surprising things that happened during the early project meetings was that the participating teachers asked us to run a session on learning theories. In retrospect, perhaps, we should not have been so surprised. We had, after all, stressed that feedback functioned formatively only if the information fed back to the learner was used by the learner in improving performance. But whilst one can work out after the event whether or not any feedback has had the desired effect, what the teachers needed was to be able to give their students feedback that they knew in advance was going to be useful. To do that they needed to build up models of how students learn.

So the teachers came to take greater care in selecting tasks, questions, and other prompts, to ensure that the responses made by students actually "put on the table" the ideas which they bring to a learning task. The key to effective learning is to then find ways to help students restructure their knowledge to build in new and more powerful ideas. In the KMOFAP classrooms, as the teachers came to listen more attentively to the students' responses, they began to appreciate more fully that learning is not a process of passive reception of knowledge, but one in which the learners must be active in creating their own understandings.

These ideas reflect some of the main principles of the constructivist view of learning – to start where the students are and to involve the students actively in the process. It became clear to the teachers that, no matter what the pressure to achieve good test and examination scores, learning cannot be done for the student; it has to be done by the student.

Students came to understand what counted as good work through a focus on the criteria and on their exemplification. Sometimes this was done through focused whole-class discussion around a particular example; at others it was achieved through students using criteria to assess the work of their peers. The activities, by encouraging students to review their work in the light of the goals and criteria, were helping them to develop meta-cognitive approaches to learning.

Finally, the involvement of students both in whole-class dialogue and in peer-group discussions, all within a change in the classroom culture to which all four activities contributed, were creating more a more rich community of learners where the social learning of students would become more salient and effective.

A learning environment and changes of role

There are also deeper issues here. A learning environment has to be "engineered" to involve students more actively in the tasks. The emphasis has to be on the students doing the thinking and making that thinking public. As one teacher said:

> There was a definite transition at some point, from focusing on what I was putting into the process, to what the students were contributing. It became obvious that one way to make a significant sustainable change was to get the students doing more of the thinking. I then began to search for ways to make the learning process more transparent to the students. Indeed, I now spend my time looking for ways to get students to take responsibility for their learning and at the same time making the learning more collaborative.
>
> Tom, Riverside School

This teacher had changed his role, from presenter of content to leader of an exploration and development of ideas in which all students were involved. One of the striking features of the project was the way in which, in the early stages, many spoke about the new approach as "scary", because they felt that they were losing control of their classes. Toward the end of the project, they described this same process not as a loss of control, but one of sharing responsibility for the class's learning with the class – exactly the same process, but viewed from two very different perspectives.

The learning environment envisaged requires a classroom culture that may well be unfamiliar and disconcerting for both teachers and students. The effect of the innovations implemented by our teachers was to change the rules, usually implicit, that govern the behaviours that are expected and seen as legitimate by teachers and by students. As Perrenoud (1991) put it:

> Every teacher who wants to practice formative assessment must reconstruct the teaching contract so as to counteract the habits acquired by his pupils.

For the students, they have to change from behaving as passive recipients of the knowledge offered to becoming active learners who could take responsibility for their own learning. These students became more aware of when they were learning, and when they were not. One class, who were subsequently taught by a teacher not emphasising assessment for learning, surprised that teacher by complaining: "Look, we've told you we don't understand this. Why are you going on to the next topic?".

What has been happening here is that everybody's role expectations, *i.e.* what teachers and students think that being a teacher or being a student requires you to do, have been altered. Whilst it can seem daunting to undertake such changes, they do not have to happen suddenly. Changes with the KMOFAP teachers came slowly and steadily, as experience developed and confidence grew in the use of the various strategies for enriching feedback and interaction.

Further research

In our 1998 review, we listed a number of issues for study by further research. The first issue was the extent to which the context of any study is artificial so that generalisability of the results cannot be guaranteed. This reservation was one of the reasons why we developed the KMOFAP work and now it can be applied to the generalisability of the findings of that study. Our experience of seeing other schools base their own innovations on the KMOFAP results is that a sustained commitment over at least two years is needed, that evaluation and feedback have to be built into any plan, and that any teachers involved need strong support, both from colleagues and from their school leadership.

A second research interest arose from a surprising feature – that the research we studied seemed to pay no attention to issues relating to race, class and gender; these issues still await exploration. A third area for further enquiry is that of beliefs and assumptions about learning theory. Both the assumptions about learning underlying the curriculum and pedagogy, the beliefs of teachers about learning, about their roles as assessors and about the "abilities" and prospects of their students, will affect their interpretations of their students' learning work, and will thereby determine the quality of their formative assessment. A parallel enquiry is needed into the perceptions and beliefs held by students about themselves as learners, and into their experience of the changes that follow from innovations in formative assessment.

A fourth area is the effect on practice of the content knowledge, and the pedagogical content knowledge, that teachers deploy in their school subjects. Issues for enquiry would be the way in which these resources underlie each teacher's composition and presentation of the learning work, and the interpretative frameworks that he or she uses in responding to the evidence provided by feedback from students.

The social setting of a classroom, the community it forms, and the quality of the interactions within that community, all have strong effects in such innovations as better classroom dialogue and peer- and self-assessment. Matters to be studied here would the nature of the social setting in the classroom, as influenced both by the divisions of responsibility between learners and teachers in formative assessment, and by the constraints of the wider school system.

Two further issues now seem important. One is the tensions and possible synergies between teachers' own assessments and the assessment results and methods required by society. The other is the need to co-ordinate all of the above issues in a comprehensive theoretical framework linking assessment in classrooms to issues of pedagogy and curriculum – a task which remains to be tackled.

RESEARCH AND PRACTICE

Why did it work?

At one level, our story was now complete. A basis in research had led to a successful innovation and the publication of its outcomes proved as popular as the original report of the research (Black *et al.*, 2002, 2003). However, we were surprised that it had been so successful in promoting quite radical changes in teachers' practice, and wondered whether lessons could be learnt from it about the notoriously difficult problem of turning research into practice.

One factor that appears to have been important is the credibility that we brought as researchers to the process. In their project diaries, several of the teachers commented that it was our espousal of these ideas, as much as the ideas themselves, that persuaded them to engage with the project: where educational research is concerned, the facts do not necessarily speak for themselves. Part of that credibility is that we chose to work with teachers in the three subjects, English, mathematics and science when, in each of these, one or two members of the team had expertise and reputations in the subject community. Thus, when specific issues, such as "Is this an appropriate question for exploring students ideas about the concept of photosynthesis?" arose, we could discuss them seriously.

A further relevant factor about the content is that the ideas had an intrinsic acceptability to the teachers. We were talking about improving learning in the classroom, which was central to their professional identities, as opposed to bureaucratic measures such as target-setting. One feature of our review was that most of it was concerned with such issues as students' perceptions, peer- and self-assessment, and the role of feedback in a pedagogy focused on learning. Thus it helped to take the emphasis in formative assessment studies away from *systems,* with its emphasis on the formative-summative interface, and re-locate it on classroom *processes.*

Linked to the previous factor is that in our choice to concentrate on the classroom processes, we had decided to live with the external constraints operating at the formative-summative interface: the failed attempts to change the *system,* in the 80s and 90s in England, were set aside. Whilst it might have been merely prudent to not try again to tilt at windmills, the more fundamental strength was that it was at the level chosen, that of the core of learning, that formative work stakes its claim for attention. Furthermore, given that any change has to work out in teachers' practical action, this is where reform should always have started. The evidence of learning gains, from the literature review and from our project, restates and reinforces the claim for priority of formative work that earlier policy recommendations (DES, 1988) tried in vain to establish. The debate about how policy should secure optimum synergy between teachers' formative, teachers' summative, and external assessments is still unresolved, but the new salience of work on formative assessment has now shifted the balance of the arguments.

The process strategy

In our development model, we attended to both the content and the process of teacher development (Reeves *et al.*, 2001). We attended to the process of professional development through an acknowledgement that teachers need time, freedom, and support from colleagues, in order to reflect critically upon and to develop their practice (Lee, 2005), whilst offering also practical strategies and techniques about how to begin the process. By themselves, however, these are not enough. Teachers also need concrete ideas about the directions in which they can productively take their practice, and thus there is a need for work on the professional development of teachers to pay specific attention to subject-specific dimensions of teacher learning (Wilson and Berne, 1999).

One of the key assumptions of the project was that if the promise of formative assessment was to be realised, traditional research designs – in which teachers are "told" what to do by researchers – would not be appropriate. We argued that a process of supported development was an essential next step. In such a process, the teachers in their classrooms had to work out the answers to many of the practical questions that the research evidence could not answer. The issues had to be reformulated in collaboration with them, where possible in relation to fundamental insights, and certainly in terms that could make sense to their peers in ordinary classrooms.

The key feature of the INSET sessions was the development of action plans. Since we were aware from other studies that effective implementation of formative assessment requires teachers to re-negotiate the "learning contract" that they had evolved with their students (Brousseau, 1984; Perrenoud, 1991), we decided that implementing formative assessment would best be done at the beginning of a new school year. For the first six months of the project (January 1999 to July 1999), therefore, we encouraged the teachers to experiment with some of the strategies and techniques suggested by the research, such as rich questioning, comment-only marking, sharing criteria with learners, and student peer- and self-assessment. Each teacher was then asked to draw up an action plan of the practices they wished to develop and to identify a single focal class with whom these strategies would be introduced at the start of the new school year in September 1999. Details of these plans can be found in Black *et al*. (2003). As the teachers explored the relevance of formative assessment for their own practice, they transformed ideas from the research and from other teachers into new ideas, strategies and techniques, and these were in turn communicated to teachers, creating a "snowball" effect. As we have introduced these ideas to more and more teachers outside the project, we have become better at communicating the key ideas.

Through our work with teachers, we have come to understand more clearly how the task of applying research into practice is much more than a simple process of "translating" the findings of researchers into the classroom. The teachers in our project were engaged in a process of knowledge creation, albeit of a distinct kind, and possibly relevant only in the settings in which they work (Hargreaves, 1999). We stressed this feature of our approach with the teachers right from the outset of the project. We discovered later that some of them did not, at that stage, believe us: they thought that we knew exactly what we wanted them to do but were leaving them to work it out for themselves. As they came to know us better, they realised that, at the level of everyday classroom practice, we really did not know what to do.

Making research practical

Whilst we do not believe that all educational research should be useful, we do believe strongly that the majority of research in education should be undertaken with a view to improving educational provision – research in what Stokes (1997) calls "Pasteur's quadrant". And although we do not yet know everything about "what works" in teaching, we believe that there is a substantial consensus on the kinds of classrooms that promote the best learning. What we know much less about is how to get this to happen.

Researching how teachers take on research, adapt it, and make it their own is much more difficult than researching the effects of different curricula, of class sizes, or of the contribution of classroom assistants. While we do not know as much as we would like to know about effective professional development, if we adopt "the balance of probabilities" rather than "beyond reasonable doubt" as our burden of proof, then educational research has much to say. When policy without evidence meets development with some evidence, development should prevail. Thus we take issue with the stance of some policy makers who appear to want large-scale research conducted to the highest standards of analytic rationality, but the findings of which are also relevant to policy. It may often be the case that these two goals are, in fact, incompatible.

References

Black, P. and D. Wiliam (1998a), "Assessment and Classroom Learning", *Assessment in Education,* Vol. 5, pp. 7-71.

Black, P. and D. Wiliam (1998b), *Inside the Black Box: Raising Standards through Classroom Assessment.* See also *Phi Delta Kappan,* Vol. 80, pp. 139-148.

Black, P. and D. Wiliam (2003), "In Praise of Educational Research: Formative Assessment", *British Educational Research Journal*, Vol. 29(5), pp. 623-637.

Black, P. et al. (2002), *Working inside the Black Box: Assessment for Learning in the Classroom*, Department of Education and Professional Studies, King's College, London.

Black, P. et al. (2003), *Assessment for Learning: Putting it into Practice*, Open University Press, Buckingham, United Kingdom.

Brousseau, G. (1984), "The Crucial Role of the Didactical Contract in the Analysis and Construction of Situations in Teaching and Learning Mathematics" in H.-G. Steiner (ed.), *Theory of Mathematics Education: ICME 5 Topic Area and Miniconference*, Institut für Didaktik der Mathematik der Universität Bielefeld, Bielefeld, Germany, pp. 110-119.

Butler, R. (1988), "Enhancing and Undermining Intrinsic Motivation; the Effects of Task-involving and Ego-involving Evaluation on Interest and Performance", *British Journal of Educational Psychology,* vol. 58, pp. 1-14.

Crooks, T.J. (1988), "The Impact of Classroom Evaluation Practices on Students", *Review of Educational Research,* Vol. 58, pp. 438-481.

DES (1988), *Task Group on Assessment and Testing: A Report*, Department of Education and Science and the Welsh Office, London.

Flyvbjerg, B. (2001), *Making Social Science Matter: Why Social Inquiry Fails and how it can Succeed again*, Cambridge University Press, Cambridge UK.

Foos, P.W., J.J. Mora and S. Tkacz (1994), "Student Study Techniques and the Generation Effect", *Journal of Educational Psychology,* Vol. 86, pp. 567-576.

Fuchs, L.S. and D. Fuchs (1986), "Effects of Systematic Formative Evaluation: a Meta-Analysis", *Exceptional Children*, Vol. 53, pp. 199-208.

Hargreaves, D.H. (1999), "The Knowledge Creating School", *British Journal of Educational Studies*, Vol. 47, pp. 122-144.

King, A. (1992), "Facilitating Elaborative Learning through Guided Student-generated Questioning", *Educational Psychologist,* Vol. 27, pp. 111-126.

Kluger, A.N. and A. DeNisi (1996), "The Effects of Feedback Interventions on Performance: A Historical Review, a Meta-Analysis, and a Preliminary Feedback Intervention Theory", *Psychological Bulletin,* Vol. 119, pp. 254-284.

Lee, C. (2005), "Studying Changes in the Practice of Two Teachers", *International Journal of Teacher Development*, in press.

Natriello, G. (1987), "The Impact of Evaluation Processes on Students", *Educational Psychologist,* Vol. 22, pp. 155-175.

Perrenoud, P. (1991), "Towards a Pragmatic Approach to Formative Evaluation", in P. Weston (ed.), *Assessment of Pupils Achievement: Motivation and School Success*, Swets and Zeitlinger, Amsterdam, pp. 79-101.

Ramaprasad, A. (1983), "On the Definition of Feedback", *Behavioral Science,* Vol. 28, pp. 4-13.

Reeves, J., J. McCall and B. MacGilchrist (2001), "Change Leadership: Planning, Conceptualization and Perception", in J. MacBeath and P. Mortimore (eds.), *Improving school effectiveness,* Open University Press, Buckingham UK, pp. 122-137.

Rowe, M.B. (1974), "Wait Time and Rewards as Instructional Variables, their Influence on Language, Logic and Fate Control", *Journal of Research in Science Teaching*, Vol. 11, pp. 81-94.

Sadler, R. (1989), "Formative Assessment and the Design of Instructional Systems", *Instructional Science,* Vol. 18, pp. 119-144.

Sadler, R. (1998), "Formative Assessment: Revisiting the Territory", *Assessment in Education*, Vol. 5, pp. 77-84.

Stokes, D.E. (1997), *Pasteur's Quadrant: Basic Science and Technological Innovation*, Brookings Institution Press, Washington DC.

Toulmin, S. (2001), *Return to Reason*, Harvard University Press, Cambridge MA.

Vispoel, W.P. and J.R. Austin (1995), "Success and Failure in Junior High School: A Critical Incident Approach to Understanding Students' Attributional Beliefs", *American Educational Research Journal,* Vol. 33, pp. 377-412.

White, B.Y. and J.R. Frederiksen (1998), "Inquiry, Modeling, and Metacognition: Making Science Accessible to all Students", *Cognition and Instruction*, Vol. 16, pp. 3-118.

Wiliam, D. (2003), "The Impact of Educational Research on Mathematics Education" in A. Bishop, M.A. Clements, C. Keitel, J. Kilpatrick and F.K.S. Leung (eds.), *Second International Handbook of Mathematics Education*, Kluwer Academic Publishers, Dordrecht Netherlands, pp. 469-488.

Wiliam, D. *et al.* (2004), "Teachers Developing Assessment for Learning: Impact on Student Achievement", *Assessment in Education,* Vol. 11, pp.49-65.

Wilson, S.M. and J. Berne (1999), "Teacher Learning and the Acquisition of Professional Knowledge: An Examination of Research on Contemporary Professional Development", in A. Iran-Nejad and P.D. Pearson (eds.), *Review of Research in Education,* American Educational Research Association, Washington DC, pp. 173-209.

Formative Assessment of Learning: A Review of Publications in French

by

Linda Allal and Lucie Mottier Lopez
University of Geneva

The concept of "formative evaluation" was introduced by Scriven (1967) in an article on the evaluation of educational programmes (curricula, methods, instructional material). For Scriven, formative evaluation aims at providing data that permit successive adaptations of a new programme during the phases of its development and its implementation. Bloom (1968) quickly incorporated the idea of formative evaluation – applied to student learning – into his newly defined model of mastery learning. The characteristics of this function of evaluation were spelled out in considerable detail in subsequent publications (Bloom, 1976; Bloom, Hasting and Madaus, 1971). Over the years, an extensive literature has accumulated in English concerning formative assessment (the term "assessment" having progressively replaced "evaluation" when the object is student learning in the classroom). This literature is well-known to educational researchers in many areas of the world. On the other hand, the work carried out and published in other languages (French, German, Spanish, etc.) is relatively unknown in the English-language community. The present review is aimed at fostering international dissemination of work on formative assessment published in French over the past 25 years.[1]

Our review is based on publications by researchers and assessment specialists in France and in the French-speaking regions of Belgium, Canada, and Switzerland. To carry out the review we constructed a database composed of over 100 journal articles published in the major French-language journal in the area of assessment. We also consulted a number of key books, especially those resulting from conferences organised by the French-language associations on assessment. The review is focused on formative assessment of student learning in elementary and secondary school settings but takes into account developments in other contexts

---

[1] We thank Janet Looney for inviting us to prepare this review in the context of an OECD/CERI project on "What works?" in the area of formative assessment of student learning. The development of the review benefited from exchanges we had in Geneva and Paris.

(particularly teacher training and higher education) that have influenced the conception and practice of formative assessment in the classroom. The first part of the review describes the material on which the review is based, its origin and coverage. The second part defines the major conceptual orientations of formative assessment in the French-language literature. The third part presents a classification of the types of empirical research that have been carried out on formative assessment.

COVERAGE OF THE REVIEW

Our database is composed of articles appearing in the journal *Mesure et évaluation en éducation* (*Measurement and Assessment in Education*).[2] The journal, initially entitled *Mesure en éducation*, was founded in 1978 by professionals in charge of school examinations in Québec. Several years later, university specialists in measurement and assessment took on a major role in the editorial board and the present title of the journal was adopted. In 1986, the editorial board was enlarged to include two sub-committees, one composed of members from universities and research centers in Québec, the other of members from European universities and research institutions in Belgium, France and Switzerland. It is worth noting that *Mesure et évaluation en éducation* is the only international, peer-reviewed journal published in French which specialises in questions of educational assessment.

From the beginning, the journal was sponsored by an active Québec association: the *Association Professionnelle de Mesure en Éducation*, which became the *Association pour le Développement de la Mesure et de l'Évaluation en Éducation*. In 1985, a parallel association was created in Europe: *Association pour le Développement des Méthodologies d'Évaluation en Éducation*. Although the two associations share the same acronym (ADMEE), their names differ in one slight but significant respect: the word *mesure* in the Canadian version is replaced by *méthodologies* in the European version. These choices are a reflection of cultural attitudes toward the concept of measurement in the research communities of the two continents. While in Canada, measurement and assessment (or evaluation) go hand in hand, in much of French-speaking Europe, there is a tendency to prefer qualitative assessment without the operations of quantification associated with measurement (for a discussion of this question, see Allal, 1997). Despite these differences, the two ADMEE associations have closely collaborated in the edition of a common journal. The annual conferences of each association attract a wide range of researchers, professionals and practitioners who work

---

[2] In contrast with English where the term "assessment" has replaced "evaluation" when the object is student learning, the word *évaluation* is used in French both for student assessment and for programme evaluation.

in the area of educational assessment, including participants and keynote speakers from the other side of the Atlantic. In addition, several joint conferences between the two associations have been held.

The database used for this review is composed of 105 articles published in the journal *Mesure et évaluation en éducation* between 1978 and 2002.[3] It includes articles that deal directly with formative assessment or that address issues of importance for formative assessment (*e.g.*, articles on observation methods or on new means of summative assessment that have implications for formative assessment). For each article in the database, a summary was made of the theoretical orientations that were presented and the empirical research that was reported. A coding scheme was applied to facilitate identification of various theoretical and empirical dimensions.

In addition, we examined the chapters appearing in six edited books that resulted from ADMEE conferences on assessment: Allal, Cardinet and Perrenoud (1979), De Ketele (1986), Depover and Noël (1999), Figari and Achouche (2001), Laveault (1992), Weiss, 1991. We also consulted two edited books (Grégoire, 1996a; Hivon, 1993) presenting work from symposia on assessment organised by another French-language network (*Réseau Éducation et Formation*), as well as several other well-known books in the field (Allal, Bain and Perrenoud, 1993; Bélair, 1999; Bonniol and Vial, 1997; Cardinet, 1986a, 1986b; Hadji, 1989, 1997; Huberman, 1988; Louis, 1999; Perrenoud, 1998a; Scallon, 2000).

CONCEPTUALISATION OF FORMATIVE ASSESSMENT

The initial conception of formative assessment proposed by Bloom has been enlarged in several directions by researchers working in French. After a presentation of the main orientations of this enlargement, four successive developments in French-language research on formative assessment will be described.

Enlarging the conception of formative assessment

In the initial conception of mastery learning proposed by Bloom (1968; Bloom *et al.*, 1971), an instructional unit is divided into several successive phases. First of all, teaching/learning activities are undertaken in relation with the objectives of the unit. Once these activities have been completed, a

---

[3] The construction of the database was facilitated by the existence of a CD-Rom which contains all issues of the journal from 1978 through 1998. This material was completed by the issues appearing between 1998 and 2002, which is the year corresponding to the most recent issues of the journal.

formative assessment, usually a paper-pencil test, is proposed to the students. The results of the test provide feedback to the teacher and students and are used to define appropriate corrective measures for students who have not yet mastered the instructional objectives. Correctives can take various forms: additional exercises, different types of instructional material (*e.g.*, verbal vs. visual representations), small-group discussions, one-to-one tutoring, computer-based tasks, but in all these cases the aim remains the *remediation of learning difficulties* identified by formative assessment. Each of the phases (teaching, testing, remediation) is planned, prepared and managed by the teacher who attempts to assure that all the students will master the objectives of the unit.

A number of publications in French have contributed to an enlargement of the conception of formative assessment. One of the earliest formulations appeared in an article by Audibert (1980) which proposed a "non-specialist's" view of formative assessment. Formative assessment, he wrote, "takes place day by day and allows the teacher and the student to adapt their respective actions to the teaching/learning situation in question. It is thus, for them, a privileged occasion for conscious reflection on their experience (*prise de conscience de leur vécu*), for objectivation in action". (p. 62)[4] Several authors (in particular, Allal, 1979, 1988; Perrenoud, 1998b) have systematically contrasted the characteristics of an enlarged perspective of formative assessment with those of the approach initially defined by Bloom. The major points of contrast are presented in Table 1.

Rather than considering formative assessment as a specific event that occurs after a phase of teaching, the enlarged perspective advocates the integration of formative assessment within each instructional activity. This integration requires a diversification of the means of assessment. In addition to paper-pencil tests, quizzes or worksheets designed to verify whether students understood the content of a lesson, assessment is carried out informally by direct teacher observation, by exchanges among students (reciprocal assessment) at various points during an instructional activity, and by whole-class discussions that allow students to present different ways of understanding a task or of carrying out an activity.

---

[4] The French-language quotations in this paper are translated by the authors of this review. We indicate in parentheses expressions in French that are difficult to translate in a fully appropriate way.

Table 1. Bloom's initial conception vs. an enlarged conception of formative assessment (FA)

Bloom's initial conception	An enlarged conception
- Insertion of FA after a phase of teaching - Use of formative tests - Feedback + correction → remediation - Management of FA by the teacher - Mastery of objectives by all students - Remediation benefits the students who were assessed	- Integration of FA in all learning situations - Use of varied means of data collection - Feedback + adaptation of instruction → regulation - Active student involvement in FA - Differentiation of instruction and, to some extent, of objectives - Regulation at 2 levels: for the students assessed, for future students (continuing instructional improvement)

Source: Authors.

In the enlarged perspective of formative assessment developed in French-language publications, the idea of *remediation* of learning difficulties (feedback + correction) is replaced by the broader concept of *regulation* of learning (feedback + adaptation). This transformation emerged initially in a paper by Cardinet (1977) whose conception of regulation was inspired by cybernetic systems analysis. A distinction was subsequently made between three modalities of regulation associated with formative assessment (Allal, 1979, 1988):

1. *Interactive regulation* occurs when formative assessment is based on the interactions of the student with the other components of the instructional activity, that is, with the teacher, with other students and/or with material allowing self-regulated learning. The integration of different forms of interactive regulation within an instructional activity allows continuing adaptations of learning as it takes place. Interactive regulation contributes to the progression of student learning by providing feedback and guidance that stimulate student involvement at each step of instruction.

2. *Retroactive regulation* occurs when a formative assessment is conducted after completion of a phase of teaching and allows identification of the instructional objectives attained or not attained by each student. The feedback from the assessment leads to the selection of means for correcting or overcoming learning difficulties encountered by some students. It corresponds to the notion of remediation present in the initial conception of formative assessment defined by Bloom.

3. *Proactive regulation* occurs when different sources of information allow the preparation of new instructional activities

designed to take into account differences among students. It is linked to concerns with the differentiation of instruction so as to insure enrichment and consolidation according to student needs, rather than focusing on remediation of learning difficulties.

Innovative approaches to formative assessment often combine these three types of regulation. Instructional activities are designed to include several forms of interactive regulation based on informal means of assessment (observation, discussion). More structured means of formative assessment (tests, written productions, oral examination) are introduced periodically to allow for retroactive regulation of difficulties that were not resolved by the informal interactive regulations. In addition, proactive regulation takes into account all available information so as to insure that future activities are better adapted, from the outset, to the needs of the students; in other words, differentiation of instruction is planned, rather than being just added on, after observing difficulties.

In Bloom's initial conception of formative assessment, the teacher (or sometimes, the curriculum developer) assumes responsibility for the planning and management of each assessment operation: preparation of a formative test, analysis and interpretation of the results, proposal of appropriate remediations. In an enlarged conception, external regulation (by the teacher, by the test, by remedial material) is redefined as scaffolding that assists students' development of self-regulation. This means fostering the active involvement of students in formative assessment through procedures of self-assessment, reciprocal peer-assessment, and joint teacher-student assessment (Allal, 1999).

One further point of comparison needs to be mentioned. The basic aim of mastery learning is that formative assessment, followed by feedback and correction, will allow all (or virtually all) students to attain the instructional objectives. In the perspective proposed in the French-language literature, a much greater emphasis is given to the differentiation of instruction. Although it is accepted that basic objectives (*e.g.*, learning to read) must be mastered by all students, questions are raised about the possible adaptation of the objective to better take into account student cultural experiences and personal interests. The idea is expressed, for instance, that there may be several ways of "being a reader", such as reading to act, reading to get the "gist", reading to understand in depth, reading to communicate. In this perspective, formative assessment aims at identifying qualitative differences among students that need to be taken into account in the choice of reading material, in the tasks used for assessment, in the regulations fostered in class. For example, structured activities of peer interaction about a text may allow confrontations among students who have different approaches to reading.

A final direction of enlargement has resulted from work with classroom teachers, and particularly secondary teachers who are often faced with important constraints on the time and resources available for formative assessment (Allal and Schwartz, 1996). In this context it was found useful to differentiate two complementary levels of formative assessment. Level 1 concerns formative assessment that directly benefits the students who are assessed, as proposed in the basic Bloom model. Level 2 concerns situations where formative assessment data are used to inform teacher planning of future instructional activities proposed to *new* groups of students. When teachers are unable to carry out level 1 regulations (*e.g.*, due to lack of time or other obstacles), they should nevertheless be encouraged to carry out level 2 regulations, which in the long run can lead to systemic improvement of instruction.

Since the initial publications by Bloom and his collaborators, the conception of formative assessment has of course evolved in the English-language literature. For instance, in the review by Black and Wiliam (1998), the concept of feedback is described as a "system" that operates with four components:

- Data on the student's actual level.
- Data on a reference level.
- A mechanism for comparing the levels.
- A mechanism used to alter the gap.

The concept of regulation in the French-language literature includes these four components but emphasises the importance of additional factors linked to the processes intervening in attempts to "alter the gap". These processes are reflected in:

- The actions actually carried out by the teacher and the students to alter the gap.
- The degree of active student involvement in these actions.
- The uses students make of tools and resources present in the instructional environment to adapt or enrich their learning activity.
- The meaning attributed by students and teachers to the various aspects of assessment.
- The ways in which teachers and students negotiate assessment (talk about criteria, discuss requirements, construct shared understandings about what is expected).

The conceptualisation of regulation as the essential attribute of formative assessment has benefited from the contributions of a large number of French-language publications drawing on a diversity of theoretical perspectives, which are discussed subsequently in this paper (Allal, 1979, 1988, 1993; Cardinet, 1977, 1983; Hadji, 1989; Laveault, 1999; Nunziati, 1990; Perrenoud, 1991, 1993b, 1998b; Scallon, 2000; Schneuwly and Bain, 1993; Vial, 2001; Weiss, 1993).

Four developments in the evolution of work on formative assessment

It is possible to identify four major developments in the evolution of the conception of formative assessment in the French-language literature. These developments are presented in the order of their emergence. Each new development has attempted to overcome certain limitations of prior perspectives. It is important to note, however, that new developments have led to successive re-conceptualisations of formative assessment integrating prior contributions, rather than to the disappearance of earlier viewpoints.

Focus on instrumentation

French-language researchers initially adopted the focus on instrumentation that characterised formative assessment from the outset. The *Handbook on Formative and Summative Evaluation of Student Learning*, published in 1971 by Bloom and his coworkers, served as a model for the development of instruments for formative assessment (tables of objectives coordinated with formative tests and remediation activities). Several collections of instruments were published in different subject matter areas (*e.g.*, Marchandisse and Blampain, 1974; Tourneur, Noël and Honclaire, 1975) and general guidelines for the construction of criterion-referenced tests were established (Racine, 1982). More advanced instrumentation was subsequently developed in the form of computer-based item banks and systems of "tailored testing" allowing diagnostic error analysis (*e.g.*, Dassa, 1988; De Campos, 1990; Leclercq, 1980; Séguin, 1984). The dissemination of these forms of instrumentation helped to transform the conceptions and practices of formative assessment but also raised theoretical questions. Objections emerged about a "technology" of assessment that risked being cut off from theoretical reflection about the processes of learning and teaching (see in particular, Bain, 1988, on the "instrumental illusion" of the classical approaches to formative assessment). In response, Scallon (1988) defended instrumentation of formative assessment and argued that instrument development can take into account the aims and contextual constraints of classroom instruction.

Search for theoretical frameworks

At a conference of Swiss and Belgian researchers held in Geneva in 1978, a call was formulated for more in-depth theoretical grounding of formative assessment. The search for theories that can offer conceptual orientation for conducting assessment has been pursued since then in several different directions in the French-language literature.

During the Geneva conference, Allal (1979) outlined the differences between Bloom's conception based on a neo-behaviorist model of learning and a more constructivist approach to formative assessment based on Piagetian and other cognitive theories of learning. Several conference papers and subsequent articles described the implications of a constructivist conception for specific subject matters, such as mathematics (Brun, 1979; Thouin, 1993), French (Weiss, 1979), sciences (Thouin, 1982). Further reflection on this theme was proposed by Crahay (1986) who developed the argument that a constructivist perspective is necessary but nevertheless insufficient for the definition of optimal procedures of formative assessment.

Certain preoccupations of the constructivist perspective, such as the identification of learning processes and strategies that account for observed responses, have received renewed treatment in the light of contemporary theories of cognitive psychology. Implications were drawn from these theories for two major aspects of assessment: (1) the development of diagnostic models of formative assessment based on research on learning difficulties in the areas of reading (Lété, 1996) and of mathematics (Grégoire, 1996b) and the attempt to refine diagnostic assessment by use of Anderson's ACT model of declarative and procedural knowledge (Grégoire, 1999); (2) the investigation of the role of metacognitive processes in formative assessment and in self-assessment (Allal, 1993; Laveault, 1999; Scallon, 1996).

In parallel with developments of the constructivist/cognitive perspectives, new orientations were sought in theories emphasising social and philosophical dimensions of teaching and learning. Referring to work in social psychology, Cardinet (1988) proposed looking at formative assessment as a process of successful teacher-student communication about objectives, criteria, learning difficulties, etc. Using communication theory, Ouellette (1990) defined assessment as a dialogue constructed "with reference to a process of learning, as a function of interactions within an educational relationship" (p. 13). In an eclectic approach combining philosophical, social and institutional considerations, Hadji (1989) analysed formative assessment from the viewpoint of teacher-student transactions about reciprocal expectations and interpretations of assessment outcomes.

More recently, formative assessment was examined from the viewpoint of socio-cultural theories of teaching and learning. Referring to the Vygotskian concept of social mediation of learning, Allal and Pelgrims Ducrey (2000) argued that interactive formative assessment is aimed at providing scaffolding of learning in the student's zone of proximal development. This viewpoint is especially relevant for assessment situations involving teacher interactions with small groups or with individual students. We believe, however, that the theoretical framework of situated cognition and learning offers a broader perspective for conceptualising both interactive formative assessment and use of formative assessment tools in terms of teacher and student participation in the practices of a classroom community (Allal, 2002). A situated perspective was adopted by Mottier Lopez (2002) in a detailed analysis of the influence of classroom microculture on the practice of portfolio assessment with a predominantly formative aim.

Another theoretical approach to formative assessment has been proposed by French-language researchers in the areas of "didactics" (Bain, 1988; Chevallard, 1986; Garcia Debanc and Mas, 1987). This approach analyses assessment as part of a triadic system linking the teacher, the learner and the knowledge being dealt with. Emphasis is placed on how the content structures of school disciplines determine the aims, means and functions of formative assessment. Schubauer-Leoni (1991) proposed an interpretation of assessment within the framework of the "didactical contract" linking the reciprocal expectations of teacher and learners with respect to a given content area or task. Bain and Schneuwly (1993) developed the idea that, for any given instructional activity (*e.g.*, text production), it is necessary to identify relevant scientific "reference models" (*e.g.*, theories of discourse production, of language operations, of text genre) which can inform and guide formative assessment. The relationships between formative assessment and didactics were also discussed in several chapters of a book edited by Laveault (1992).

A few authors have explicitly situated formative assessment in the intersection of several theoretical perspectives. Perrenoud (1991, 1998b) argued that it is necessary to link cognitive, communicative and didactic orientations of formative assessment in a general framework of regulation that includes but goes beyond regulation due specifically to assessment. Bonniol and Vial (1997) explored the contrasting implications of cybernetic, systemic and complexity theories for the conceptualisation of formative assessment.

It is interesting to note that several recent English-language publications on classroom assessment, in particular Shepard (2000), give an important place to the implications of constructivist, socio-cultural and situated theories of learning, thereby joining major concerns of the French-language literature.

Studies of existing assessment practices in their contexts

The search for theoretical frameworks could lead to an increasingly abstract vision of formative assessment, cut off from the realities of classroom practice. This is why it is essential to articulate theoretical work with the study of how assessment is actually practiced in the classroom. Studies in this direction have dealt with several phenomena: the interplay between instrumentation and intuition in teachers' practices of formative assessment (Allal, 1983); the fundamental incompatibility between certain instruments of formative assessment and the everyday assessment practices of teachers (Weiss, 1984); the forms of teacher-student negotiation of assessment rules and norms (Chevallard, 1986); the institutional factors affecting teachers' attitudes toward inequalities of students achievement and the effect on assessment practice (Grisay, 1988); the pragmatics of actually doing formative assessment without worrying about doctrine (Perrenoud, 1991); the systemic aspects of assessment that can foster or inhibit the development of formative assessment practices (Perrenoud, 1993a). In work on formative assessment instrumentation, such as computer-based diagnostic testing, increasing emphasis is given to taking into account classroom practices and the ways of articulating instrumentation and practice (Dassa and De Cotret, 1993). Accounts of practice by teachers and teacher educators (*e.g.*, chapters by Berset, Elliott, Wegmuller in Allal, Bain and Perrenoud, 1993) have provided concrete illustrations of different forms of regulation associated with formative assessment.

Development of active student involvement in assessment

The role of the teacher remains essential for the practice of formative assessment: it is the teacher who decides what place will be given to formative assessment and the teacher's attitudes and implicit "theories" of teaching and learning have a profound impact on how formative assessment is put into practice. There is, however, increasing recognition of the importance of encouraging active student involvement in formative assessment. Nunziati (1990) and Vial (1995) developed an in-depth conceptualisation of the student's role in the formulation of assessment goals and criteria, in the conduct of interactive assessment, and in the construction of shared understanding of what assessment means. Allal (1999) proposed three different but interrelated forms of student involvement in assessment: individual self-assessment, reciprocal peer-assessment, and co-assessment entailing confrontation of teacher and student assessments. Campanale (1997) developed a detailed model of self-assessment, including metacognitive and reflexive dimensions intervening in the transformation of pedagogical practice in the context of professional development activities. Laveault (1999) expanded the conceptualisation of self-assessment by the inclusion of motivational regulations, in addition to cognitive and metacognitive regulations. A common theme in the French-language literature is that interactive formative assessment, between peers and between teacher and students, constitutes a framework of social mediation that fosters the student's increasing capacity to carry out more autonomous self-assessment and self-regulated learning. Frameworks for practicing various forms of self/peer/joint teacher-student assessment have been elaborated and applied in classroom settings (*e.g.*, Doyon, 1992; Doyon and Juneau, 1991). It is needs to be recognised, however, that various dilemmas and pitfalls can occur when teachers encourage student involvement in assessment and things do not turn out as planned (Allal, 1999).

EMPIRICAL RESEARCH ON FORMATIVE ASSESSMENT

This part of our review analyses the empirical research presented in French-language publications on formative assessment. It is based primarily on the journal articles in the database we constructed, but takes into account examples of research presented in the books we consulted. Publications of empirical research have been classified in three major categories: (1) experimental studies of the effects of formative assessment; (2) development of instruments and procedures of formative assessment; (3) studies of teachers' attitudes and practices of formative assessment. The classification of publications in these categories allows a rough estimation of the relative amount of research conduced in each category. It is not possible, however, to arrive at a rigorous quantification since many articles contain elements relevant to several categories.

Experimental research on the effects of formative assessment

In the English-language literature, experimental or quasi-experimental research designed to determine the effects of formative assessment on student learning is relatively widespread, as attested by existing reviews (*e.g.*, Black and Wiliam,1998) and by meta-analyses of the effects of mastery learning which includes formative assessment as a key component (*e.g.*, Block and Burns, 1976; Slavin, 1987). This type of investigation has not found an equivalent place in the French-language literature. Of the 105 articles in our database, only two present experimental vs. control group comparisons of the effects of formative assessment on student learning. One of the studies was based on a design comparing mastery learning (with formative assessment) in two history classes to traditional instruction carried out by the same teachers in two matched history classes of a Geneva high school (Huberman, Juge and Hari, 1985). The results showed a positive effect the first trimester but this effect was not maintained subsequently in the second and third trimesters. Various factors which limited the effectiveness of mastery learning – principally institutional constraints and student tendency to make the minimum effort needed for passing a grade – are discussed in the article. The second study (Gagné and Thouin, 1991), conducted in three French-speaking Ontario high schools, concerned a formative assessment procedure focused on the correction of spelling mistakes (lexical and grammatical) in student texts. Experimental and control classes were compared with respect to pretest-posttest gains on a spelling test and on a scale measuring student attitudes with respect to assessment. The results showed a relatively small effect of formative assessment on spelling scores but a substantial improvement of student attitudes toward assessment. In addition to these two studies, there is a brief reference in an article by Dassa (1988) to a quasi-experimental study carried out in Québec which compared three ways of using computer-based diagnostic assessment tools. Positive effect sizes are reported (0.56 for achievement in French and in mathematics) but the article gives little information on the experimentation and is devoted primarily to a critical discussion of the problems linked to the integration of diagnostic technology in classroom teaching.

In the books we consulted, we identified only one experimental study of the effects of formative assessment on student learning. Del'Guidice (1999) presented an investigation in which five groups of 4th-grade students received different types of diagnostic assessment and regulation. The results of these groups were compared to those of a matched control group on several tasks of geometry (calculation of areas). The author stated that the integration of formative assessment in learning situations had a beneficial effect on immediate learning and on transfer. His master's and doctoral thesis were cited but no data were presented in the book chapter.

Development of formative assessment instruments and procedures

Articles on instrument development have appeared regularly in the journal Mesure et évaluation en éducation since its creation. Many of the articles pertain, however, to the development of measurement instruments for research or for summative assessment, or concern instruments that are ill-defined with respect to their function. We were able to identify only a limited number of articles (around a half-dozen) which present empirical evidence of the validation of formative assessment instruments. One type of instrumentation stands out because it was the object of a substantial number of studies by Canadian researchers, namely the development of diagnostic instruments for error analysis and regulation of learning in the area of mathematics. Research in this area includes a variety of approaches: research comparing different models of diagnostic test construction, including estimation of reliability, information on validity, indications about conditions of application (Bertrand et al., 1985); qualitative analysis of computer-based error diagnostics and their didactical validity (Dassa and

De Cotret, 1993; De Campos, 1990); critical reflections about the place of computerised systems of diagnostic testing, such as adaptive testing and performance-responsive drill and practice (Dassa, 1988; Dassa and Vazquez-Abad, 1992). Computer-based diagnostic instrumentation in the area of text revision has also been developed (Laurier, 1996) and extended to student self-assessment and self-regulation (Coen and Gurtner, 1999).

In addition to research on instrument validation, there are various articles (about a half-dozen) which present empirical evidence about the use and implementation of formative assessment procedures. Examples include: a study by Scallon (1985) of how students use a diagnostic assessment guide for multiplication and their attitudes toward this type of assessment; the analysis by Allal *et al.* (1987) of the self-assessment and reciprocal peer-assessment behaviors that occur in mathematics games in 2nd and 3rd grades; an investigation by Derycke (1998) comparing two types of instrumentation – a criterion-referenced checklist and a portfolio – used for student follow-up when changing teachers (*suivi pédagogique*); a study by Richard, Godbout and Picard (2000) of a team sport assessment procedure that was applied in several activities (soccer, volley ball).

The journal and the book chapters we consulted also include a sizeable number of publications (over 25) presenting formative assessment instruments or procedures that have been developed in collaborative research with teachers, either in the context of teacher education and professional development or in work on curriculum reforms. These articles include conceptual justifications and references to practice but do not offer any systematic empirical evidence regarding applications in the classroom. Examples include: the classroom assessment guide presented by Descoteaux and Lirette (1983); the kits (*trousses*) developed by Cazabon (1991) for formative assessment in language learning; the Learning portfolio (*dossier d'apprentissage*) described by Simon and Forgette-Giroux (1993).

Studies of teacher attitudes and practices of formative assessment in the classroom

Investigations of how formative assessment functions in classroom settings are based primarily on three sources of information. The first includes action-research projects involving collaboration between researchers and teachers. Projects in Switzerland showed that detailed diagnostic instruments developed by researchers were not compatible with classroom practice (Weiss, 1984) and tended to reinforce recognition of the role of interactive formative assessment in the classroom (Cardinet, 1983). Subsequent projects (*e.g.*, Schwartz and Allal, 2000) were inserted in professional development programmes designed to accompany teachers in their attempts to conceptualise and put into practice their personal versions of formative assessment. In Canada, action-research projects were undertaken to develop formative assessment instruments in a constructivist and interactionist perspective for mathematics (Thouin, 1993) and for science instruction (Thouin, 1995). Instruments of various types were developed with teachers, tried out in their classes and shared with other practitioners. Another project allowed successive reformulations of teachers' projects for transforming their assessment practices in a more formative perspective (Desrosiers, Godbout and Marzouk, 1992).

A second source of information comes from studies based on teachers' responses to attitude scales, questionnaires or interviews. Standard instrument development methodology was used by two groups of Canadian researchers to validate scales for measuring teacher beliefs and attitudes about assessment and student learning (Gadbois *et al.*, 1991; Louis and Trahan, 1995). But, beyond the initial validation studies, investigations using the scales have not been reported in subsequent journal articles. On the other side of the Atlantic, a questionnaire survey, addressed to 113 Belgian elementary school teachers, showed that teachers were generally favorable to formative assessment but that there was often a gap between espoused beliefs and classroom practice (Van Nieuwenhoven and Jonnaert, 1994). Using questionnaires and interviews, Campanale (1997) found a positive evolution of teacher conceptions of learning and assessment during a professional development programme that gave an important place to self-assessment of practice. A less encouraging result was found in a study of student perceptions of assessment in 6th to 8th grades in Québec; responses to a questionnaire showed little evidence that students encountered formative assessment experiences (Bercier-Larivière and Forgette-Giroux, 1995).

A third source of information on assessment practice consists in detailed descriptions formulated by teachers and teacher educators of their own practices. Examples include the formative assessment procedures developed by Elliott (1993) for beginning reading, by Berset Fougerand (1993) for writing and spelling and by Wegmuller (1993) for activities of text production. Despite the anecdotal nature of these reports, they provide evidence that teachers who are interested in formative assessment can develop a wide range of procedures involving different forms of regulation and active student implication. There are also a number of books based largely on teachers' experiences with respect to formative perspectives for correcting or assessing student work (Groupe EVA, 1991; Veslin and Veslin, 1992) and the development of active student participation in assessment (Doyon and Juneau, 1991).

Conclusion

The French-language publications on formative assessment have contributed to a significant enlargement of the conception of formative assessment. The central idea of this conception is the regulation of teaching and learning through informal, interactive assessment and through the use of instruments that are adapted to classroom practice. The work by French-language researchers has led to a diversification and enrichment of the ways of carrying out formative assessment. Theoretical proposals have often been influenced by intensive contacts with teachers, through curriculum development projects, through teacher education programmes, through school reform movements. There has not, on the other hand, been a systematic concern for verification of the impact of formative assessment on student learning. Very little controlled experimental work has been conducted. Instrument development has not been sufficiently integrated into long-term research projects. Studies of practice are episodic and dispersed in different settings, which makes it difficult to identify patterns or trends. In summary, the theoretical promise of French-language work on formative assessment is in need of considerably more empirical grounding. This is a major challenge for the researchers of this community in the coming decades.

References

Allal, L. (1979), "Stratégies d'évaluation formative : conceptions psycho-pédagogiques et modalités d'application" in L. Allal, J. Cardinet and P. Perrenoud (eds.), *L'évaluation formative dans un enseignement différencié*, Peter Lang, Bern, pp. 153-183.

Allal, L. (1983), "Évaluation formative : entre l'intuition et l'instrumentation", *Mesure et évaluation en éducation,* Vol. 6, pp. 37-57.

Allal, L. (1988), "Vers un élargissement de la pédagogie de maîtrise : processus de régulation interactive, rétroactive et proactive" in M. Huberman (ed.), *Assurer la réussite des apprentissages scolaires ? Les propositions de la pédagogie de maîtrise*, Delachaux et Niestlé, Neuchâtel, pp. 86-126.

Allal, L. (1993), "Régulations métacognitives" in L. Allal, D. Bain and P. Perrenoud (eds.), *L'évaluation formative et didactique du français*, Delachaux et Niestlé, Neuchâtel, pp. 81-98.

Allal, L. (1997), "La mesure : variations culturelles sur le thème ADMEE", *Mesure et évaluation en éducation,* Vol. 19, pp. 1-4.

Allal, L. (1999), "Impliquer l'apprenant dans les processus d'évaluation : promesses et pièges de l'autoévaluation" in C. Depover and B. Noël (eds.), *L'évaluation des compétences et des processus cognitifs : modèles, pratiques et contextes*, De Boeck, Brussels, pp. 35-56.

Allal, L. (2002), "L'évaluation dans le contexte de l'apprentissage situé : peut-on concevoir l'évaluation comme un acte de participation à une communauté de pratiques ?", Conference for the 15th symposium of ADMEE-EUROPE, Université de Lausanne, September.

Allal, L., E. Baeriswyl, M. Tra Bach and E. Wegmuller (1987), "Le jeu comme situation d'auto-évaluation", *Mesure et évaluation en éducation,* Vol. 10, pp. 47-64.

Allal, L., D. Bain and P. Perrenoud (eds.) (1993), *L'évaluation formative et didactique du français*, Delachaux et Niestlé, Neuchâtel.

Allal, L., J. Cardinet and P. Perrenoud (eds.) (1979), *L'évaluation formative dans un enseignement différencié*, Lang, Bern.

Allal, L. and G. Pelgrims Ducrey (2000), "Assessment *of* – or *in* – the zone of proximal development", *Learning and Instruction,* Vol. 10, pp. 137-152.

Allal, L. and G. Schwartz (1996), "Quelle place pour l'évaluation formative dans l'enseignement au cycle d'orientation ?", *CO Infos,* No. 178, pp. 5-8.

Audibert, S. (1980), "En d'autres mots … l'évaluation des apprentissages !", *Mesure et évaluation en éducation,* Vol. 3, pp. 59-64.

Bain, D. (1988), "L'évaluation formative fait fausse route", *Mesure et évaluation en éducation,* Vol. 10, pp. 23-32.

Bain, D. and B. Schneuwly (1993), "Pour une évaluation formative intégrée dans la pédagogie du français : de la nécessité et de l'utilité de modèles de référence" in L. Allal, D. Bain and P. Perrenoud (eds.), *L'évaluation formative et didactique du français*, Delachaux et Niestlé, Neuchâtel, pp. 51-79.

Bélair, L. (1999), *L'évaluation dans l'école : nouvelles pratiques*, ESF, Paris.

Bercier-Larivière, M. and R. Forgette-Giroux (1995), "L'évaluation des apprentissages telle que perçue par des élèves de 6, 7 et 8e années", *Mesure et évaluation en éducation*, Vol. 18, pp. 37-58.

Berset Fougerand, B. (1993), "Écrire ... à haute voix : intégration de l'orthographe dans la production écrite" in L. Allal, D. Bain and P. Perrenoud (eds.), *L'évaluation formative et didactique du français*, Delachaux et Niestlé, Neuchâtel, pp. 171-196.

Bertrand, R., M. Tremblay-Desrochers, M. Morin and J. Roberge-Brassard (1985), "Analyse comparative de trois modèles d'instruments diagnostiques en mathématiques", *Mesure et évaluation en éducation*, Vol. 8, pp. 5-41.

Black, P. and D. Wiliam (1998), "Assessment and Classroom Learning", *Assessment in Education*, 5(1), pp. 7-74.

Block, J. and R. Burns (1976), "Mastery Learning", *Review of Research in Education*, 4, pp. 3-49.

Bloom, B.S. (1968), "Learning for Mastery", *Evaluation Comment*, 1(2), pp. 1-12.

Bloom, B.S. (1976), *Human Characteristics and School Learning*, McGraw-Hill, New York.

Bloom, B.S., J.T. Hasting and G.F. Madaus (1971), *Handbook on Formative and Summative Evaluation of Student Learning*, McGraw-Hill Book Co, New York.

Bonniol, J.-J. and M. Vial (1997), *Les modèles de l'évaluation*, De Boeck, Brussels.

Brun, J. (1979), "L'évaluation formative dans un enseignement différencié de mathématiques", in L. Allal, J. Cardinet and P. Perrenoud (eds.), *L'évaluation formative dans un enseignement différencié*, Peter Lang, Bern, pp. 170-181.

Campanale, F. (1997), "Auto-évaluation et transformation de pratiques pédagogiques", *Mesure et évaluation en éducation*, Vol. 20, pp. 1-24.

Cardinet, J. (1977), *Objectifs éducatifs et évaluation individualisée* (second edition, Report No. R77.05), Institut Romand de Recherches et de Documentation Pédagogiques, Neuchâtel.

Cardinet, J. (1983), "Quelques directions de progrès possibles pour l'appréciation du travail des élèves", *Mesure et évaluation en éducation,* Vol. 6, pp. 5-35.

Cardinet, J. (1986a), *Évaluation scolaire et mesure*, De Boeck, Brussels.

Cardinet, J. (1986b), *Évaluation scolaire et pratique*, De Boeck, Brussels.

Cardinet, J. (1988), "La maîtrise, communication réussie" in M. Huberman (ed.), *Assurer la réussite des apprentissages scolaires ? Les propositions de la pédagogie de maîtrise*, Delachaux et Niestlé, Neuchâtel, pp. 155-195.

Cazabon, B. (1991), "L'évaluation formative de la communication : l'intégration des composantes", *Mesure et évaluation en éducation,* Vol. 14, pp. 5-22.

Chevallard, Y. (1986), "Vers une analyse didactique des faits d'évaluation" in J.-M. De Ketele (ed.), *L'évaluation : approche descriptive ou prescriptive ?*, De Boeck, Brussels, pp. 31-59.

Coen, P.F. and J.L. Gurtner (1999), "Processus cognitifs en jeu dans une tâche d'écriture assistée par le logiciel AutoéVal" in C. Depover and B. Noël (ed.), *L'évaluation des compétences et des processus cognitifs : modèles, pratiques et contextes*, De Boeck, Brussels, pp. 239-254.

Crahay, M. (1986), "Évaluation formative et théorie constructiviste du développement" in J.-M. De Ketele (ed.), *L'évaluation: approche descriptive ou prescriptive ?*, De Boeck, Brussels, pp. 135-187.

Dassa, C. (1988), "L'intégration du diagnostic pédagogique aux apprentissages scolaires : de la théorie à la pratique", *Mesure et évaluation en éducation,* Vol. 11, pp. 7-26.

Dassa, C. and S.R. De Cotret (1993), "Validation d'un système informatisé de diagnostic en mathématiques au secondaire : une approche centrée sur l'analyse didactique", *Mesure et évaluation en éducation,* Vol. 16, pp. 5-26.

Dassa, C. and J. Vazquez-Abad (1992), "De l'évaluation informatisée à l'intervention pédagogique", *Mesure et évaluation en éducation,* Vol. 15, pp. 17-24.

De Campos, M. (1990), "Outil diagnostique et enseignement assisté par ordinateur", *Mesure et évaluation en éducation,* Vol. 13, pp. 55-69.

De Ketele J.-M. (1986) (ed.), *L'évaluation : approche descriptive ou prescriptive ?*, De Boeck, Brussels.

Del'Guidice, J. (1999), "L'évaluation-régulation, vecteur des transferts d'apprentissage" in C. Depover and B. Noël (eds.), *L'évaluation des compétences et des processus cognitifs : modèles, pratiques et contextes*, De Boeck, Brussels, pp. 99-114.

Depover, C. and B. Noël (eds.) (1999), *L'évaluation des compétences et des processus cognitifs : modèles, pratiques et contextes*, De Boeck, Brussels.

Derycke, M. (1998), "Suivi pédagogique ; grille critériée et dossier d'apprentissage", *Mesure et évaluation en éducation*, Vol. 20, pp. 33-53.

Descoteaux, M-S. and N. Lirette (1983), "Présentation du guide d'évaluation en classe", *Mesure et évaluation en éducation*, Vol. 6, pp. 123-133.

Desrosiers, P., P. Godbout and A. Marzouk (1992), "Des pistes pour soutenir la transformation des pratiques évaluatives" in D. Laveault (ed.), *Les pratiques d'évaluation en éducation*, Éditions de l'ADMÉÉ, Montreal, pp. 139-150.

Doyon, C. (1992), "Une pratique d'autoévaluation des apprentissages au primaire" in D. Laveault (ed.), *Les pratiques d'évaluation en éducation*, M Editeur, Montmagny, Québec, pp. 75-86.

Doyon, C. and R. Juneau (1991), *Faire participer l'élève à l'évaluation de ses apprentissages*, Beauchemin, Laval, Québec.

Elliott, N. (1993), "En observant l'apprenti-lecteur" in L. Allal, D. Bain and P. Perrenoud (eds.), *L'évaluation formative et didactique du français*, Delachaux et Niestlé, Neuchâtel, pp. 145-160.

Figari, G. and M. Achouche (2001), *L'activité évaluative réinterrogée*, De Boeck, Brussels.

Gadbois, L., R. Burelle, C. Parent and S.P. Séguin (1991), "Un instrument de mesure des croyances et attitudes des enseignants à l'égard des pratiques d'évaluation formative des apprentissages de leurs élèves", *Mesure et évaluation en éducation*, Vol. 14, pp. 5-24.

Gagné, F. and M. Thouin (1991), "L'évaluation formative des apprentissages en orthographe et attitude des élèves à l'égard de l'évaluation", *Mesure et évaluation en éducation*, Vol. 14, pp. 5-16.

Garcia-Debanc, C. and M. Mas (1987), "Évaluation des productions écrites des élèves", *Enjeux*, Vol. 11, pp. 108-122.

Grégoire, J. (ed.) (1996a), *Évaluer les apprentissages. Les apports de la psychologie cognitive*, De Boeck, Brussels.

Grégoire, J. (1996b), "Quelle démarche d'évaluation diagnostique des troubles d'apprentissage en mathématique ?", *Évaluer les apprentissages. Les apports de la psychologie cognitive*, De Boeck, Brussels, pp. 19-37.

Grégoire, J. (1999), "Que peut apporter la psychologie cognitive à l'évaluation formative et à l'évaluation diagnostique?" in C. Depover and B. Noël (eds.), *L'évaluation des compétences et des processus cognitifs : modèles, pratiques et contextes*, De Boeck, Brussels, pp. 17-33.

Grisay, A. (1988), "La pédagogie de maîtrise face aux rationalités inégalitaires des systèmes d'enseignement" in M. Huberman (ed.), *Maîtriser les processus d'apprentissage. Fondements et perspectives de la pédagogie de maîtrise*, Delachaux et Niestlé, Paris, pp. 235-265.

Groupe EVA (1991), *Évaluer les écrits à l'école primaire*, Hachette, Paris.

Hadji, C. (1989), *L'évaluation, règles du jeu, des intentions aux outils*, Éditions ESF, Paris.

Hadji, C. (1997), *L'évaluation démystifiée*, ESF, Paris.

Hivon, R. (ed.) (1993), *L'évaluation des apprentissages. Réflexions, nouvelles tendances et formation*, Éditions du CRP, Université de Sherbrooke, Québec.

Huberman, M. (ed.) (1988), *Assurer la réussite des apprentissages scolaires ? Les propositions de la pédagogie de maîtrise*, Delachaux et Niestlé, Neuchâtel.

Huberman, M., P.A. Juge and P.A. Hari (1985), "La pédagogie de maîtrise : une évaluation instructive au niveau gymnasial", *Mesure et évaluation en éducation*, Vol. 8, pp. 43-82.

Laurier, M. (1996), "Pour un diagnostic informatisé en révision de texte", *Mesure et évaluation en éducation*, Vol. 18, pp. 85-106.

Laveault, D. (ed.) (1992), *Les pratiques d'évaluation en éducation*, Éditions de l'ADMÉÉ, Montreal.

Laveault, D. (1999), "Autoévaluation et régulation des apprentissages" in C. Depover and B. Noël (ed.), *L'évaluation des compétences et des processus cognitifs : modèles, pratiques et contextes*, De Boeck, Brussels, pp. 57-79.

Leclercq, D. (1980), "Computerised Tailored Testing: Structured and Calibrated Item Banks for Summative and Formative Evaluation", *European Journal of Education*, Vol. 15(3), pp. 251-260.

Lété, B. (1996), "La remédiation des difficultés de lecture par la rétroaction verbale sur ordinateur" in J. Grégoire (ed.), *Évaluer les apprentissages: les apports de la psychologie cognitive*, De Boeck University, Brussels, pp. 133-155.

Louis, R. (1999), *L'évaluation des apprentissages en classe: théorie et pratique*, Éditions Études Vivantes, Laval.

Louis, R. and M. Trahan (1995), "Une mesure des croyances des enseignants titulaires du primaire relative à trois approches d'évaluation des apprentissage", *Mesure et évaluation en éducation,* Vol. 17, pp. 61-88.

Marchandisse, G. and D. Blampain (1974), *Techniques d'évaluation formative en langue maternelle*, ministère de l'Éducation nationale de la Culture française, Brussels.

Mottier Lopez, L. (2002), "Interroger la pratique du portfolio en situation scolaire dans une perspective 'située' de l'apprentissage", Paper for the 15th symposium of ADMEE-EUROPE, Université de Lausanne, September.

Nunziati, G. (1990), "Pour construire un dispositif d'évaluation formatrice", *Cahiers Pédagogiques*, No. 280, pp. 48-64.

Ouellette, L.-M. (1990), "La communication comme support théorique à l'évaluation", *Mesure et évaluation en éducation*, Vol. 13, pp. 5-22.

Perrenoud, P. (1991), "Pour une approche pragmatique de l'évaluation formative", *Mesure et évaluation en éducation*, Vol. 13, pp. 49-81.

Perrenoud, P. (1993a), "Touche pas à mon évaluation ! Une approche systémique du changement", *Mesure et évaluation en éducation*, Vol. 16, pp. 107-132.

Perrenoud, P. (1993b), "Vers des démarches didactiques favorisant une régulation individualisée des apprentissages" in L. Allal, D. Bain and P. Perrenoud (eds.), *L'évaluation formative et didactique du français*, Delachaux et Niestlé, Neuchâtel, pp. 31-50.

Perrenoud, P. (1998a), *L'évaluation des élèves. De la fabrication de l'excellence à la régulation des apprentissages. Entre deux logiques*, De Boeck, Brussels.

Perrenoud, P. (1998b), "From Formative Evaluation to a Controlled Regulation of Learning Processes. Towards a Wider Conceptual Field", *Assessment in Education*, 5(1), pp. 85-102.

Racine, S.B. (1982), "La validité et la fidélité dans la mesure critériée", *Mesure et évaluation en éducation*, Vol. 5, pp. 92-110.

Richard, J-F., P. Godbout and Y. Picard (2000), "La validation d'une procédure d'évaluation formative en jeux et sports collectifs", *Mesure et évaluation en éducation*, Vol. 23, pp. 43-67.

Scallon, G. (1985), "La participation des élèves au diagnostic pédagogique : exploration avec des élèves de 4e secondaire en mathématiques", *Mesure et évaluation en éducation*, Vol. 8, pp. 5-44.

Scallon, G. (1988), "Plaidoyer pour une méthodologie instrumentée d'évaluation formative", *Mesure et évaluation en éducation*, Vol. 11, pp. 43-55.

Scallon, G. (1996), "Évaluation formative et psychologie cognitive : mouvances et tendances" in G. Grégoire (ed.), *Évaluer les apprentissages. Les apports de la psychologie cognitive*, De Boeck, Brussels, pp. 159-173.

Scallon, G. (2000), *L'évaluation formative*, Éditions du Renouveau Pédagogique Inc, Saint-Laurent, Québec.

Schneuwly, B. and D. Bain (1993), "Mécanismes de régulation des activités textuelles : stratégies d'intervention dans les séquences didactiques" in L. Allal, D. Bain and P. Perrenoud (eds.), *L'évaluation formative et didactique du français*, Delachaux et Niestlé, Neuchâtel, pp. 219-238.

Schubauer-Leoni, M.-L. (1991), "L'évaluation didactique: une affaire contractuelle" in J. Weiss (ed.), *L'évaluation : problème de communication*, DelVal, Cousset, pp. 79-95.

Schwartz, G. and L. Allal (2000), *Vers une pratique de l'évaluation formative dans le secondaire I: Analyses d'expériences menées au cycle d'orientation de Genève*, Développement et innovation pédagogique au cycle d'orientation, Geneva.

Scriven, M. (1967), "The Methodology of Evaluation", *AERA Monograph Series on Evaluation*, 1, pp. 39-83.

Séguin, S.P. (1984), "L'utilisation des micro-ordinateurs pour l'évaluation des apprentissages : quelques perspectives d'avenir", *Mesure et évaluation en éducation*, Vol. 7, pp. 53-64.

Shepard, L. (2000), "The Role of Assessment in a Learning Culture", *Educational Researcher*, 29(7), pp. 1-14.

Simon, M. and R. Forgette-Giroux (1993), "Vers une utilisation rationnelle du dossier d'apprentissage", *Mesure et évaluation en éducation*, Vol. 16, pp. 27-40.

Slavin, R.E. (1987), "Mastery Learning Reconsidered", *Review of Educational Research*, 57, pp. 175-213.

Thouin, M. (1982), "La définition des objectifs et l'évaluation dans le domaine affectif, quelques éléments de réflexion", *Mesure et évaluation en éducation*, Vol. 5, pp. 31-34.

Thouin, M. (1993), "L'évaluation des apprentissages en mathématiques : une perspective constructiviste", *Mesure et évaluation en éducation*, Vol. 16, pp. 47-64.

Thouin, M. (1995), "Le développement d'instruments de mesure des apprentissages en sciences de la nature au primaire", *Mesure et évaluation en éducation*, Vol. 16, pp. 95-123.

Tourneur, Y., Y. Noël and B. Honclaire (1975), *Liste des objectifs, épreuves d'évaluation et outils de rattrapage en mathématiques*, ministère de l'Éducation nationale et de la Culture française, Brussels.

Van Nieuwenhoven, C. and P. Jonnaert (1994), "Une approche des représentations des enseignants du primaire à propos de l'évaluation", *Mesure et évaluation en éducation*, Vol. 16, pp. 41-79.

Veslin, O. and J. Veslin (1992), *Corriger des copies: évaluer pour former*, Hachette, Paris.

Vial, M. (1995), "Nature et fonction de l'auto-évaluation dans le dispositif de formation", *Revue française de pédagogie*, No. 112, pp. 69-76.

Vial, M. (2001), "Évaluation et régulation" in G. Figari and M. Achouche (eds.), *L'activité évaluative réinterrogée*, De Boeck, Brussels, pp. 68-78.

Wegmuller, E. (1993), "Et s'ils apprenaient à écrire en connaissance de cause! L'ovniprésence de l'évaluation formative" in L. Allal, D. Bain and P. Perrenoud (eds.), *L'évaluation formative et didactique du français*, Delachaux et Niestlé, Neuchâtel, pp. 197-218.

Weiss, J. (1979), "L'évaluation formative dans un enseignement différencié du français: une conception de la formation à dépasser" in L. Allal, J. Cardinet and P. Perrenoud (eds.), *L'évaluation formative dans un enseignement différencié*, Peter Lang, Bern, pp. 194-202.

Weiss, J. (1984), "Heurs et malheurs d'un instrument d'évaluation", *Mesure et évaluation en éducation*, Vol. 7, pp. 31-42.

Weiss, J. (ed.) (1991), *Évaluation : problème de communication*, DelVal, Cousset, Suisse.

Weiss, J. (1993), "Interaction formative et régulation didactique" in L. Allal, D. Bain and P. Perrenoud (eds.), *L'évaluation formative et didactique du français*, Delachaux et Niestlé, Neuchâtel, pp. 113-122.

Formative Assessment in Classrooms: A Review of the Empirical German Literature
by
Olaf Köller, University of Erlangen-Nuremberg

INTRODUCTION AND DATABASES

Germany has a long tradition of philosophers and educational reformers who proposed alternative education (so-called *Reformpädagogik*) as a more appropriate approach to teaching that meets students' needs for competence, autonomy and self-determination. Beyond other features, alternative education has emphasised that teachers should be aware of how they provide feedback to students, as feedback indicating personal growth to students will foster their learning and motivational development. Although there has been growing consensus across centuries and decades in Germany that the kind of feedback determines whether students achieve cognitive, emotional and motivational growth, systematic research on this issue has been conducted in relatively few German studies. In particular, there has been very little systematic empirical research on formative assessment in Black and Wiliam's (1998) sense. These authors interpret formative assessment "as encompassing all those activities undertaken by teachers, and/or by their students, which provide information to be used as feedback to modify the teaching and learning activities in which they are engaged". (Black and Wiliam, 1998, p. 7-8)

Databases

The literature review covers the time period from 1980 until 2003. The search was conducted by several means. The first approach was to search using key words in two German databases, PSYNDEX and FIS-BILDUNG. While the first one contains the more psychologically-oriented literature (similar to PsychInfo), the second one mainly encompasses work in the fields of education or pedagogy (like ERIC). This search was of limited success because formative assessment is not a common concept in the German literature. More general descriptors (*e.g.*, assessment, feedback) resulted in more data that could be handled for this review. In addition, contents of several German journals that publish empirical studies in the field of education and/or instruction were scanned. These journals were (translations in parentheses):

- *Zeitschrift für Pädagogik* (Journal of pedagogy).

- *Zeitschrift für Erziehungswissenschaft* (Journal of educational science).
- *Unterrichtswissenschaft* (Research on instruction).
- *Zeitschrift für Pädagogische Psychologie* (Journal of educational psychology).
- *Zeitschrift für Entwicklungspsychologie und Pädagogische Psychologie* (Journal of developmental and educational psychology).
- *Psychologie in Erziehung und Unterricht* (Psychology in education and instruction).

In addition, a citation search of relevant articles in the above-mentioned journals was conducted. The resulting literature yielded more than 150 articles and book chapters. The body of this paper reviews selected theoretical papers and empirical studies of outstanding relevance to this report (rather than reviewing all articles located in these three search modes).

HISTORICAL ROOTS OF FORMATIVE ASSESSMENT IN GERMANY

Concepts of alternative education (*Reformpädagogik*) have been the most important historical roots of formative assessment in German classrooms. Hellmich and Teigler (1992) argue that particularly the works by Montessori, Freinet, Kerschensteiner and Steiner have been very influential.[1] In contrast to traditional teacher-directed approaches, these authors have highlighted students' needs for autonomy and self-determination.[2]

In *Montessori's pedagogy*, the teacher acts more or less in the background and becomes a careful observer and individual counsellor of the students, providing help to optimise their knowledge acquisition. The principles of autonomy, self-action and self-control which encourage students to assess their learning progress are of particular importance. *Freinet's pedagogy* places a strong emphasis on self-assessment. Students should learn to define their own projects, to assess their learning progress and whether they have reached their goals in these projects. Tools for

---

[1] Particularly Steiner's approach has led to the foundation of the so-called Waldorf-schools. These schools belong to private educational sector but all school leaving certificates are equivalent to those provided by public schools.

[2] For the purpose of this review, however, we will concentrate on the impact of alternative education on feedback processes in classrooms. More general descriptions of alternative education, particularly of the work by Freinet, Montessori, and Steiner can be found in Hellmich and Teigler (1992).

formative assessment in this sense are student week plans, diaries and working materials that allow students to assess and correct their own work.

The *Waldorf-pedagogy*, based on *Steiner's work*, has called for the abolishment of marks. Proponents of this approach have also argued against the German practice of requiring students who have received poor grades to repeat school years. *Kerschensteiner* proposed the advantages of self-assessments not only for the evaluation of final results but also for each working or learning step in school. Students from Waldorf-schools do not get any marks until the end of lower secondary level (grade 10) and remedial measures are conducted for poor achieving students so that they do not have to repeat a school year.

After World War II, concepts of alternative education felt into desuetude and it was not until the 1960s that alternative education was rediscovered and brought into the debate on educational reforms (*Bildungsreform*). Furthermore a strong critique of grades emerged in this period, because several empirical studies demonstrated that the psychometric properties (objectivity, reliability, and validity) of grades were quite poor (see Ingenkamp, 1971 for an overview). Educational reformers called for:

- The abolishment of grades.
- More standardised tests as measures of summative assessment instead of grades.
- More individualised feedback.
- Process-oriented instead of product-oriented diagnosis.
- More remedial measures for low-achieving students.
- A stronger emphasis on encouraging and motivating teaching.

Consequently several alternative tools for student assessment were proposed, all of which had a more formative as opposed to a summative character.

MEASURES OF ALTERNATIVE ASSESSMENT IN GERMAN SCHOOLS

The term "alternative assessment" is used here to illustrate that some of the measures presented below are important assessment tools beyond marks but are not really formative.

Diagnostic forms

Diagnostic forms (*Diagnosebögen*, cf. Ingenkamp, 1985) provide detailed information about learning success and allow a much more differentiated assessment than grades. Interestingly they were firstly introduced in German classrooms in 1915 and rediscovered in the last 30 years. Teachers in comprehensive schools have used these measures of formative assessment.

Major goals of using diagnostic forms are (cf. Winter, 1991):

- Assessment of social learning outcomes.
- Differentiated feedback information for both students and parents.
- Awareness of individual learning progress and growth in ability.
- Information which helps to optimise knowledge acquisition and to initiate remedial measures for low-achieving students.

Proponents have argued that teachers should use diagnostic assessment after each instruction unit for each student. However, teachers as well as school administrators have declined diagnostic testing that is too time-consuming. Consequently these measures disappeared from German classrooms in the 1980s.

Learning reports

Teachers typically complete learning reports (*Lernberichte*, cf. Lübke, 1996) twice a year. They are alternative form of summative assessment and combine information about social and cognitive learning outcomes. The learning reports contain both individual assessments and evaluations of the total class. Each student and the whole class receive advice on how to optimise motivational and cognitive development.

Diaries on learning success

Diaries (*Lerntagebücher*, Herrmann and Höfer, 1999) provide opportunities for students to reflect on their own learning processes and to detect and correct deficits over time. Diaries thus serve as a tool for autonomous and self-regulated learning. The advantages of diaries include:

- Opportunities for individual reflections.
- Opportunities for communication among students about achievement or learning goals.
- Help in preparing for final examinations (cf. Herrmann and Höfer, 1999).

Student week plans

Student week plans (*Wochenarbeitspläne*) are based upon Freinet's work. Typically, the week plans are used in elementary schools where teachers have more degrees of freedom with respect to their assessment practice. The week plan allows students to check whether they have reached their goals and solved all problems during the previous lessons across one week. The idea is that students become much more aware of their achievement levels and learn to be open to criticism (if they have not reached their aims). The week plan always includes an individual growth curve demonstrating the achievements during the week.

Portfolio

Portfolios are particularly useful in co-operative learning settings (cf. Herold and Landherr, 2001) because they allow students to evaluate their own impact on group-results. Students not only rate their behaviour within the group behaviour but also have to justify their ratings. Typically the ratings are discussed among all group members.

Some empirical evidence for the effectiveness of measures of alternative assessment

In recent years, a few German researchers have conducted empirical studies on assessment (see Grunder and Bohl, 2001 for an overview). Köller and Trautwein (2003) examined the use of alternative assessment measure in five comprehensive schools. They compared math and science achievement of 8th graders from these schools with 8th graders who had been tested with the same instruments in the TIMS study. Achievement scores of these five schools were above average (compared to the nationally representative TIMS study), suggesting that strategies of alternative assessment might have had positive effects on learning outcomes.

MARKS VS. VERBAL REPORTS AS ASSESSMENT MEASURES

In 1970, the Conference of Federal Ministers of Education (*Kultusminister-Konferenz*) decided that marks should be substituted by verbal reports in primary schools, at least in grades 1 and 2. This decision was intended to individualise education.

Again, major goals of this reform were:

- Avoiding pressure to achieve.
- Promoting cooperation instead of competition.

- Reducing social disparities and preventing declines in the achievement levels of disadvantaged students.
- Individual support.
- Assessment based on individual progress instead of social comparisons.

Empirical studies of the implementation and practice of verbal reports in elementary schools, however, showed that the reform was not working as hoped. For example, Benner and Ramseger (1985) conducted a content analysis of about 450 verbal reports. Four different types of verbal reports could be identified:

- *Normative reports* assessed the students based upon criteria defined in curricula and text books.
- *Nice reports* were highly encouraging but failed to obtain any information on the real achievement level, deficits and developmental potential of the student.
- *Descriptive reports* provided a clear picture of the students' achievement levels but ignored any information of students' progress in the different subjects.
- Finally, *developmental reports* had a truly formative character in that they described progress and deficits and how these deficits could be eliminated. Note that only this type represents a measure of formative assessment to any extent.

Valtin (cf. Valtin, 2002; Wagner and Valtin, 2003) analysed the effects of different types of assessment (marks vs. verbal reports) on the development of educational outcomes in elementary school. Her panel comprised 241 children from East and West Berlin who were tested several times, individually or in groups, from grade 2 to grade 4. Outcomes were attitude toward learning and toward school subjects, academic self-concept, achievement motivation, test anxiety, intelligence, and academic achievement in mathematics and German. Contrary to her prediction students did not profit notably from verbal reports.

One reason for these disappointing findings might be that the teachers in Valtin's study only practiced formative assessment when writing the reports but not in everyday situations in the classroom. The work of Rheinberg in particular (cf. Rheinberg and Krug, 1999) has demonstrated that formative assessment during ordinary lessons can have huge effects on motivation. His approach is described in the next section.

ADDITIONAL STUDIES IN GERMANY ON FORMATIVE ASSESSMENT

Some studies have systematically investigated effects of feedback processes on student characteristics. Interestingly, this research has been mainly carried out by psychological researchers who have been strongly influenced by American researchers on motivation such as Atkinson and McClelland. Major proponents in Germany included Heckhausen (1989), Rheinberg (Rheinberg and Krug, 1999), and Meyer (Meyer and Plöger, 1979). Heckhausen and Rheinberg established the concept of teacher's frame of reference (individual vs. social). In their studies, teachers using an individual frame of reference provided temporal feedback to students and emphasised improvement, whereas teachers with a social frame of reference assessed their students' accomplishments on the basis of comparisons with others. Meyer's research focused on the paradoxical effects of praise and blame, that is, he investigated situations in which teacher's praise (blame) led the student to think that he or she must be stupid (bright).

Teachers' reference norms: the work by Rheinberg

There is a long international research tradition investigating the effects of different types of feedback based on individual or social comparisons. Ames (1992) noted that social comparisons are encouraged by the frequent allocation of grades that rank-order students along a single continuum based on performance in the same task, by the public announcement of results, and by competitive learning environments that emphasise the importance of outperforming other students. In a strong critique of such competitive environments, Covington (1992) argued that competition reduces levels of academic achievement and undermines self-worth. Marsh (1991) further argues that competition and social comparison processes are likely to be stronger in highly selective school settings, thus exacerbating the negative effects on variables like academic self-concept or self-esteem.

In order to establish alternative frames of reference in the classroom, teachers can emphasise improvement, effort, and learning (individual frame of reference), rather than grades, ability differences, and outperforming classmates (social frame of reference). Concerning the important role of different types of comparisons, the German motivational psychologist Rheinberg (1980, 1999; also see Rheinberg and Krug, 1999) has established the concept of teachers' reference norms which has substantial theoretical overlap with major ideas of goal theory as proposed by Nicholls (1984). Based on research in motivation conducted by McClelland (cf. McClelland et al., 1953) or Heckhausen (1989), Rheinberg defined teacher's reference norm as a standard to which individual achievements are compared. Such standards can be based upon different frames of reference. Comparing individual achievements with prior achievements constitutes an individual reference norm, while comparing students' achievements with those of their class mates defines a social reference norm. The advantage of an individual perspective is that students directly register any improvement in their achievements, and can thus bolster their academic self-concept.

An important aspect of Rheinberg's work is that he not only distinguishes between the two types of teacher feedback, but that he also argues that teachers with a social reference norm typically present tasks of the same difficulty level to all students to obtain valid information about inter-individual differences. Holding the difficulty levels constant allows teachers to attribute students' achievement differences to ability. Furthermore teachers with a social reference norm believe that ability differences among students are highly stable across time. Therefore, poor achieving students will always show poor accomplishments, while bright students will always perform well in school.

Teachers with an individual reference norm prefer a quite different perspective, in that they judge their students based on prior achievement levels. Achievement gains over time are praised, stagnation or regression is blamed. There is no doubt, that an individual reference norm can be easily applied in everyday lessons, when students work on tasks by themselves. Table 1 summarises the differences between teachers with a social reference norm and those with an individual reference norm (see Rheinberg, 1980, p. 123 and Rheinberg, 1999, p. 44).

Table 1. Differences between teachers with an individual (IRN) and a social reference norm (SRN)

Variable	SRN	IRN
Comparisons	Cross-sectional, among students	Longitudinal, within students
Individualisation	Individualised instruction, assigning different task to students with different achievement levels	Longitudinal, within students
Causal attributions	More frequent, primarily time-constant factors (*e.g.*, ability), internal attributions of success and failure	Less frequent, preference for time-variant causes (persistence, concentration, attention); internal attributions of success, external or at least internal and variable attributions of failure
Feedback	Based on social comparison, emphasising the rank of each student within a class	Based on temporal comparisons, emphasising individual progress and growth

Source: Taken from Rheinberg (1980), p. 123 and Rheinberg (1999), p. 44 (slightly modified).

Rheinberg and colleagues have conducted many experimental studies investigating the effects of different reference norms on student outcomes, two of which are presented subsequently (see Mischo and Rheinberg, 1995 and Köller, 2004, for more complete overviews of studies investigating effects of reference norms on educational outcomes). Additionally an article by Lüdtke and Köller (2002) is described since these authors provided evidence for the effectiveness of an individual reference norm on students' academic self-concepts based upon two large German field studies with samples sizes of N = 3 992 and N = 2 150 students from grades 7 and 8, respectively.

Krug and Lecybyl (1999a)

These authors conducted an experiment on the effects of different reference norms (individual vs. social). Participants included 44 students from two classes of a vocational school. Students in both classes had the same teacher in social sciences. In one class, however, this teacher used an individual reference norm over a period of eight weeks, while she used a social reference norm in the other class. Dependent variables included observer ratings of students' understanding of the content taught, achievement tests, the teacher-students-relationship, students' participation, and how much students liked the lessons. The findings were quite mixed, that is, students in the individual reference norm condition had higher values on some of the outcome measures, while no differences occurred on the other measures. Note, however, that no dependent variable had a higher mean in the social reference norm condition.

Krug and Lecybyl (1999b)

Krug and Lecybyl conducted a second study similar to the first, but distinguished between low, middle and high-achieving students. Again the sample included students (17 in class 1 and 19 in class 2) from two classes of a vocational school and the teacher was the same in both conditions. Again, positive effects of an individual reference norm on several outcome measures were observed. These effects, however, were largest for poor achieving students.

Lüdtke and Köller (2002)

The two studies of these authors were inspired by Marsh's (1987) work on the big-fish-little-pond-effect (BFLPE). The BFLPE describes the phenomenon that equally able students have lower academic self-concepts in classes or schools where the average achievement level is higher than in classes or schools where the average achievement level is lower. Social comparison theory (Festinger, 1954) provides a theoretical framework explaining the BFLPE: students are inherently more likely to make social comparisons with higher-achieving students – thus leading to lower academic self-concepts — in high-ability classes than in low-ability classes. In their study, Lüdtke and Köller investigated the effects of teacher feedback on the BFLPE in large samples of secondary level students (see above). The basic assumption was that the BFLPE would be smaller in classes in which teachers strongly emphasise improvement, effort, and learning (individual reference norm). The authors, however, found that the negative BFLPE was observable in all classes but that there was an additional positive effect of an individual reference norm on academic self-concept.

Paradoxical effects of praise and blame: the work by Meyer

It is a common belief that positive teacher feedback (praise) during regular lessons has positive rather than negative effects on student characteristics such as motivation, self-esteem and learning. Negative feedback (blame) is usually expected to have the opposite effects. However, Meyer (1982, 1992; also see Meyer *et al.*, 1979), a German researcher in the field of motivation, has conducted a series of experiments showing that praise and blame can have counter-intuitive effects on students self-evaluations, meaning that praise can, under some special circumstances, reduce ones self-perceptions of ability, whereas blame can increase such self-perceptions. From his attributional point of view, the effects of teacher praise depend on a student's interpretation. If praise is attributed to ability, the student's self-perceptions of ability may increase. If praise is attributed to effort, the student's self-perception of ability may even decrease (if the perception of high effort is perceived as an indicator of low ability, particularly after simple tasks). Thus, praise does not always lead to a perception of high ability, and blame does not necessarily lead to a low estimation of ability. Such findings were first reported by Meyer and colleagues (Meyer *et al.*, 1979). Effort attributions were assumed to be the intervening variables (Meyer, 1992). The general method has been to present participants with a scenario in which two students receive feedback for an identical outcome. One student is praised (or criticised), the other receives neutral feedback, for instance: "Peter and Paul have each got 7 out of 10 problems right. The teacher gives Paul neutral feedback, 'You've got seven problems right, Paul.' However, he praises Peter: 'Well done, Peter!'". In the failure conditions, praise is usually replaced by blame: "Well, that wasn't very good, Peter!". Participants are then asked to judge the ability of both protagonists (see Meyer *et al.*, 1979).

It has to be admitted that this scenario method tends to assess rather unrealistic interaction sequences. However, some studies with more realistic settings, either experimental (Meyer, Mittag and Engler, 1986) or field studies (Tacke and Linder, 1981), have also shown paradoxical effects of praise and blame (see Pikowsky, 1988). Rheinberg and Weich (1988) were able to show that paradoxical ability attributions were even made spontaneously when identical achievements were sanctioned in different ways. Meyer *et al.* (1986) showed that paradoxical inferences are not restricted to ability attributions in scenario studies but even have effects on students' self-concept of ability. In their study, students who were praised inferred lower task-specific competence than students who received neutral feedback.

The level of cognitive development seems to be a moderator of such paradoxical effects: Barker and Graham (1987) found that the apparently paradoxical effects of praise and criticism occur more frequently as a function of increasing age. Whereas 4- to 5-year-olds always inferred that praise indicated high ability and high effort, paradoxical effects began to appear among 11- to 12-year-olds.

To summarise the research on praise and blame has clearly shown that teachers' feedback can have paradoxical effects in that praise has negative effects, while the consequences of blame could be positive. These findings do not necessarily devaluate such feedback as a helpful formative measure but argue for caution in daily situations in which feedback is provided.

SUMMARY AND SOME REMARKS ON FUTURE DIRECTIONS IN RESEARCH ON FORMATIVE ASSESSMENT IN GERMANY

The previous sections of this literature report have shown that there is not very much German research on effects of formative assessment on educational outcomes. This is surprising to some extent, because there are many approaches of formative assessment described in the German literature. These approaches have not been sufficiently evaluated. Despite this lack of research, there are currently some very interesting videotape studies for several subjects (*i.e.*, English, math, and science) that may facilitate insight into the assessment practices of German teachers and the way in which they affect learning. Within the TIMS study (Stigler *et al.*, 1996) 100 German math lessons were videotaped. All these videos can be coded with respect to teachers' assessment practices. Similar studies are currently conducted for physics (project head: Prof. Dr. Manfred Prenzel from the Institute for Science Education) and English (project head: Prof. Dr. Eckard Klime, German Institute for International Educational Research). All studies collect not only video data but also achievement as well as motivation, social and other data. Therefore it will be possible to analyse the relationships between assessment styles and all educational outcomes.

References

Ames, C. (1992), "Classroom Goals, Structures, and Student Motivation", *Journal of Educational Psychology*, Vol. 84, pp. 261-271.

Barker, G.P. and S. Graham (1987), "Developmental Study of Praise and Blame as Attributional Cues", *Journal of Educational Psychology*, Vol. 79, pp. 62-66.

Baumert, J., R.H. Lehmann *et al.* (1997), "TIMSS: Mathematisch-naturwissenschaftlicher Unterricht im internationalen Vergleich", Leske + Budrich, Opladen.

Benner, D. and J. Ramseger (1985), "Zwischen Zifferenzensur und pädagogischem Entwicklungsbericht. Zeugnisse ohne Noten in der Grundschule", *Zeitschrift für Pädagogik*, Vol. 31, pp. 151-174.

Black, P. and D. Wiliam (1998), "Assessment and Classroom Learning", *Assessment in Education*, Vol. 5, pp. 7-74.

Covington, M.V. (1992), "Making the Grade: A Self-worth Perspective on Motivation and School Reform", Cambridge University Press.

Deutsches PISA-Konsortium (ed.) (2001), "PISA 2000. Basiskompetenzen von Schülerinnen und Schülern im internationalen Vergleich", Leske + Budrich, Opladen.

Deutsches PISA-Konsortium (ed.) (2002), "PISA 2000. Die Länder der Bundesrepublik Deutschland im Vergleich", Leske + Budrich, Opladen.

Deutsches PISA-Konsortium (ed.) (2003), "PISA 2000. Ein differenzierter Blick auf die Länder der Bundesrepublik Deutschland", Leske + Budrich, Opladen.

Festinger, L. (1954), "A Theory of Social Comparison Processes", *Human Relations*, 7, pp. 117-140.

Grunder, H.-U. and T. Bohl (eds.) (2001), *Neue Formen der Leistungsbeurteilung*, Schneider, Hohengehren.

Heckhausen, H. (1989), *Motivation und Handeln*, Springer, Berlin.

Hellmich, A. and P. Teigler (eds.) (1992), *Montessori-, Freinet-, Waldorfpädagogik*, Beltz, Weinheim.

Herold, M. and B. Landherr (2001), *Selbstorganisiertes Lernen: SOL; ein systemischer Ansatz für Unterricht*, Schneider, Hohengehren.

Herrmann, J. and C. Höfer (1999), *Evaluation in der Schule – Unterrichtsevaluation*, Bertelsmann Stiftung, Gütersloh.

Ingenkamp, K. (1971), *Die Fragwürdigkeit der Zensurengebung*, Beltz, Weinheim.

Ingenkamp, K. (1985), *Lehrbuch der Pädagogischen Diagnostik*, Beltz, Weinheim.

Köller, O. (2004), *Konsequenzen von Leistungsgruppierungen*, Waxmann, Münster.

Köller, O. and U. Trautwein (eds.) (2003), *Schulqualität und Schülerleistung. Evaluationsstudie über innovative Schulentwicklung an fünf hessischen Gesamtschulen*, Juventa, Weinheim.

Krug, S. and R. Lecybyl. (1999a), "Die Wirkung experimentell variierten Lehrerverhaltens auf Unterrichtswahrnehmung, Lernbereitschaft und Leistung von Schülern" in F. Rheinberg and S. Krug (eds.), *Motivationsförderung im Schulalltag*, Hogrefe, Göttingen, pp. 81-94.

Krug, S. and R. Lecybyl, R. (1999b), "Die Veränderung von Einstellung, Mitarbeit und Lernleistung im Verlauf einer bezugsnormspezifischen Motivationsintervention" in F. Rheinberg and S. Krug (eds.), *Motivationsförderung im Schulalltag*, Hogrefe, Göttingen, pp. 95-114.

Lübke, S.-I. (1996), *Schule ohne Noten*, Leske + Budrich, Opladen.

Lüdtke, O. and O. Köller (2002), "Individuelle Bezugsnormorientierung und soziale Vergleiche im Mathematikunterricht: Der Einfluss unterschiedlicher Referenzrahmen auf das fachspezifische Selbstkonzept der Begabung", *Zeitschrift für Entwicklungspsychologie und Pädagogische Psychologie*, Vol. 34, pp. 156-166.

Marsh, H.W. (1987), "The Big-fish-little-pond Effect on Academic Self-concept", *Journal of Educational Psychology*, Vol. 79, pp. 280-295.

Marsh, H.W. (1991), "The Failure of High-ability High Schools to Deliver Academic Benefits: The Importance of Academic Self-concept and Educational Aspirations", *American Educational Research Journal*, Vol. 28, pp. 445-480.

McClelland, D.C., J.W. Atkinson, R.A. Clark and E.L. Lowell (1953), *The Achievement Motive*, Appleton-Century-Crofts, New York.

Meyer, W.-U. (1982), "Indirect Communications about Perceived Ability Estimates", *Journal of Educational Psychology*, Vol. 74, pp. 888-897.

Meyer, W.-U. (1992), "Paradoxical Effects of Praise and Criticism on Perceived Ability", *European Review of Social Psychology*, Vol. 3, pp. 259-283.

Meyer, W.-U., M. Bachmann, U. Biermann, M. Hempelmann, F.-O. Plöger and H. Spiller (1979), "The Informational Value of Praise and Blame on Perceptions of Ability", *Journal of Educational Psychology*, Vol. 71, pp. 259-268.

Meyer, W.-U., W. Mittag and U. Engler (1986), "Some Effects of Praise and Blame on Perceived Ability and Affect", *Social Cognition*, Vol. 4, pp. 293-308.

Meyer, W.-U. and F.-O. Plöger (1979), "Scheinbar paradoxe Wirkungen von Lob und Tadel auf die wahrgenommene eigene Begabung" in S.H. Filipp (ed.), *Selbstkonzept-Forschung*, Klett, Stuttgart, pp. 221-236.

Mischo, C. and F. Rheinberg (1995), "Erziehungsziele von Lehrern und individuelle Bezugsnormender Leistungsbewertung", *Zeitschrift für Pädagogische Psychologie*, Vol. 9, pp. 139-151.

Nicholls, J.G. (1984), "Achievement Motivation: Conceptions of Ability, Subjective Experience, Task Choice, and Performance", *Psychological Review*, Vol. 91, pp. 328-346.

Pikowsky, B. (1988), "Lob im Unterricht: Lehrer- und Schülerkognitionen", *Zeitschrift für Pädagogische Psychologie*, Vol. 2, pp. 251-258.

Rheinberg, F. (1980), *Leistungsbewertung und Lernmotivation*, Hogrefe, Göttingen.

Rheinberg, F. (1999), "Trainings auf der Basis eines kognitiven Motivationsmodells" in F. Rheinberg and S. Krug (eds.), *Motivationsförderung im Schulalltag*, Hogrefe, Göttingen, 2, pp. 36-52.

Rheinberg, F. and S. Krug (eds.) (1999), *Motivationsförderung im Schulalltag*, Hogrefe, Göttingen, 2.

Rheinberg, F. and K.W. Weich (1988), "Wie gefährlich ist Lob? Eine Untersuchung zum 'paradoxen Effekt' von Lehrersanktionen", *Zeitschrift für Pädagogische Psychologie*, Vol. 2, pp. 227-233.

Stigler, J.W., P. Gonzales, T. Kawanaka, S. Knoll and A. Serrano (1996), "The TIMSS Videotape Classroom Study: Methods and Preliminary Findings", Prepared for the National Center for Education Statistics, U.S. Department of Education, Los Angeles, CA.

Tacke, G. and F. Linder (1981), "Der Einfluss individualisierenden Lehrerverhaltens auf das Selbstkonzept von Schülern", *Zeitschrift für Entwicklungspsychologie und Pädagogische Psychologie*, Vol. 13, pp. 190-193.

Valtin, R. (2002), *Was ist ein gutes Zeugnis? Noten und verbale Beurteilungen auf dem Prüfstand*, Juventa, Weinheim.

Wagner, C. and R. Valtin (2003), "Noten oder Verbalbeurteilungen? Die Wirkung unterschiedlicher Bewertungsformen auf die schulische Entwicklung von Grundschulkindern", *Zeitschrift für Entwicklungspsychologie und Pädagogische Psychologie*, Vol. 35, pp. 27-36.

Winter, F. (1991), *Schüler lernen Selbstbewertung*, Peter Lang, Frankfurt.

Also available in the CERI collection

Internationalisation and Trade in Higher Education – *Opportunities and Challenges*
250 pages • September 2004 • ISBN: 92-64-01504-3 • 50 euros

Quality and Recognition in Higher Education – *The Cross-border Challenge*
203 pages • July 2004 • ISBN: 92-64-01508-6 • 30 euros

Innovation in the Knowledge Economy – *Implications for Education and Learning*
Knowledge Management series
96 pages • May 2004 • ISBN: 92-64-10560-3 • 21 euros

Equity in Education – *Students with Disabilities, Learning Difficulties and Disadvantages*
165 pages • May 2004 • ISBN: 92-64-10368-6 • 40 euros

Disability in Higher Education
168 pages • December 2003 • ISBN: 92-64-10505-0 • 24 euros

Measuring Knowledge Management in the Business Sector: First Steps
Knowledge Management series
219 pages • December 2003 • ISBN: 92-64-10026-1 • 40 euros

New Challenges for Educational Research
Knowledge Management series
146 pages • August 2003 • ISBN: 92-64-10030-X • 21 euros

Networks of Innovation – *Towards New Models for Managing Schools and Systems*
Schooling for Tomorrow series
182 pages • June 2003 • ISBN: 92-64-10034-2 • 25 euros

Understanding the Brain – *Towards a New Learning Science*
115 pages • July 2002 • ISBN: 92-64-19734-6 • 23 euros

www.oecd.org/bookshop

OECD PUBLICATIONS, 2, rue André-Pascal, 75775 PARIS CEDEX 16
PRINTED IN FRANCE
(96 2005 02 1 P) ISBN 92-64-00739-3 – No. 53869 2005